Of Such Is the Kingdom

A Practical Theology of Disability

Summer Kinard

ANCIENT FAITH PUBLISHING
CHESTERTON, INDIANA

Of Such Is the Kingdom: A Practical Theology of Disability
Copyright ©2019 Summer Kinard

Published by:
    Ancient Faith Publishing
    A Division of Ancient Faith Ministries
    P.O. Box 748
    Chesterton, IN 46304

All Old Testament quotations, unless otherwise identified, are from the Orthodox Study Bible, © 2008 by St. Athanasius Academy of Orthodox Theology (published by Thomas Nelson, Inc., Nashville, Tennessee) and are used by permission. New Testament quotations are from the New King James Version of the Bible, © 1982 by Thomas Nelson, Inc., and are used by permission.

ISBN: 978-1-944967-61-1

Printed in the United States of America

Library of Congress Control Number:2019950085

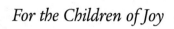

For the Children of Joy

And they brought unto him also infants, that he would touch them: but when his disciples saw it, they rebuked them. But Jesus called them unto him, and said, Suffer little children to come unto me, and forbid them not: for of such is the kingdom of God. Verily I say unto you, Whosoever shall not receive the kingdom of God as a little child shall in no wise enter therein.

—LUKE 18:15–17 KJV

Contents

Of Such Is the Kingdom of God

W HEN I WAS GROWING UP as an undiagnosed autistic girl, it didn't take me long to realize when I embarrassed someone. Some people were uncomfortable with my inability to speak easily or understandably, or with my intense and long silences. When I learned to read, they were uncomfortable with the way my different brain helped me see the meanings of complicated passages well beyond my years. Everything I read about God stuck to the forefront of my understanding of the world, and I embarrassed people by seeming to think God was right there with us. I couldn't go anywhere or do anything without knowing God was with me. I was encouraged by the love and patient teaching of my two grandmothers and two great-grandmothers, who prayed for children and took extra time to tell me how to behave and what things meant.

When those grandmothers and great-grandmothers told me about God, they introduced me to God as a refuge. In the world I was an embarrassment, but with God, I was loved and called to a purpose. I grew up and out of the disability part of my different kind of brain by leaning on God and asking Him to teach me. I knew from an early age that I didn't understand a lot about the world. I read in the Bible that God is a teacher who gives wisdom to anyone who asks, so I asked Him. I begged God to teach me, and from the time I received a Bible at the age of ten, I studied every scrap of Scripture or the Fathers I could find. In autistic terms, God became my lifelong "area of interest." But more than that, I was consumed by a burning love for God and the unshakable and simple sense of His presence with us.

That's why, when I grew up and had my own autistic children and entered the Orthodox Church, I wasn't surprised when the men and women who most readily accepted us were the grandparents serving as ushers, kitchen helpers, bookstore organizers, choir members, and friends. Like my grandmothers and great-grandmothers before them, these men and women reached out to us and showed us with simple patience how to live the life of faith. Because it was easy for me to see God at work in them, I asked them whenever I had challenges or questions. Through them, I was introduced to friends of all ages who followed their good example and welcomed us and loved us, even though sometimes we had unusual needs or questions.

I have experienced welcome both as a parent of children with disabilities and as an adult with a neurological difference. Even though I speak English fluently now and have done so for decades, my old weaknesses show themselves when I try to speak the languages of my fellow Orthodox Christians. Yet, time and again I have been shown grace as I struggle through dyslexia and apraxia at the side of the choir rehearsal, touching my lips with my fingers to help them make the words I need to say in Greek or another language of chant.

Uncountable times, the kind eyes of ushers have chased the tears out of my eyes when they stop me to say they're glad we're here and they love our children, even when I'm on my way out to take a melting-down child to a quiet space. I have had the joy of watching my daughter, formerly almost silent, come out of her shell to play Mary Magdalene in an Easter pageant with the encouragement of our youth director. I have had the joy of seeing my nonverbal sons, after many weary hours of us holding them up to God in therapies, come to say, "In the name of the Father and the Son and the Holy Spirit" while they make their crosses.

The kindness and patience and prayerful presence of my fellow Orthodox Christians are virtues that have made my struggles into virtues too, because they have made a way for me to share what God has given me. Their welcome and their flexibility in learning to bring us into the life of the Church have given my children that precious gift I was given as a child: to know that God is with them, and they are called for a purpose. In fact, as we will see in this book, God has given some people disabilities for their salvation and the salvation of the whole Church.

When I began the process of writing this book three years ago, I was facing the prospect of teaching my fully nonverbal youngest son about the life of faith. I remember standing at the icon corner after we received the results of his earliest evaluations—the ones that showed him at the bottom of the scale of communication ability, among other challenges—and looking from my dear son to the cross on the wall. Here was a child given to me by God, a miracle child whose severe birth defect had saved his life from an even worse birth defect, and a group of experts handed me a page with a few pictures on it and the advice, "Maybe he will eventually be able to associate these pictures with things he wants."

But the images of what I wanted for him were right in front of me on the icon wall. I wanted my boy to know God. The old fire that had been with me since my own childhood rose up, and I told God, "You taught Saint Anthony to read in the desert with the help of angels. You have taught countless saints who had no one but You. You teach him to read. You put Your Word in his heart. Write Yourself there." A few days later, my totally nonverbal son spelled on his magnet board, "Hodegetria," the name of the icon of the Theotokos, "She Who Shows the Way," from an iconography video he liked to watch. A couple of days after that, he wrote us a request when he wanted to go outside. God was already with my son, but that moment, that sign when he spelled out our help from the Theotokos, made me realize that God was at work in my son's *disability*.

There have been many struggles in each of my children's lives that have challenged me to look for the mercy of God reaching us right where we were, but my eyes had been opened with that simple word on the magnet board. I started to look for places where my family's autism revealed God's grace at work. After a few months of participating in my son's cutting-edge speech therapy, I began adapting his interventions for use in church. I found myself making lots of connections with other Orthodox parents of children with disabilities, especially once I shared resources such as visual schedules for the Divine Liturgy and nonverbal prayer aids. I found that families were facing a wide range of challenges and degrees of welcome into the life of the Church.

Some of the families had been welcomed and felt close to God despite the hardships they faced. Many of them were overwhelmed not only with the struggles to meet their children's needs, but with a sense of isolation from the church community and from God. As I listened and walked with my brothers and sisters in the Orthodox special-needs community, I noticed a great need for resources to help families with disabilities* to understand themselves within the saving love of God in the Church. A great need exists for teaching that is accessible and practical and, above all, in touch with the intimate love of God, who is saving us in the Church.

Like the parents who brought their children for Jesus to bless, many parents felt that they were rebuked in their attempts to bring their children to God. Some of these families had encountered misunderstanding like I met in some of the people around me when I was growing up. Some of these families had been treated as though they or their children were an embarrassment to God. And some had encountered welcome that gives right glory to God and opens the way of salvation for the whole Body of the Church. That's why this book is titled *Of Such Is the Kingdom*.

We live in a time when living with disabilities is more probable than ever, in part because we have medical interventions that help fragile life to thrive, and in part because the structure of society has changed so that some formerly hidden disabilities have been brought to light. One in every five persons lives with a disability. Yet, just as communities bear the burden of illness, families bear the burden of disabilities. There is no way to speak of a child who eats through a feeding tube without speaking of his family who feeds him, or of a girl who communicates with a speech output device without speaking of the parents who taught her to use it, or of children with hearing

---

* I use the shorthand "families with disabilities" to refer to families that include one or more members (whether parents or children) who have any kind of disability.

and sight impairments without the families who guide them through the sighted and hearing worlds. Throughout this book, I will speak of *families with disabilities* in order to reflect the truth that for every child born with a disability, an entire family is fundamentally reoriented around that disability.[1]

Families with disabilities are often singled out for blame and excluded. The challenges of living with disability often make church life difficult to engage for such families, especially when the disability is invisible. Invisible disabilities such as neurodivergence (e.g., autism, ADHD, and learning disabilities) and chronic conditions (e.g., Crohn's disease, arthritis, food allergies, genetic syndromes, and celiac disease) isolate families from the broader community and, tellingly, from church communities. This book will address welcome for persons and families with all types of disabilities, with special focus on ways to include these most-excluded groups. This is because, as I researched for this book, I found that persons and families with the types of disabilities that cause social and communication challenges also encounter the greatest challenges to inclusion in the Church.[2] Families of children with invisible disabilities such as autism are far less likely to ever set foot in a church than families with no disability or with visible disabilities such as mobility challenges, blindness, or Down syndrome.

We recognize the lack of inclusion in this case by taking note of the people missing from our services. This means that we can only see the degree of the problem of welcome by counting the people who aren't showing up in church. As the Association of Religion Data Archives reports, "The odds of a child with autism never attending religious services [are] nearly twice as high as compared to children with no chronic health conditions."[3] Studies vary about attendance for families who try to go but get rebuffed from church communities, but many families with an autistic member stop going to church because there is no tangible mercy extended to them to help them attend.[4] No formal studies show how these numbers are reflected specifically in the Orthodox Church, but this overall trend holds steady across Christian denominations. The Assembly of Canonical Orthodox Bishops of the United States of America calls us to work to overcome the barriers, or handicaps, to inclusion by focusing on how God relates to us:

> Handicaps are in fact the barriers that we create for people with disabilities by excluding them socially and physically. There are many persons with disabilities even in our own parishes; nevertheless, our parishes have not reached out sufficiently to adults and children with disabilities in its [sic] ministry. Indeed, the reality of disability is often shrouded in silence or shame because the presence of disability challenges basic assumptions and stereotypes. Therefore, it would be useful for us to recall the fundamental theological principles that should guide our pastoral ministry and practical response as we realize our mission as Church to be a welcoming communion. "God shows no partiality." (Gal. 2.6) "For the Lord does not see as we see; we see the outward appearance, but the Lord looks at the heart." (1 Sam. 16:7)[5]

One out of every five persons in the world has a disability. If we want to reverse the trend of people leaving the Orthodox Church as they enter adulthood, the exclusion of families with disabilities, especially invisible disabilities, adds to the demographic concerns that are symptoms of a need to recenter church culture.

Yet it is not concern about church growth that has inspired the writing of this book, but the desire to help each of us welcome others as Christ has welcomed us (Rom. 15:7). Full inclusion of families with disabilities into the life of the Orthodox Church is the stuff of the Kingdom of God, because we are all members of the same Body of Christ, whether or not we live with a disability in our family. When we learn how to welcome everyone into the Orthodox Church, with the help of our Tradition, one another, and the practical exercises and resources in this book and the accompanying website, we will learn to live with the humility of children whom God welcomes—not as embarrassments, but as His own beloved creation.

Why a Practical Theology of Disability?

Years before I became a mother to five autistic children, I was walking alongside my student, who drove a motorized wheelchair along a sidewalk on our university campus. She was the brightest in her class, and we were discussing a fine point in one of the works of St. Gregory of Nyssa as we went. We paused as a car slowed beside us and a young man got out to stand in front of us.

"May we help you?" I asked.

"Miss," he said to my student, "if you will believe in Jesus, you can stand up out of that wheelchair and walk."

My jaw dropped. A hundred rebukes came to mind. *How dare he attack this woman, who has devoted her life to studying the Lord, as though she lacked faith?* Thankfully, before I could draw breath to tell the man what I thought, my student spoke up.

"Sir," she said, "this wheelchair is an answer to my prayers. I know Jesus, and He gave me this wheelchair so I can fulfill the call He has placed on my life."

As I began to write this book, hundreds of passages from the Bible and the Fathers came to mind, pointing to the grace of God. But my student's quick and grace-filled words that day also come to mind. We need a *practical* theology of disability so that we can give a word in season and an answer to the hope that is in us, right in the midst of the challenges of life. We need a *practical* theology of disability so that we can give thanks in everything that God has brought into our lives. Like my student so many years ago, we have to know what God is like not only in our heads, but in our daily lives and in the real, sacred, disabled bodies God has given us in the Church for our salvation.

Structure
This book is a practical theology of disability in several senses. First, I have kept the chapters short and included bullet points and discussion questions at the end of each one. This is so that you can read this book with more ease and greater understanding in your family, book group, church school class, seminar, ministry class, or as a whole church community.

Second, I am applying the truths of the patristic tradition to questions and challenges that arise from life with disabilities. Because I have read the Fathers and the Bible for over three decades with my unusual brain, I have noticed patterns of grace that I hope will offer healing and examples of virtue for each of you and your communities. I have brought these patterns forward as simply and plainly as I could so that they might encourage you.

Third, this book not only tells you about God and disabilities but invites you to practice thinking about disability and welcome in a God-centered way. Each section of the book includes chapters that invite you to reflect on real stories from your fellow Orthodox Christians. You will also be asked to reflect on key biblical passages with discussion questions and insights from the Fathers. In some sections, I also introduce prayer strategies that fit particularly well into family life with disabilities.

Finally, this book is practical because I have gathered resources and best practices from other Orthodox Christians who welcome families with disabilities in their homes and churches. Every story here is shared with the blessing of a priest in the hope of encouraging and building one another up in faith.

The sections of the book are centered around four parts of Orthodox Christian life that are in reality all interwoven at all times. For the purpose of taking a closer look at some of the important ideas that will help us grow in Christ, I have broken up the topics into these focus areas:

KAIROS: *God's Time Reveals*

First, I will talk about how we can know the meaning of our bodies by taking a view from God's time. Here we will also take apart some of the confusing ideas we might have about disabilities and illnesses and make a beginning on welcome. We look at Christ as our model in this section and see how our baptisms change the way we experience suffering from disabilities.

THEOSIS: *Becoming Like God in Weakness*

Next, I talk about our salvation, becoming like God through participation in the sacraments, prayers, and virtues. God became human so that we might become like Him and so that we might encounter Him through our senses. I offer a theological reading of attention and learning and lay out some best practices for teaching to and praying with people with disabilities.

KENOSIS: *Self-Emptying Disables the Disability*

This section will dig more deeply into how virtues—ways we imitate Christ—make us like God and also show how we can minister to each other. We will see what grace looks like when it's poured out on and from Orthodox Christians with disabilities. Not only do we exercise virtue through serving our disabled fellow Christians, but we also experience the grace of their ministries to others. The highest virtue is the greatest gift of the Holy Spirit, love.

KOINONIA: *The Iconic Community*

The community of the Church is an icon of God's love that bears one another's burdens. A community that acts like God lives with them will welcome families with special needs. In this section, we will talk about best practices for building a community that includes families with disabilities.

This book will show you how to see God in life with disabilities. It will show you how to fully include families living with disabilities into your church community. It will show you how to develop faith practices that will put you in the habit of knowing that God sees you and is with you. It will apply the ancient wisdom of the Church about our salvation to the questions raised by living fully in a church with disabilities among her members. Above all, this book will help you to see how God is already with us in this work, for it is God's presence with us that gives us hope.

SUMMARY

» Disabilities do not embarrass God. Rather, they are for our salvation and to reveal the glory of God.

» We must remove the barriers from families with disabilities so that they can enter the full life of the Church. We do this for the sake of God, who welcomes us and who has made us for His glory.

» Families with invisible disabilities face the most obstacles to inclusion.

» The book is structured to be used in groups. The sections are: God's Time Reveals (Kairos), Becoming Like God in Weakness (Theosis), Self-Emptying Disables the Disability (Kenosis), and The Iconic Community (Koinonia).

REFLECTION QUESTIONS

1. Handicaps are barriers to accessibility or inclusion that we can change or remove. Wheelchair ramps are an example of an accommodation that removes the handicap of not being able to get up steps. What are some disabilities you've heard of? What are some handicaps that you can help overcome?

2. The bishops have asked us to focus on the fact that God shows no partiality. Yet, we might be in the habit of ignoring the needs of families with disabilities who come to our churches. What are some ways that you can treat people as equal sharers in the grace of God?

3. Do you think less of people who cannot communicate well? Thinking about someone who speaks another language might help you to accept people with communication challenges. If you wanted to welcome that person, you would try to learn his or her language, too. Ask the Holy Spirit to help

you understand, just as He taught all people on the Day of Pentecost.

4. What are you hoping to learn in studying with this book? Talk with your priest about your ideas and questions, and ask him for guidance in praying as you study.

PART ONE

Kairos

"It is time for the Lord to act."

CHAPTER I

God's Time Reveals

A T THE END OF ORTHROS, just before the Divine Liturgy begins, the deacon says to the priest or bishop, "It is time for the Lord to act." God, who is simple[6] and beyond time, is always who He is, but we experience a transformation of time at this moment, when the world teeters on the cusp of eternity, when we draw a breath and catch the fragrance of the breath of God.[7] When we step into the Divine Liturgy, time is watered through with eternity. Christ is with us, and suddenly, we know His presence more fully than at any other time in our lives.[8] It's with that beautiful foretaste of God's time that we start this book, because we see the beauty of disabled bodies in our churches in the light of eternity-in-time. When God acts, we learn that disability of body does not hinder grace entering the soul.[9]

It's important to start our inquiry about the theology of disability with a look at God's appointed time, the time when God acts, for several reasons:

» First, doing so sets our thoughts in the perspective of all of salvation history.

» Second, when we reason from God's time, we see that God is already acting in the lives of the people He has drawn to church. This realization cuts off any temptation to judge or shame or exclude families with disabilities, because we realize that the God who made all people is here among us.

» Third, we know that living with disabilities places demands on time, and we must learn new ways to minister to people whose additional needs extend over their entire lives.

We do not know how we will be in the resurrection, but we know that even now disabilities do not hinder the grace of God from entering our souls. When we work together in love for the whole community of God's Church, we remove handicaps to the Church's disabled members. When we act in love for God and our neighbors, we become part of the heavenly Church.

Always Taking Place

In the Divine Liturgy, we experience a foretaste of heaven. The resurrected Lord is among us, and, as St. John of Kronstadt tells us, "we celebrate, in the risen Christ, the universal resurrection from the dead."[10] In Christ's presence, we are who we are meant to be. This is because time in the Divine Liturgy is Resurrection time, time akin to the physical but also to the spiritual, resurrected body of Christ. Saint Gregory of Nyssa describes this now and always and not-yet time in his sister St. Macrina's words: "Although it is always taking place, it has not yet taken place."[11] In the Divine Liturgy we are present not only in the way we have been and in the way we are, but also in a foretaste of how we will be. This is a bodily truth, not only a spiritual one, and it applies to disabled bodies as well as abled ones.

To be who God has made us to be is the hope of all

Christians, and it is a balm to Christians with disabilities in particular. This is because persons with disabilities are frequently treated as though they are persons whom God did not will, as though their existence were somehow outside of God's Providence. That sort of misguided treatment is due to the discomfort that people feel when faced with a person whose very existence highlights human frailty. People don't like to be confronted with their own frailty, and often they lash out at or push away people who remind them that being made by God and receiving God's grace is by no means a guarantee of bodily health and an easy life. Yet every Christian belongs in the Divine Liturgy. Every Christian, including the disabled Christian, is who God has made him to be when he steps or is carried or is wheeled into the presence of Christ.

We start with God's time because of this hard truth that is made plain when we step into the presence of God: everything we have, including our disabilities, is given to us by our loving God, for our salvation. This salvation is not only personal salvation but the salvation of the whole Body of Christ that is the Church. The suffering of a member is but part of the suffering of Christ. It is wrong to draw away from the suffering members, because as a Body we must treat kindly what is weak or in need of special care (see 1 Cor. 12:22–26). This hard truth, that we are who God has made us to be in the Divine Liturgy, is also a source of great joy. Just as every member of the Body ought to bear the burdens of the rest, so every member shares the joy of Christ's presence with us. The sharing of Resurrection time and of burden and of joy is accomplished in love, and this book will explore the practical ways that love calls us to be knit together as one Body.

> Indeed, the reality of disability is often shrouded in silence
> or shame because the presence of disability challenges basic
> assumptions and stereotypes.[12]

The time when God acts shows us who we are and exposes our secret fears and our common joys. It also reveals misleading and nonsense questions about disability for what they are. These are the questions that do not bear good fruit, because they are asked on false premises.[13]

Chief among these misleading questions is the question that the disciples asked about the man born blind: "Who sinned, this man or his parents, that he was born blind?" (John 9:1). This question usually comes about slyly, by asking in fear and often smugness about the cause of the disability with which someone was born. Whoever asks such a question believes that she can avoid disability by being smarter or better at following rules than persons with disabilities or their families. Of course, someone who asks such a question implies that a parent of a child with a birth defect or neurological condition caused the disability somehow. Even worse, the asker believes disability, and perhaps the person who has it, to be an evil, something not from God. The asker cannot understand evil apart from being deprived of doing what one pleases and cannot see the blessing for the whole Church that comes with the inclusion of a Christian with disabilities.

The second biggest nonsense question is usually presented as a challenge. "If you had faith, you would not be disabled." Of course, this statement is true in one sense, that if we all lived in faith with God, people with disabilities would live as though they had no disabilities. Our love for one another would not be hindered by inequalities created from our own false worship of ideas and forms that are not God. But in the usual way it is intended, the statement is really a question. "Did not this disability come upon you because you fail to believe?" That hidden question reveals the anxiety of people facing their mortality in fear when they see the weakness of a fellow Christian. It is as though they see in their disabled neighbor a reminder of their own weakness and ask, "Can I avoid death by believing?" The answer, of course, is no. We are all going to die. But all of us, disabled and abled together, are united with Christ, who is risen from the dead, who is trampling down death by death and has granted life to those in the tombs. Fr. John Chryssavgis writes,

> Our ministry to children and adults with disability presents us with more than a chance to serve our neighbor. It presents us with a challenge to our culture where worldly image (rather than God's image) is a priority, where ideal perfection is valued and weakness disdained, and where virtues alone are emphasized and failures are concealed. It is a witness to the centrality and visibility of the Cross in our lives and in our intentions.[14]

Families with disabilities are excluded from the full life of the Church when others treat them as though their disability were due to lack of faith. But a person with a disability who comes to church is already living the resurrection life in foretaste spiritually, even though he still suffers weakness in body or mind. He has stepped into the time when God acts, Resurrection time, which gives us a foretaste of eternity in the Kingdom of God.

This matters to us, because faith teaches us to reason from the Resurrection when we want to know how to treat one another and how to live in our own bodies. Just as the judgment at the last resurrection shows us that how we treat one another is how we treat the Lord (see Matt. 25:31–46), so it shows us that how we live in our bodies should reflect our resurrection goal of communion with God and one another. The Fathers tell us that people with disabilities are not excluded from the presence of God in the resurrection. Rather, it is in our very weakness that Christ's strength is made perfect.[15]

Reasoning from the Resurrection

In order to act and discern well, the pattern of tradition tells us, we must know what we are aiming toward. For human relationships and knowledge of human nature, we look to Christ, our Alpha and Omega, who will raise us up on the last day. This life is only a small part of the eternal life, and our bodies now are only the beginning of what they will become in eternal life with God. Since we know that all of our relationships will be restored in heaven, we begin to live in restored relationships now. Since we know that all of our bodies will be in full communion with God in the resurrection, we honor the body now.

The holiness bestowed on every one of us in baptism and chrismation is the beginning, and we honor what we do not yet see as well when in faith we confess the "one holy catholic and apostolic Church" and "the resurrection of the dead and the life of the age to come."[16] We do not know what our resurrected bodies will look like, but we know that we will be like Christ when He appears (1 John 3:2). We know that after His Resurrection the Lord remained circumscribed in His body so that His disciples could touch His hands and feet.[17] The resurrected Christ was still fully God and fully human, and He still had the properties of human nature. But what does our Lord's example mean for those of us with disabilities? There is a tendency to rest our hopes on our own understandings of what resurrected bodies might be like. This tendency can lead us to overlook the holiness of the people before us now if we make the mistake of trusting in our own understandings about a fully restored, holy body, rather than following Christ's command to love one another as He loves us. The reliance on one's own imagination leads to misleading questions and attitudes, not because we are always wholly wrong in our imaginations, but because even holy imagination must be submitted to Christ.

Thus there are two usual paths of misguided imaginings, those of able-bodied people and those of people born with disabilities. Those who are born with disabilities might not be able to conceive of a way of knowing God without their disabilities, because for them, disability is part of their way of salvation. It is as disabled persons that they have always known and loved and followed God.

When people without disabilities or who remember a time without them wistfully speak of the resurrection for people with disabilities, they usually express a desire that the disability will be gone. To those without disabilities, their way of knowing God has never been with disabled bodies. They imagine an ideal resurrected body that is free from disabilities, because they cannot conceive knowing God fully otherwise.

It's true that no one will be disabled in the resurrection, but what exactly that means is still mysterious.[18] Perhaps in the resurrection, God the "Almighty Artist" will remake those of us with disabilities whole in an ideal but recognizable way, without bodily sign of our lifetime disability.[19] Perhaps we will bear in our bodies the marks of our disabilities as trophies of virtues that we practiced and that others in the Church practiced on our behalf.[20] The Fathers teach us that all inequalities will be gone, but we have no certainty about what that means bodily. The Fathers mean that anything that keeps us from the fullness of communion with God will be gone, but we already know that God can give grace to every soul He creates. There is nothing on heaven or on earth or under the earth able to separate us from the love of God in Christ Jesus our Lord (Rom. 8:38–39).

These bodies are like seeds that will rise to a new glory that we cannot yet imagine (John 12:24). But we know that when we rise again, we will be like the Lord. The Lord bore the wounds of His Passion in His resurrected body. Yet, His body was not disabled in His Resurrection by having been nailed to the Cross. He conquered death in His body and rose in it. It may be that in ways we cannot understand, we are both brought into wholeness in the resurrection and also still show some signs in our bodies of the limitations that we lived with in this life.

Whether we are mended in the resurrection so that every sign of disability fades in an ideal version of ourselves, or whether we bear some marks of our disabilities—but without limiting communion with God and one another because of God's grace—we know that these very bodies, whether they be disabled in any way or fully abled and healthy, are the ones that will rise again. This means that we ought to treat one another now with the full dignity that we will be able to perceive then, when all of our earthly vices and sins will no longer cloud our eyes to the image of God in one another. What will certainly be removed is shame and inability to cling to God in love. We will love our neighbors as ourselves, and God will be all in all. Nothing can stop grace entering the soul, and in the resurrection we will all be filled with the love of God.

Adapted for Joy

People often wish that those with disabilities should be free of them in the resurrection, but another question is hidden in the wish for an end to bodily suffering or struggle. Sometimes people mistake the resurrection as a transfer to a disembodied state. But the change that will come is not from bodies to no bodies, but rather from our bodies now, which are adapted for the struggle for virtue, to these same bodies once they are adapted to the experience of joy. This is why St. Augustine reminds us:

> What is required to ensure the soul's blessedness, then, is not an escape from any kind of body whatsoever but the acquisition of an incorruptible body. And what incorruptible body could be better adapted to the joy of those who rise again than the one in which they groaned when it was corruptible?[21]

In the resurrection, these bodies in which we struggle will be adapted for fullness of joy. So in foretaste all bodies, including disabled ones, experience the Divine Liturgy, where we encounter the presence of Christ. When we make adaptations for Orthodox Christians to come to church, we are not only making room for them to get in the door—which is an important first step!—but we must adapt our welcome with the aim of sharing the full joy of the Lord. All of us will experience the full joy of God's presence when these very bodies are transformed in the resurrection. If we can make room and bend a little toward bearing one another's burdens, we will adapt now for resurrection joy in the Lord. We will experience the joy of the Lord in foretaste as we welcome people with disabled bodies into the full life of the Body of Christ, the Church.

Prayer Shows Us the Image of God in Disabled Persons

Please tell people that there is more to us bringing our child to church than praying for immediate healing.
—AN ORTHODOX CHRISTIAN MOTHER OF A DISABLED CHILD

When you pray for children and adults who live with disabilities, there is nothing wrong with asking God to give them perfect health. But there are many other benefits to request in prayer as well, so that God will adapt their bodies and the Body of the Church for joy. Remember that the person before you is already who God has made them to be. Her disabled body is already the seed of her eternal, resurrected body, a body that God deems worthy of saving and bringing into fullness of joy. Approach persons with disabilities in prayer the way you would any other Christian—with the love of God, with trust in the healing presence of God, and with sensitivity to their needs. Some of the things you might ask in prayer for people with disabilities include:

» Consolation from the Holy Spirit
» Peace of heart and mind
» Good access to the best medical care
» Good options for the next best steps for them and their families
» Provision for all of their needs
» Virtue to prosper in their struggles
» Hope and faith and love
» Kindness from others wherever they go

» That the goodness and love and glory of God be revealed in and through their lives
» Protection from harm
» For the love of Christ to shine in their hearts

When we pray, we are not alone, because the Holy Spirit is always praying with us (see Rom. 8:15–17). We can also ask the holy unmercenary physicians to pray for our loved ones and church members living with disabilities. There are many holy unmercenaries recognized by the Orthodox Church and many other saints also known to help especially with healings. Some of the holy unmercenaries are Sts. Cosmas and Damian, St. Panteleimon, St. Luke of Crimea, Sts. Cyrus and John, St. Anastasia the Healer, St. Thallelaius, St. Samson, St. Hermolaus, St. Diomedes, St. Hermione, and Sts. Zenaida and Philonella. If you are unsure how to pray for someone with a disability, ask these saints to pray for them, too. Their wisdom and love will guide your requests to the Lord.

Summary

» When we gather for the Divine Liturgy, we experience both the Cross of Christ and a foretaste of the resurrection.

» Reasoning from the resurrection shows us that the usual misleading questions about persons and families with disabilities are not rooted in the way God acts. We have to trust in God and look to Christ for our model of how to love one another now, because the resurrected Lord tells us we will all be one in His love when we are resurrected.

» We become more of who we will be when we enter God's time, the foretaste of the resurrection, in the Divine Liturgy. Our bodies in which we struggle now, even if they are disabled, will be adapted for joy in the resurrection.

» Our treatment of one another should honor the gift of how God made us as we experience the foretaste of the resurrection. That means we should not exclude people with disabilities from church but should do all we can to bring them into the anticipation of this future joy that we will all share.

» When we pray for people with disabilities, we should also keep the fullness of God's time in mind. We should pray for the full person and the full lives of the families who come to us with disabled members, because God, who can and will restore us all, is already fitting us for joy.

REFLECTION QUESTIONS

1. What makes you uncomfortable about people with disabilities? Do your feelings change when you remember the Cross and Resurrection of our Lord?

2. Have you thought before about Christ's presence in the Divine Liturgy bringing joy to us (blessing us) as we are now? What aspect of your life reminds you of what God made you to be and calls you to be when you enter Christ's presence? Which characteristic of a loved one with a disability seems different if you look at him in Christ's presence?

3. Reasoning from the resurrection is like steering a ship or a vehicle based on your final destination. What would change for you if you tried to live now as you will live in the resurrection?

4. What are some prayers you pray when you are going through a hard time? What are some prayers you pray when you are happy? Have you thought of praying the same way on behalf of families with disabilities in your church?

CHAPTER 2

Illness versus Disability

*Each of us is born the way that we are—with the gifts that
we all have, as well as with the weaknesses that we all
have—"in order that God's works might be revealed in us."*
—Fr. John Chryssavgis[22]

WHATEVER WE HAVE IS GIVEN to us for our salvation.
God does not create evil. God works all things together
for good. So how do we talk about God being with us in sickness and disability? When the Fathers talk about sickness,
they reason about it with the same pattern that they use to
talk about evil. Evil does not exist as a thing in itself, but
rather evil comes from a falling away from good. This idea is
called the *privation* theory of evil. It means simply that God
makes good out of nothing, and anything that isn't good has
turned away from God back toward nothing. It's good news
to us, because there is no opposing force to God. There is only
one God, the Father and the Son and the Holy Spirit.

With sickness, the reasoning is similar. God creates health,
and sickness is a falling away from health. This idea is the
privation theory of illness. It means that God makes us for
perfect health, but we sometimes get sick because we are out

of balance with the good, or we experience illness because some other problem is affecting us. Sin is a common human problem that has knocked us off course so that we die. That common human sin sometimes causes each of us to get sick, whether or not we personally acted out of balance with the good in such a way as to provoke illness. Sickness sometimes has particular causes, like overeating that leads to indigestion, or substance abuses that cause bodily damage. At other times sickness has general causes, like catching a cold even though you wash your hands well, or developing a dangerous disease through no fault of your own. The roadmap for exploring illness as it relates to God tells us that sickness is due to a set of wrong turns, either by our own fault or simply because humans as a whole have curved off the narrow road of health that God intended.

When we turn from looking at illness to looking at disability, we see some important differences. First, unlike illnesses that come and go, disabilities are often present from the beginning of life and are usually permanent. Unlike sickness, which we all experience, only about twenty percent of people are disabled, though most people who are not personally affected will have a loved one who is.[23] Most disabilities are not within a family's control, either, so when we talk about disabilities we do not focus on avoiding sin to prevent them.

Sickness is part of the human condition common to all, whereas disability is a limitation borne in the bodies of only some of us. The teaching of the Church takes these differences into account, emphasizing that disabilities are given to us in order to reveal God's work among us in a variety of ways, including spiritual consolations, opportunities for virtue, or healings both spiritual and physical.

What to Make of the Scriptural Examples

One of the challenges of living as faithful Christians with disabilities is that our scriptural examples are mostly people whom Jesus or His disciples healed. Though there are other examples, which we will examine below, the people in our churches are most familiar with the healing stories. The pattern of the stories that has stuck in common memory is that a person with a disability encountered Jesus, who healed the person, told them to sin no more, and often commended the person for having great faith, as well.

But does being born with disabilities, or otherwise acquiring them and living with them our whole lives, mean that Christians today lack faith? Or is something else going on? After all, God doesn't change, so healings should occur as frequently now as they did at the time of the Apostles. Has a lack of humility blocked God's work, in the same way that the villagers of Jesus' hometown blocked Him from healing many there (Matt. 13:58, Mark 6:5)? Are we arrogant now? Have we forgotten God? These are some of the misguided ideas that people offer to defend a certain way of seeing God's Providence when it comes to disabilities. But what parent, even a parent with only a little faith, would not give everything she has, would not humble herself or suffer any humiliation, on behalf of her child?

In fact, these questions about the cause of disabilities are not based in the character of God at all; rather, they put God to the test. (See Deut. 6:16; Matt. 4:7; Luke 4:12.) These questions imply the following: that disabilities persist for lack of faith, that they persist because we are unwilling to humble ourselves, and that they persist because we have forgotten to ask God for help. But the real trouble here is that the questioners have set up a test for God by trying to explain why God doesn't immediately and totally heal all disabilities in the expected way. "If you are really God," they say in their hearts, "you will heal this person entirely and immediately."

But along with setting up this test for God, they set a test for their fellow human: "If you really believe in God, God will heal you entirely and immediately." Thus they add a test within a test: "If you really believe in God, and if God is really God, you will be healed immediately." Without realizing it, a person who thinks thus has rejected the Kingdom of God and not loved either God or his neighbor.

Saint Anthony the Great helps us out of this sort of trouble with an insightful reality check. "For to work signs is not ours. That is the Savior's doing," he tells us, with the understanding that we neither control nor know why God heals some people through signs and miracles.[24] But what are we to do, if we cannot summon miracles at a whim? We are to pursue virtues, not to rebuff one another because a miracle of a particular kind is not given.

Though Christ heals us in both soul and sometimes also in body, and though praying for healing is good, our work as Christians is to follow the commandments of God and to love God with all we have, and our neighbors as ourselves. In fact, St. Anthony tells us that this lifelong struggle in prayer and obedience is more important to our salvation (becoming like God) than whether we receive or even participate in miracles:

> Wherefore to those who boast of their miracles and not of their virtues, saying: *Lord, have we not cast out devils in thy name and wrought many miracles in thy name?* he answered: *Amen, I say to you I know you not.* For the Lord knows not the ways of the unholy.[25]

This need for holiness above miracles is what we should remember when we hear or read about miracles of healing and the ancient sermons on the subject. The Fathers sometimes conflated disability with sickness as the results of sinful living in order to warn their listeners away from poor choices. Still, they taught that the gospel stories about healing were lessons for everyone on how to live in virtue. This struggle for virtues, both then and now, is fueled by the consoling Holy Spirit, who brings us benefits, even in our disabilities, in the same way that Christ bedewed the three children in the fiery furnace.[26] Disability is the fiery trial that bears witness to the presence of Christ with us.

Disabilities and the Value of Virtues

Sermons on the paralytic (or paralytics) in the gospels demonstrate these trends.[27] Saint Gregory Palamas teaches about the spiritual meaning of the healing of the paralytics "as a pattern for virtue."[28] The healings of the blind men also are a call to "follow the light which illumines both soul and body,"[29] now that our minds have been opened to the truth of the Resurrection just as their eyes were opened. Saint Cyril of Jerusalem's "Sermon on the Paralytic" focuses on how Christ heals him so that he (the paralytic) can imitate His (Christ's) virtues.[30] The sermon centers on the beautiful spiritual meaning of the litter, or bed, that Christ told the paralytic to take up.[31] Saint Cyril draws a connection between the healed man using the bed to carry away old inclinations to sin—the passions—and Christ's Cross as the bed in the Song of Songs—His Passion that heals and redirects our misguided passions. We come to see the bed that the paralytic took up to follow the Lord as a metaphor for the Cross.

Whether or not we are healed in body as well as soul, the metaphor stands, for Christ "is a versatile doctor, sometimes healing the soul first, and then the body, sometimes following the reverse order."[32] Even if bodily healing is not fulfilled in this lifetime (as is true for most of us living with disabilities), yet we are to take up that bed, that cross of imitating Christ, and "let the soul rule the body and not be at the beck and call of animal instincts."[33] By "animal instincts," St. Cyril means our desires for bodily goods and power over others. No matter our disabilities or our abilities to move and reason, this healing of Christ is still available to our souls. (We will talk more about how disabilities affect learning and the freedom of our wills in the sections on Theosis and Kenosis.)

Another trend in the ancient teaching calls not only the persons living with disabilities but also the community around them to seek to live virtuously. When we encounter persons with disabilities, we are to treat them with the honor with which we would treat the Lord and to welcome them as though we are entertaining "angels unawares" (Heb. 13:2).[34]

Faith with Disabilities

Regarding the healing of persons with disabilities in Scripture, notable exceptions to the biblical pattern are Jacob, who became disabled as a result of wrestling with God, and the Apostle Paul, whose "thorn in the flesh" was given him along with Christ's words, "My grace is sufficient for you, for my power is made perfect in weakness" (2 Cor. 12:9). These examples are relevant to the chief message about the meaning of disabilities. These were two great figures of faith who became disabled *after* they had experienced encounters with God and believed.

Just as disabilities feed the disillusionment with the body that is a precursor to the virtues,[35] so these heroes of the faith experienced pain in their bodies to remind them to rely on God. Disability was given as a gift and a sign to these men, in the same way that disability was removed from others in the healings in the Gospels. All ideas of self-sufficiency were stripped away from Jacob by that hip stricken by God and from Paul by that thorn in the flesh. Through those signs they remembered that knowing God and loving Him were more important than the power He had given them. The disabilities in their cases gave them what they needed for their salvation.

When Samson had been rendered blind, God returned his extraordinary strength without returning to him his sight. This is another example of someone doing the will of God while disabled. I point out these three—Jacob, Samson, and the Apostle Paul—as examples because each of them was known for his extraordinary faith in God. We have to lay aside the idea that faith always cures disabilities, because we can have faith *and* disabilities. Sometimes God gives us signs of healing that we receive in faith, but most often God gives us signs of our need of Him. That is what faith reveals to us: the true desire and need of our hearts and whole beings to commune with God. We need God and should set our hearts on Him, whether we believe with or without disabilities.

Suffering shifts our focus from only enjoying our bodies to enjoying the God who made us so that, as St. Gregory Palamas said, "the affliction [disability] is a remedy from God."[36] Disabilities are afflictions that heal. Because the presence of God in the Divine Liturgy transforms time and space and the entirety of daily life of the community of God,[37] disability shows us that God is never gone from us, no matter how much we suffer. The love of God works through our brokenness just as God worked with Jacob and Samson and the Apostle Paul.

God's Time Reveals

It is impossible that the creation of any man would be superfluous in a universe where not even the creation of a single leaf of a tree is superfluous.

—St. Augustine[38]

As our prayers tell us, God is everywhere present and fills all things.[39] As St. Cyril of Jerusalem tells us, "Whatever the Holy Spirit touches is hallowed and changed."[40] Even if we did not have other witnesses from the Tradition, these two statements would be sufficient to show us that Christians with disabilities are holy. We know furthermore that the people whom God has made with disabilities are not superfluous, and that God's strength is made perfect in weakness. This is how people with disabilities reveal the glory of God. The glory of God is not far off but is interwoven in our daily life, and suffering, like His presence, is interwoven with every part of the universe.

In his book *Everywhere Present*, Fr. Stephen Freeman diagnoses the trouble with seeing a separation between the secular world and the world that God inhabits:

> The two-storey universe is another way of describing a secular culture. The word *secular* should never be confused with *atheist*. Instead it refers to a separation between our daily life and God.[41]

Rather, we should understand that our Faith is grounded in an understanding of the world as a one-storey universe, where God and the saints and the living and dead are all together.

We dwell in this one-storey universe when we enter into God's time. Time and space have been transformed in the Eucharist, the time when God acts, and the entire Church and our communities carry that transformed reality into the world.

Disabilities are a gift of witness to that world where God is with us. They are an opportunity to partake of heavenly joy in foretaste, for the God of heaven is with us. To embrace a person with disabilities fully into the Orthodox Church, we have to lay aside all illusions of a secular space or time that is separated from God. Truly, God invites us into His Kingdom, where it is time for the Lord to act. That is why disabilities are afflictions that heal not only the person but also the community, for we cannot love God, whom we have not seen, unless we love our disabled brothers and sisters, whom we have seen. We can only see their holiness by welcoming them into the Church, where the Holy Spirit touches and hallows them. We can only be holy by following the commandments to love God and our neighbors.

Theosis, Not Theodicy

Making the most of the time, because the days are evil.

—EPH. 5:16

This view of disability as a call to holiness in God's time is the reason the question we Orthodox ask is not, "Why do bad things happen to good people?" but, "How is this disability for our salvation, and not only the salvation of each person, but also the whole Body of Christ?" We live in God's time and God's space—in short, in God's world—and we have entered Christ's own suffering in baptism.[42] When we are united to Christ in His suffering, we receive the benefits of

His Resurrection and healing as well. We are not separated from God in a world apart from Him, but we are here in the time when God acts. There is nothing to stop the Savior from healing us. He is not absent or far away. But the fact that our disabilities remain, that we members of His Body still suffer under them, shows us that we need these struggles yet for our salvation.

Summary

» In the Church, some of the confusion and stereotypes that prevent inclusion of families with disabilities stem from treating disabilities in the same way as curable illnesses. But the teaching of the Church is a bit different in emphasis for disabilities.

» Rather than focusing on falling away from health and the need for repentance, disabilities are treated as an affliction that heals.

» The scriptural accounts of persons with disabilities are not always about signs of healing. Some notable exceptions— Jacob, Samson, and the Apostle Paul—were given disabilities as signs rather than receiving healings as signs.

» The trouble with signs is that we cannot perform them. They're God's work, while our work is to strive for holiness through virtues like obeying God and loving Him and our neighbor. There is no reason ever to accuse someone with disabilities for lack of faith. God gives disabilities to people with faith sometimes, sometimes even as a sign.

» We live in a one-storey universe where time and space are filled with God, who is everywhere present, and the transformed time of the Divine Liturgy carries over into our daily lives. Because of this, there is no boundary to living faithfully even with disabilities. Our disabled bodies are holy, too.

» Orthodox Christians do not worry about theodicy—Why do bad things happen to good people?—because of this transformed time and the presence of God. Rather, since we have all entered Christ's saving suffering in baptism, our question is, "How is this gift of disability for our salvation both as persons and as the community of the Body of Christ?"

REFLECTION QUESTIONS

1. In the Psalms and many historical teachings of the Church, afflictions like disabilities are seen as a source of humility that can open our hearts to God. Christ humbled Himself for our salvation so that nothing we face can separate us from the love of God. Yet the serpent in the Garden of Eden took his affliction as an opportunity to be prouder and more jealous than before. Affliction, then, does not on its own produce misery or humility or love, but it reveals the disposition of hearts. What kind of habits and ways of thinking might lead to a heart that grows humbler and more loving in the face of the burdens of disabilities?

2. Galatians 2:20 says, "I have been crucified with Christ; it is no longer I who live, but Christ who lives in me; and the life I now live in the flesh I live by faith in the Son of God, who loved me and gave himself for me" (RSV). How does disability show us what it is like to be crucified with Christ? If Christ lives in us, how does this reality change how we view the world and each other?

3. Knowing that we live in a world that is filled with the presence of God is absolutely necessary for living faithfully with disabilities. Spiritual consolation comes to us in the

suffering like the dew of Christ's presence kept the three holy children safe in the fiery furnace. We are made by God and are growing toward Him. Read this passage from a poem by Rainer Maria Rilke. Does it help you see yourself as someone whom God loves and has made for holiness?

> *Be modest now, like a thing*
> *ripened until it is real,*
> *so that he who began it all*
> *can feel you when he reaches for you.*[43]

CHAPTER 3

SPOTLIGHT
A Church That Won't Ask Me to Leave

This chapter is based on an interview with an autistic Orthodox Christian who wishes to be identified only as Garrison.[44]

When Garrison's daughter was six or eight years old, he asked a question: "Where are all the severely disabled children?"

Garrison's daughter had spina bifida. As a nurse and as a father, Garrison knew that she was not the only severely disabled child in his community. But he didn't see the other children at church.

"Where are they?"

He asked his pastor. The answers, to Garrison, sounded like excuses rather than reasons. So he asked again. His pastor told him that children with disabilities didn't want to come, because they were bitter toward God for how they were created. Or their parents didn't want to bring them, because they were angry with God.

But Garrison was there. He wasn't angry. His daughter was there. She wasn't bitter. He knew other families with disabled kids, and they weren't angry or bitter.

So Garrison kept asking. He asked, and he asked, until he was asked to leave the parish.

And that happened at the next church he attended, and the next.

A Question That Wouldn't Go Away

He wasn't asked to leave because of his autism—at least not directly. Although he hadn't yet been diagnosed when his daughter was born, he had been autistic all his life. And before his daughter was born, he was a valued member of his congregation.

But because of his autism, he didn't understand the subtle ways that social norms are communicated. And because of his autism, he didn't know how to tell when people didn't want to hear his question any more. He couldn't read body language or tone of voice. He understood words, and he believed what people told him.

So when people told him that his daughter was welcome at church, that they wanted her to be there, he believed them.

He believed that the churches wanted people with disabilities to attend.

So he kept asking his question: Where are they?

And he kept being asked to leave.

Finally, he gave up looking for another church.

But he didn't give up looking for an answer to his question: Where are the severely disabled children? Why aren't they in church?

Autism and Understanding

Being diagnosed with autism helped Garrison find an answer to his question. As he learned about himself and the way he relates to other people, he realized that every human needs to be included. It's the most important need we have.

When you violate social norms, other people pull away. This teaches you how you ought to behave and what you need to do to be included.

Most parents of severely disabled children get the message.

But a disability isn't something you can change. So parents learn to leave their severely disabled child at home, to make other people more comfortable. Maybe they find someone else to look after their child while they go to church. Maybe they quit going. But they understand that, when people at church say, "We welcome everyone," what they sometimes mean is, "We want to welcome everyone. But we don't. We only welcome you if you are like us."

Garrison, of course, didn't get the unspoken message. "I was oblivious," he admits.

Because he was oblivious, he brought his daughter to church. He sent her to Sunday school. But the Sunday school teachers planned activities she couldn't participate in. They didn't include her. Perhaps they wanted to include Garrison's daughter, but they didn't know how. Since they didn't explicitly discuss how to include her, implicit exclusion was the result. Garrison's daughter knew her teachers were uncomfortable. And people don't like to go where they make other people uncomfortable.

"You make them 'other,' and they stay away," Garrison explains, "and you don't have to feel guilty."

Finding the Orthodox Church
For two years, Garrison was without a church to attend. And then his son found the Orthodox Church and invited him to go along.

"I sat through one Vespers service. I had been trying to understand my whole life what worship was. At the end of Vespers, I told my son, 'You found it. That was worship.'"

True worship was something that Garrison was looking for. But there was something else he wanted, too.

"I'm looking for a church that won't ask me to leave."

After so many years, he was afraid of being rejected. And so, after he joined the Orthodox Church, he spent most of every service in the basement instead of in the nave.

He told himself that he was hiding to avoid hurting other people. And that was part of it, of course. He'd been told over and over that he'd hurt and offended other people because he didn't always follow social expectations. And he believed it.

But he was also afraid of being hurt. And, most especially, he was afraid of the chalice.

"At the chalice, I'm not in control," he explained. "At the chalice, God is not in control. It's not about control. Communion. It's about communion. I was afraid of that."

His wife and his priest are helping him through his fears. Whether he's in the basement or in the nave, he comes to church.

A Question Answered

Since becoming Orthodox, Garrison doesn't ask why there aren't severely disabled children at church. It's not because he's afraid to ask. He doesn't need to ask. He knows.

They don't come because they aren't sought.

Garrison thinks about the story of the man whose friends carried him with them when they went to see Jesus. And when they couldn't get into the house where Jesus was, they hauled him up to the roof. They made a hole in the roof and let him down through the hole. There wasn't a ramp. There was no elevator. There was only a desire to include their friend.

That desire is what's missing for Garrison's daughter. If she is to be included in the local Orthodox church, Garrison explains, "people have to seek her out, befriend her."

To bring people with disabilities into the church, you have to go where they are and spend time with them on their turf. You have to build relationships with them. You have to be a friend.

Not because they might someday go to church with you. Not because of anything they might do for you.

But only because of love.

DISCUSSION QUESTIONS

1. The story of Jesus healing a paralyzed man is in three of the gospels, with the detail that the friends lowered the man through the roof in two of the stories. Read Matthew 9:2–8, Mark 2:1–12, and Luke 5:17–26. What was Jesus' reaction? What was the crowd's reaction?

2. Why is it unusual to see people with disabilities in church? What are some ways that you could welcome a family like Garrison's?

3. What would it take for your family to feel welcome in church?

CHAPTER 4

A Closer Look at the Gospel

DISTRACTIONS OR KINGDOM BEARERS?

T HIS BOOK IS TITLED *Of Such Is the Kingdom* not only because it is addressed primarily to parents and church communities of children with disabilities, but because a great throng of little ones is waiting to be blessed in church life. They are waiting for us, like the disciples of Jesus, to remove the hindrances we have mistakenly put in place. Let's look at one of the ways we hinder families with disabilities from entering fully into the life of the Church: We see them as distractions.

Let's take a closer look at the passage in the Gospel of Luke where Jesus blesses the children and commands the disciples to allow them to come. This event happened after Jesus had performed amazing miracles and even raised the dead. It comes at the end of the story of Jesus' ministry, just before Palm Sunday and the week leading to His Passion. As such, it makes up part of a shift from glorious miracles to a focus on humility and teaching in preparation for the awesome events of the Crucifixion and Resurrection.

Just before the passage on blessing children, Jesus tells the story of the Pharisee and tax collector. Jesus ends His teaching by saying, "for every one who exalts himself will be humbled, but he who humbles himself will be exalted" (Luke 18:14). Next come the children in a three-verse passage. Immediately after our passage, the rich ruler approaches Jesus and asks what he should do to inherit eternal life. He goes away saddened at the cost asked of him. Jesus then begins to teach His disciples about the mysteries of the Cross, which they don't understand at that time. He heals a blind man on the road, whom the disciples told to leave Jesus alone, just like they had rebuked the children. The series of events shifts with the story of Zacchaeus, which takes us straight into the first Holy Week.

This context is important, because it shows us that Jesus blessed the children as a teaching and a sign. This blessing was an act at the height of Jesus' popularity, when His marvelous works were drawing crowds of thousands. Yet, even though they had seen Jesus raise the dead and heal the sick, the disciples rebuked the parents bringing the children, as well as the blind man who asked Jesus for healing along the road. Why is that? And what can we learn from their mistake and Jesus' teaching?

One of the ways we practice theology is to read our lives through the stories in the holy Tradition. When we do so, we can spot the patterns of mercy that God has set out for our salvation. For the rest of this chapter, read through this gospel passage and engage the reflection questions. Here is the passage in a modern translation (Luke 18:15–17 RSV):

> Now they were bringing even infants to him that he might touch them; and when the disciples saw it, they rebuked them. But Jesus called them to him, saying, "Let the children come to

OF SUCH IS THE KINGDOM

me, and do not hinder them; for to such belongs the kingdom of God. Truly I say to you, whoever does not receive the kingdom of God like a child shall not enter it."

And in the older King James Version:

> And they brought unto him also infants, that he would touch them: but when his disciples saw it, they rebuked them. But Jesus called them unto him, and said, "Suffer little children to come unto me, and forbid them not: for of such is the kingdom of God. Verily I say unto you, Whosoever shall not receive the kingdom of God as a little child shall in no wise enter therein."

REFLECTION QUESTIONS

1. Why would the disciples rebuke the parents bringing children to Jesus to be blessed? Did they think Jesus had more important things to do? What did Jesus say was important?

2. Jesus was teaching about humility when we read that the parents brought their children for Jesus to lay His hands on them in blessing. Even so, the disciples didn't understand that the Lord wanted to bless the children. Did the disciples think they were protecting Jesus from distraction?

3. Do we try to protect God from the distraction of children with disabilities?

4. God is not distracted by little ones. He wants us to become like children. In what ways does disability humble your family?

5. Are you like the Pharisee or the rich young ruler, unable to see yourself apart from behaving decorously or building wealth? Have you ever thought that the children with disabilities aren't as good as you in God's sight? Have you

ever thought of the children with disabilities as costing too much?

6. What do you think the Kingdom of God is like?

7. How does our Divine Liturgy show us the Kingdom? Notice all the places that the Kingdom is mentioned.

8. Imagine you are a child in the Gospel. Who brings you to be blessed by the Lord? How do you feel about meeting the Lord? Would your feelings change if you were disabled?

9. Imagine you are a parent in the Gospel. How do you feel about the disciples who tell you to go away? What drives you to keep asking for a blessing until Jesus comes?

CHAPTER 5

Making a Good Beginning

SOCIAL SCRIPTS FOR WELCOMING FAMILIES WITH DISABILITIES

RECENTLY I SPOKE WITH AN Orthodox Christian friend who was incapacitated for several months by an accident where she severely injured both of her legs. She told me that she was overawed at the outpouring of love and help from her community. People kept showing up for her family. They brought prayer books, mobility aids, food, prayers, and kindness. Since I know that two members of her family are autistic, I asked her how the people showed up to help with the challenges that arise with autism. She was quiet before admitting that there was no support for autism like there had been for her injury.

"Part of it is that nobody knows what to do," she said. This friend is a fixture in her local parish, one of the people who likes to pitch in to get things done, and she was speaking from a place of compassion. As we talked, we realized that most people are waiting to help one another, but they don't know where to start.

There is great mercy in making a beginning. Saint Anthony

is credited with saying, "Every day I say to myself: Today I will begin." The tenth hour of St. John Chrysostom's prayers for every hour of the day teaches us to pray, "O Lord my God, even if I had not done anything good before Thee, do Thou help me, in Thy grace, to make a good beginning."[45] If we don't know where to begin, let us ask God as James advises: "If any of you lacks wisdom, let him ask God, who gives to all men generously and without reproaching, and it will be given him" (James 1:5). Perhaps we have not known how to welcome. This chapter is an opportunity to begin.

We need to find ways to begin in three areas: First, we need to learn how to greet people with disabilities so that we honor the image of God in them and share the love of Christ with them. Second, we need to learn how to offer help when a person comes to us with chronic needs rather than acute illnesses. Third, we need to learn how to ask for help, both from one another and the saints.

Greetings and Offering to Help

One of the best greetings to hear when you arrive in the narthex of the church is, "Welcome. I'm so glad you're here." When I have spoken with families with special needs, including those with extreme challenges, every one of them has told me that the kindness of greeters encouraged them to continue the hard work of bringing their family to church. As I mentioned in the introduction, I have felt acceptance for my own family from the greeters who have met us when we came into the church building. Families with special needs spend more time than most going in and out of the church services and church building, and the interactions they have in these times of transition can have dramatic effects on their experience of God.

Beginning to Greet Visitors with Disabilities

Look at them with love, the way you would look at a holy icon. You might need to practice, but looking at each person with the intention of loving God will be good for you and for the people who come in the door.

Don't touch them unless you're asked to do so or unless they reach out to you first. This isn't to be cold. It's because many disabilities make touch confusing or dangerous, for reasons including fragile hands or balance or sensory-processing differences. If people arrive in wheelchairs, they will feel more comfortable if they or their designated caregiver are the only persons moving them.

Welcome them with standard greetings. "Good morning," "Good evening," and "Welcome" are good beginnings. Add, "I'm so glad you're here." People are at the church because God has called them to be there. Don't turn them away.

Welcome Scripts for Regular Attendees

Use all of the greetings above, plus:

» If the person or family with disabilities attends regularly, or if you can see some of their needs right away, offer to help them as well as greet them. For instance, if there are prayer books at the back of the church, offer to carry some in for the family. If the person or family needs to take a break in an uncrowded area of the narthex or just outside the door, offer to come wave to them during the Lord's Prayer so they don't miss Communion. If they lack the coordination to light candles, or if the parents have their hands full with children, offer to light the candles for them. These are small gestures, but they demonstrate care.

» If you see a family looking stressed and you know a place

they might go in the church to have a peaceful space to calm down, quietly mention the space to them and silently make sure they can get there. Meltdowns from over-whelmed family members are never helped by touches from strangers or extra noise. Preparing the way for them will help them use their strategies to gather themselves again more easily.

» Whenever the church calendar includes special foods to accompany feasts or fasts, offer to bring those foods to the families with disabilities. It's much harder to find the many hours needed to make breads and cookies and bird rolls and vasilopitas when a family member requires constant care and vigilance. If you're not a baker or a cook, you might buy the special ingredients to drop them by. Even if you cannot bring foods to someone, you can bring special blessed basil and grapes to them from the feast days. You can make a big difference if you take an extra thirty minutes a few times a year to bring the foods that help to build our shared community life.

» Pray for them. If you don't remember to pray for families with disabilities every day, at least remember them on the days when the reading is about people who suffered a disability, such as the paralytics, the blind men, the woman bent double, or others whom the Lord met and healed. God might not heal these families instantly and dramatically, but your prayers will help more grace to enter their souls, even so.

People with disabilities aren't asking you to carry all of their burdens, only to lighten them with the consolation of your loving fellowship. These small gestures of bringing prayer books, offering to help with candles, praying for them, and bringing food on special days will stand out to families with disabilities, for whom the gestures will be full of grace. We will talk more about how to help welcome people with special food needs in the Koinonia section of the book, but offering to bring food is a good beginning.

Asking for Help

Fellow members of the church may ask parents, the priest, and the saints to help them know how to welcome children with disabilities. There's no need to feel awkward about asking. If you have a family member with a disability, or if you yourself have one, you may ask for help with your needs from other adults, the priest, and the saints. But as with greetings, often it's hard to know where to begin to ask for assistance. The following suggestions may help.

Consider any distraction by another member of the church to be a prayer request. If a family with special needs catches your attention during a church service, the first thing to do is to ask God to help them. If someone looks at you or your family member with a disability in a distracting way, the first thing to do is to ask God to help them. If church members would follow only this one rule, nearly all discord over the challenges arising from disabilities would be resolved. *If you are distracted by someone, pray for them.*

If you want to know how to help a family with disabilities, keep your talk simple and find the parents or adult when it's quiet. Say simply, "I want to help you feel welcome at church because I know God loves you, and I want to love you, too." If there's a symptom that concerns you, ask about it without judgment. For instance, if a child makes loud noises sometimes, don't say, "Your daughter was really loud today and made it so no one could pray." For one thing, the second claim is not true. Anyone who has a habit of prayer would simply pray for her when she made a noise, rather than feeling kept from prayer. For another, such a statement is not actually offering help. It's blaming the family for one's own weakness.

Rather, say, "I noticed that your daughter was loud sometimes in the service. Is she uncomfortable? Is there anything I can do to help so she can participate better?" Start with "I noticed" and show that you see that the person with a disability is someone who is really there, participating in God. If you can't talk that day, wait until you see the parents or person with the disability after a service when everyone is calm, and it is quiet. Your sincere offer will keep, and if you remember the family more because you have to wait to ask, let that remembering be a sign to you that you should pray for them right then.

If you need help from members of the church for you or your family member to participate in services, keep it simple and ask when things are calm. Write an email or call the priest on a Tuesday and say, "I/My child/My family member has this condition, and we would like to be able to do the following things so we can participate in the services/Sunday school/ coffee hour." The priest will help you with the things you need as well as find people in the church who can help you with particulars.

You might have to ask several people several times for some things, particularly if you need something physical to change. Do not be discouraged by having to ask for help more than once. There are channels of proper authority in churches, but going through them does not mean that you will be turned away. It means that some things take more time to do well.

The benefit of having to ask people for help, sometimes many people, sometimes many times, is that the people will have an opportunity to learn your needs and find ways to love you by meeting them.

Whether you are a member of the church wanting to welcome families with disabilities or a member of a family with disabilities, the saints are there to help us live together in the unity of the love of Christ. Yet, though most people know how to make their cross and venerate an icon, not everyone knows how to begin to ask the saints for help. The simplest way to do so is to venerate an icon as usual and say or whisper, "Please pray for me/them. We need help. Help us for the sake of our Lord Jesus Christ." You might also look up the kontakion for the saint, sing or read it, and then ask for help for the sake of Christ, or simply ask with the usual "In the Name of the Father and the Son and the Holy Spirit," which you say when you make your cross. The saints want to help us and will not be offended if you are clumsy about beginning. They love us.

These suggestions are for making a good beginning. Your priest and members of your church and the saints will build on these beginnings. You might also look up and ask about patron saints for particular conditions, as some saints are known to especially help people facing specific challenges.

SUMMARY

» We have social scripts for helping our fellow Christians through illnesses, but few people know what to do to help Christians with permanent disabilities.

» We can focus on making a good beginning with God's help.

» Start by greeting people with disabilities sincerely, without unsolicited touch, and with offers to help with prayer books and candles. Show families where they can find quiet, uncrowded spaces to re-center if they're overwhelmed during a service.

» Bring or offer to bring special foods to community celebrations. Pray for the families that come to mind when the readings tell us about the Lord healing people with disabilities, as well as at other times.

» If someone distracts you, pray for her. Do not get angry. Consider the distraction to be a prayer request. Ask God's help for yourself and the other people.

» We all need reminders to ask for help for and from each other and the saints. To ask other people for help for yourself or to ask how you can help others, keep your request simple, on topic, and specific. Ask when everyone is calm, in a quiet area.

» To ask the saints for help, start with your usual venerations and say, "Please help me/us." Then make your cross. The saints want to help us, so start asking.

REFLECTION QUESTIONS

1. Sometimes we feel ashamed, confused, or angry. Those feelings make it hard to know what to do. Yet, those strong negative feelings are usually a symptom of wanting to make a good beginning. Can you think of times when you were angry, ashamed, or confused when you encountered a family with disabilities at church or when you tried to take your family with disabilities to a church service or event? What would be a better beginning to what happened?

2. God gives us the grace of free choices, of good and better choices, for "if the Son makes you free, you shall be free

indeed" (John 8:36). This means we don't have to dwell on the wrong turns we have made. We can ask God for help and do good turns instead. What better choices can you make toward welcome?

3. When did someone reach out to welcome you? When was a time you reached out to welcome someone with disabilities?

4. Which saints have you heard of? Do you ask them for help? Try asking them for help this week.

5. Do you know of a saint or saints who help with particular challenges? For instance, St. Paraskevi helps people with impairments to their eyes, and St. Seraphim of Sarov is a favorite saint among autistic Orthodox Christians. Consider offering icons of patron saints of different disabilities to include in your church learning areas. How do you pray with these patron saints at home?

6. Do you have a hard time remembering to ask for help? Ask God to help you make a good beginning.

CHAPTER 6

SPOTLIGHT
Welcoming the Social Stranger

The following essay is based on a talk given by Matthew and Summer Griffith as part of their church's Lenten series in 2019. They graciously allowed me to share it here because I believe that their experience and Christ-centered approach to special needs will encourage others. Read to the end, where I help connect their essay to the rest of the book with reflection questions.

Last summer we received an autism spectrum disorder (ASD) diagnosis. Our kid is on the "more typically functioning" end of the spectrum. While not wanting to make this discussion about special-needs children in the Church only about autistic kids, we cannot help but refer to it, because autism is our main point of experience. We believe that autism should work as an example for what is more generally true.[46]

We are discussing welcoming special-needs children into the Church in terms of taking in strangers in Christ's teaching on the Last Judgment in Matthew 25. So, how are special-needs children strangers? *Special needs* is actually a term that applies primarily in the education setting for children with *particular educational requirements resulting from learning difficulties, physical disability, or emotional and behavioral difficulties.* We mean to more broadly cover disability generally.

Our answer to this is that while special-needs children are not strangers from a foreign land, they are social strangers to the socially dominant expectations for what a normal human being ought to be. That's kind of a fancy way of saying that the rest of us think they're not normal. Special-needs children have the disorder, and we do not. The ASD diagnosis itself actually states this rather plainly.

What is ASD according to the *Diagnostic and Statistical Manual of Mental Disorders V*? This is our paraphrase:

» ASD has two categories of symptoms: persistent deficits in social communication/interaction *and* restricted, repetitive patterns of behavior.
» Symptoms appear early in childhood.
» "Symptoms cause clinically significant impairment in social, occupational, or other important areas of current functioning."
» Symptoms are not better explained by something else.

We want to point to three things about the diagnostic criteria. First, according to these criteria, which explicitly state something that is implicitly included in the diagnosis of other special needs, ASD is only recognized as a disorder in relation to those of us who have the capacity to participate in the dominant social manifestations of being human—schools, jobs, whatever. Those with ASD don't function well with the rest of us. To put this in a personal way, you are autistic because I am not, and people like me are in charge.

Second, this capacity in question (to participate socially), insofar as we can see, entails the cognitive and physical capacity to sustain a delusional misunderstanding of what it means to be human—namely, that a rightly ordered life is sustainable apart from God. What we mean by that is that the world prioritizes the appearance of strength, cognitive and physical, in order to sustain the delusion that death can be avoided if we just do everything right and keep ourselves properly ordered—and that's why special-needs kids must be named as disordered.

Third, for that reason, the world has a vested interest in excluding those covered by the category of special needs from what the rest of us want to call a normal human being. It may be that participating in normalcy is a defense against our fear of death. People who cannot hide their vulnerability deeply scare the rest of us, because they show us the weaknesses that we are most afraid of witnessing in ourselves.

This brings us closer to what a Christian understanding of special-needs children ought to be. We are not experts on Orthodox anthropology, so to roughly paraphrase Fr. John Behr reading Irenaeus and the Gospel according to St. John: The creation of the human being was finished when Christ died on the Cross, and we can only become human by participating in Christ's death. *What that means, and this for me is very important to understand, is that special-needs children or disabled people generally are not disordered images of the rest of us.* This is what the DSM would lead you to believe—it is a manual of *dis*orders.

Rather, what is the case is that we are all images of Christ that have been disordered by ancestral sin. Healing of those with special needs, for that reason, does not mean healing them of Down syndrome or autism or deafness or whatever so that they can be like the rest of us. Healing of those with special needs means the same as it does for all of us. All of us are healed and all of us become human by dying in Christ. By bringing us into Christ's death by baptism, the Church members each of us into Christ's body, into the path to becoming human.

Adjusting Expectations toward Christ

Here are two personally reflective thoughts on a more practical level. First, taking in the special-needs child as Christ taught us to take in strangers is painful. It hurts to have our vulnerabilities and weaknesses brought to light so that we are forced to reckon with them. However, it is completely necessary, because in this stranger, in this child, Christ has come into our presence.

An example is this: As a parent I have a certain expectation for what a reciprocal loving relationship with my child is going to look like—how he will show love for me physically and emotionally. A struggle that parents of autistic children have often endured is that these expressions of love and reciprocity that we expect of our children are foreign to their way of being. It is not merely being a rebellious teenager or whatever. God has given me a child to love who may never in this age show me the signs of love which I deeply desire from my children or may never show me love in a way that I can understand.

That does not mean that love is not there. I am thinking of kids "more autistic" than ours who can't look others in the eye, who can't bear the sensory input of touching another person. Yet this child is not a disordered image of my expectations. Welcoming this child as Christ taught demands that my desires and expectations be broken by revealing that I have been clinging to myself and not to Christ. By taking this child in, we are given an opportunity for repentance and to show mercy, bringing us closer to the self-emptying love to which we are called as Christians.

Second, along similar lines, and, I think, a common practical concern, is distraction in the church services. For a long time, I thought that my children, more specifically the one with ASD, were distracting me from my prayer in the services. But truly it is more the case that I would go into the service looking in the wrong direction. Some of you may have been distracted as well.

But stop and rephrase that thought differently: "This child's weakness and vulnerability are distracting me from God." That's crazy, right? If we ever have that thought in the Liturgy, what is being shown to us is that we were not paying attention to God in the first place. We were not praying before God but merely paying attention to our own expectations for what prayer ought to be. God has given us an opportunity to be merciful, and it is that opportunity, taking in the person of the stranger, that fulfills the Church.

Back to the Gospel

Christ came preaching the gospel to those most marginalized by their society: the poor, the broken, those shut in the prison, those who were sick, and outsiders. In the teaching on the Last Judgment, Christ is pretty clear that these are indeed the ones whom Christians must care the most about. He even goes so far as to tell His people that when they feed the poor, give water to the thirsty, clothe the naked, take in the strangers, and visit the sick and the prisoners, they have done these things to Himself. What does He mean about this?

Now in our abundance of food, we forget our hunger. In our good health, we forget we are sick. But we are hungry, and we are sick. The disease of sin permeates like a cancer of the blood. We are sick, but we use our thoughts and bodies to pretend that we are not. I just do not want to think about it. When I can get in a car and drive where I want, I pretend to myself that I am free in order to forget I am a prisoner to sin. As long as I can think of the sick, the poor, the stranger, and the prisoner as *other*, as long as I can keep them different by my own strength,

I do not have to deal with the sin and weakness within myself.

But when we go to those whom Christ taught us to visit and take in those who are different from ourselves, the truth of our own weakness is shown to us in these people who bring Christ before us. This is good news for us, because the healthy don't need a physician. In fact, Jesus removes Himself from those who think they are *other than* the other.

Let's look at 1 Corinthians 12:12–26:

> For just as the body is one and has many members, and all the members of the body, though many, are one body, so it is with Christ. For by one Spirit we were all baptized into one body— Jews or Greeks, slaves or free—and all were made to drink of one Spirit.
>
> For the body does not consist of one member but of many. If the foot should say, "Because I am not a hand, I do not belong to the body," that would not make it any less a part of the body. And if the ear should say, "Because I am not an eye, I do not belong to the body," that would not make it any less a part of the body. If the whole body were an eye, where would be the hearing? If the whole body were an ear, where would be the sense of smell? But as it is, God arranged the organs in the body, each one of them, as he chose. If all were a single organ, where would the body be? As it is, there are many parts, yet one body. The eye cannot say to the hand, "I have no need of you," nor again the head to the feet, "I have no need of you." On the contrary, the parts of the body which seem to be weaker are indispensable, and those parts of the body which we think less honorable we invest with the greater honor, and our unpresent-able parts are treated with greater modesty, which our more presentable parts do not require. But God has so composed the body, giving the greater honor to the inferior part, that there may be no discord in the body, but that the members may

have the same care for one another. If one member suffers, all suffer together; if one member is honored, all rejoice together.

At our parish we often quote St. Silouan's words, "My brother is my life." Well, this can be shown powerfully in small ways, and our parish is full of examples of those who take in our autistic son and welcome him into the Body of Christ by bearing his weakness. At the front door, Mr. John gives him an enthusiastic greeting but almost never gets one in return. Ms. Marina does not care a thing about trucks but asks him about trucks, because that's his thing. He never responds to her, but she keeps asking.

From the perspective of normal social expectation, he is either rude or autistically disordered in his inability to socially engage with others. But in the comfort of our home, he often talks about Mr. John and about what kind of trucks Ms. Marina likes. Such apparently small, unreciprocated acts of love welcome him into the Eucharist each Sunday. They are liturgical acts. If Mr. John isn't there to greet, our son notices. Ms. Elizabeth takes him to clean the wax out of the candlestands and finds other tasks in the service that teach him to participate in the life of the Church in a way that his young, autistic brain understands. And I am brought to tears by these acts of beauty and love. These are not acts of compassion or sympathy. My kid doesn't need that. They are acts of the Body being one.

REFLECTION QUESTIONS

1. Interacting with people with special needs highlights our reliance on God. In what ways do you feel more vulnerable when you are around someone with a disability? Which weaknesses do you fear for yourself? Do you think that God

needs you to have those abilities in order to love you?

2. The Griffiths' essay raises the idea that a lot of our discomfort with including people with disabilities is due to a false belief that we rely only on ourselves to have a good life. How can reaching out to people with special needs help you see that we all rely on God?

3. "Special-needs children or disabled people are not disordered images of the rest of us." Rather, we are all becoming human by entering Christ's death in baptism and becoming members of Christ's Body. This is a big idea, which we have also seen in chapter two, "Illness versus Disability," page 35. It means that we are all in this Body of Christ together, and people with disabilities, along with those without disabilities, have a common goal of becoming like Christ. The focus shifts from what we are able to do alone to how we can help the whole Body work together. How can we imitate Christ as members of His Body? How would Christ's Body the Church change if we treated disabled people like members of Christ?

4. What are some ways that you can act in love toward someone whose disability keeps him or her from meeting usual social expectations?

5. Have you lived your Christian life believing that you did not need disabled Christians in the Church in order to be saved? What would change for you if you believed that people with disabilities are people you need for your salvation?

6. Disabled people make up twenty percent of the world, but many are absent from our churches. Twenty percent is one out of every five people. Which social expectations might be keeping that twenty percent out of the Church?

PART TWO

Theosis

CHAPTER 7

Becoming Like God in Weakness

For truly One only is holy—holy, that is, by nature; yet we also are holy, not, indeed, by nature, but by participation, training, and prayer.[47]

—St. Cyril of Jerusalem

He, indeed, assumed humanity that we might become God.[48]

—St. Athanasius

Knowledge of their Maker is for men the only really happy and blessed life.[49]

—St. Athanasius

G OD BECAME HUMAN SO THAT we might become like God. Becoming like God, or *theosis*, is what we Orthodox mean when we talk about salvation. But how do we become like God? In a general sense, we become like God by imitating God and drawing near to Him so that we may be illumined by His grace and start to take on some of His characteristics.[50] Though we all have to work out our salvation in fear and trembling (Phil. 2:12),[51] God has already accomplished most of this work by drawing near to us all in the Incarnation. God has already made communion with Him possible and continues to be with us and will bring us all fully into His presence so that God is all in all.

Salvation is not a solitary endeavor, and we are never without God's help, no matter which disabilities we live with. It is important to remember that God made each of us, and to some of us He gave disabilities for the salvation of us all. God is with each of us whom He has made, hedging us in behind and before and laying His hand upon us (Ps. 139:5 NKJV), for God who began a good work in us will be faithful to complete it (Phil. 1:6).

Three ways to imitate God and draw near to Him are prayer, participation in God through the Sacraments, and imitation of Christ through practicing the virtues.[52] Prayer is how we draw near to God and know God, and this section of the book will feature several resources for praying with disabilities. Participating in the Sacraments is how we "become Christ-bearers and partakers of the divine nature."[53] Because of the importance of the Sacraments, the chapters in this section include resources on how to include families with disabilities in sacramental life.

In order to imitate Christ, we have to learn about Him and know Him, for as the apostle asks, "How are they to believe in him of whom they have never heard?" (Rom. 10:14). This presents challenges when disabilities require that people be taught in a different way that meets them where they are. In this section of the book, therefore, we will spend several chapters on how people learn and how to teach people with a wide range of disabilities. The following section of this book, "Self-Emptying Disables the Disability: Kenosis," will go into detail about imitating Christ in the virtues for people living with disabilities.

Finally, to work out our salvation as persons, families, and church communities with disabilities, we must learn to pray. The spiritual consolations that come to us in our struggles come through prayer. As St. Gregory of Nyssa puts it, "the comfort comes through participating in the Comforter."[54] Since God condescends to teach us where we are and gives us a mouth to praise Him in whichever circumstances we live, I have gathered resources in this section for helping families with disabilities to pray. It is my hope that priests and parents and spiritual fathers will find them useful in guiding persons with disabilities to be able to enter into prayer.

Happiness and Communion with God

While today we often talk about happiness as an emotion that comes and goes along with the experience of pleasure, the older meaning of happiness was to have a life perfectly suited to human nature. As St. Athanasius explains, since we humans are made in the image of God in order to know God and be with Him, "knowledge of their Maker is for men the only really happy and blessed life."[55] We are not disappointed in our need to know God in order to obtain happiness, because "all things have been filled with the knowledge of God" in the Incarnation of the Word.[56] This is why St. Ambrose, reflecting on the life of Jacob, points out that disabilities do not keep humans from the goal of happiness, which is the knowledge of God, asking, "Is it not clear that a disability cannot be an impediment to happiness?"[57]

It is common in our time for people who respect neither God nor human life[58] to claim that the lives of people with disabilities are unworthy to be lived. The presumption is that disabilities limit the enjoyment of fleeting happiness from bodily pleasures, at least from the perspective of people who have not experienced disability, and that the lack of worldly pleasures that they call happiness therefore makes life with disabilities worth less.

But we know better. The love of the community who imitates Christ can overcome handicaps to inclusion. The presence of Christ in our suffering—which is really only a part of His suffering—is filled with consolations and is working all things for our salvation. Thus true happiness, that is, the knowledge of God, is absolutely available to all persons, no matter their disabilities.

We must understand that imitating Christ will make us happy. It might not make us happy at all times *emotionally*, because every feeling has a proper season (see Eccl. 3:1), and sometimes being like Christ is unpleasant from a sensual perspective. After all, we are "always carrying in the body the death of Jesus, so that the life of Jesus may also be manifested in our bodies" (2 Cor. 4:10). But imitating Christ will make us happy by showing us that God is the perfect place for the thriving of our nature, and knowledge of God is the perfect satisfaction of our need for communion with Him.

We will all be happy in God—in other words, in the way that a fish is happy in water. A fish with a disability still needs water in the same way as a fish without disabilities, and humans with disabilities need to commune with God through sacraments, prayer, and imitation in virtues the same as humans without disabilities. "For the glory of God is the living man, and the life of man is the vision of God."[59] Our nature longs for God, who is our life,[60] and this time of our salvation is when we begin to know Him in whose presence is fullness of joy (Ps. 16:11).[61]

Summary

» *Theosis* is to become like God through communion with and imitation of Christ. We become like God through participating in the sacraments, prayer, and training in virtues.

» The chapters in this section will focus on imitating Christ through teaching, sacraments, and prayer that meet families with disabilities where they are.

» Salvation makes us happy in God even if we are disabled. Persons with disabilities are equally able to live happy lives, especially when we understand happiness as communion with God. Happiness in God does not exclude persons with disabilities. It is the joy of being in God, which is the perfect place for the thriving of our nature. Fish are happy in water, and humans are happy in God.

Reflection Questions

1. We often think of human nature as something that keeps us from doing right. But what if we look at our nature as it is when united to Christ? Saint Cyril of Jerusalem tells us, "We have been saved by the very weapons which the devil used to conquer us. The Lord took from us our likeness, that through human nature, we might be saved. He assumed our likeness that He might bestow the greater grace on that which was lacking, that sinful human nature might be made partaker in God."[62] That is to say, the weak parts of our nature as well as the strong are united to Christ as ways to know God. The next time you think, "it's only human nature" to do something wrong, ask how Christ might be

saving that very nature.

2. What are some ways that you pray? Do you share prayers with people with disabilities? If so, what do you do differently to include them in your prayer practices?

3. Have you taught someone with disabilities about the Faith? What were some of the ways you taught? If you have a disability, is there a way that you learn most easily?

4. Have you heard the rhetoric that life with disabilities is not worth living? How does happiness in God challenge that false view?

CHAPTER 8

Entering His Courts

MAKING SERVICES ACCESSIBLE TO PEOPLE WITH PHYSICAL IMPAIRMENTS

Let brotherly love continue. Do not neglect to show hospitality to strangers, for thereby some have entertained angels unawares.

—HEBREWS 13:2

Angels with Hearing Aids, Canes, and Wheelchairs

B ECAUSE OF THE MEDIA BUZZ around healings in this age and every age, we are familiar with the stereotype of faith that shows up through signs of dramatic healings. Even for Orthodox Christians, it's easy to conjure a story of crutches left behind at holy healing waters, of canes left behind at miraculous icons, of hearing aids set aside at a shrine. Truly, God is always able to heal us of every infirmity both in this life and in the age to come.

But as we saw in Chapter 2, "Illness versus Disability," God also gives us disabilities for the salvation of the whole Church. Sometimes God even gives disabilities as a sign, as we noted in several biblical examples. It would be easy to be dazzled by the stories of total healings so much that we forget that miracles point us toward the love of God. Yet it is that love of God in Christ, poured out in hospitality, that the Church teaches us to embrace when we meet someone with a disability.

A story of Abba Agathon demonstrates the model of love we should have for our brothers and sisters with disabilities. Abba Agathon meets a disabled man along the road when Abba is going into town to sell his wares. This man asks Abba Agathon to carry him into town, buy him a cake and another item, and to carry him back. All of these things Abba Agathon does without question or complaint. Once he returns the man with a disability to where he found him, the man declares a blessing on Abba Agathon and disappears. He was an angel of the Lord.[63]

When we view persons with disabilities as angels, we do so in order to recognize their dignity and holiness as members of Christ's Body, not to set them apart as other than human. The admonition to treat everyone as though they might be an angel of the Lord hearkens back to the hospitality of Abraham, who received God Himself in the visit of three angels. When we receive a brother or sister as angels, we are not saying that they aren't human, but that they are in the image of God, too. To receive someone like an angel is to receive someone from God. This is important for another reason, because, as we learn from the story of the man born blind (John 9), people are born with disabilities in order that God's works might be revealed in them.[64]

The healing work of God is to knit each member of the Body of Christ together in the Church. Whether or not healing occurs in our bodies, the healing of the one Body of Christ, the Church, comes when each person is welcomed fully into the Body as a member. As the Assembly of Canonical Orthodox Bishops of the United States of America tells us, "Disability is principally a social issue, while healing is the removal of social barriers," and "What is called for is a sense of solidarity with all members of the Church." As we turn to look at ways to include persons with disabilities in the life of the Church, therefore, we have to consider social inclusion as well as making it physically possible for everyone to enter the building.

Though not all jurisdictions within the canonical Orthodox churches in the United States have adopted standards of building accessibility, such as compliance with the Americans with Disabilities Act or other building codes, each of them assents to the guidance of the Assembly of Canonical Orthodox Bishops of the United States of America. In their statement, the bishops have advised that parishes work to include persons with disabilities in all aspects of church life, including making physical changes to buildings and entrances. Churches should include persons with disabilities as full members not only in worship, teaching, leadership, fellowship, and dignity, but also through learning about and accommodating physical needs and supports. It is in all of these things, from treating people with disabilities with "sincere love and genuine respect," to "providing curb cuts, adequate ramps, sufficient handicapped parking, wide doors and aisles to accommodate wheelchairs," that the Church is obligated "to strive for the transfiguration of all people and all things in the heavenly vision of unity."[65]

Welcome with Consideration and Respect

The only rule is sincerity and dignity; the only approach is consideration and respect.

—FR. JOHN CHRYSSAVGIS[66]

To remove handicaps, we must remove social and physical barriers to participation in the full life of the Church. "A barrier is any space too narrow, too high, too low, too unstable, or too hard to manipulate or negotiate,"[67] as well as social barriers like isolation, exclusion, and failure to communicate. When we work to include others, we will offer not only the ability to move into and through spaces freely and safely, but also "the gift of genuine friendship."[68] The following sections relate advice that will help us make a beginning in welcoming people with visible physical differences and impairments affecting mobility, sight, and hearing.

Keep in mind as you go through these suggestions that friendship is most important. Talk respectfully with the persons with disabilities and their family members when they come to church. A disability coordinator or advocate, preferably someone with a disability or who is familiar with disabilities, can be an invaluable help to church communities.[69] Even if you do not have a coordinator, you can use the scripts from Chapter 5, "Making a Good Beginning." Ask people to tell you about themselves and their needs, use the language about disabilities that they use for themselves, and accept them as fellow members of the Body of Christ.[70]

Welcoming People Who Look Different

It's important to look at someone who comes to church as though he or she is sacred and loved and welcomed, as we would welcome holy angels and Christ Himself. A church member or visitor might have a visible birth defect, unusual eye contact or expressions, missing eyes or ears, a cleft palate, a large birth mark, unusual head shape, chronic skin condition, missing or differently shaped limbs, a feeding tube or other visible medical equipment attached to him or her, or a facial structure that indicates a chromosomal difference or unusual bodily development. No matter the difference, remember that the person in front of you is made in the image of God. When God looks at that person, He sees an image of Himself. As St. John Climacus reminds us, "When we see one of our athletes in Christ in bodily suffering and [disability], let us not maliciously seek to learn the explanation of his [disability], but rather with simple and genuine love let us try to heal him as though he were part of our own body."[71]

We are to love a fellow member of the Body of Christ as though she "were a member of our own body," because indeed she is. We are all members of the one Body of Christ. We have all stepped into the sufferings of Christ in baptism, and our bodily differences, weaknesses, and disabilities are no longer a cause for shame, just as the Cross of Christ is no longer a symbol of shame but of victory, of compassion, and of our salvation.

Welcoming People with Mobility Challenges

The same ideas apply when we welcome people with mobility challenges. We must greet one another as fellow members of the Body of Christ, with kindness and respect. That means that we won't push or pull someone without her or his permission or jostle her or him or rush her or him along. Since many of our beloved senior members of the Church face mobility challenges, many people are more familiar with how to treat people with these challenges respectfully, having transferred the respect for our elders to those who have similar physical challenges. Priests might offer Holy Communion in the pews or the aisle to a person with impaired mobility. (It can help to tell the priest ahead of time if someone with a reclining mobility device or stretcher is coming so that the ushers and priest can arrange for clear access for Holy Communion.)

Though we might be most familiar with people using canes, walkers, scooters, and wheelchairs or walking slowly or with support, I have also included some special considerations for people with more severe mobility challenges. Grace enters the soul no matter how extreme our difficulties, and we must welcome people as fellow members of Christ, drawn together in His gracious love.

Tips for Welcoming People with Mobility Impairments

» Work to make your church spaces accessible for people using wheelchairs, scooters, canes, and walkers.

» Some mobility challenges are evident, and some are caused by hidden conditions and are invisible.

» Be attentive to the person, not curious about his or her disability. Someone who needs to sit down in Liturgy does not need to rehearse his or her medical history in order to be excused from standing.

» Provide places to sit or park a device out of the flow of traffic to avoid bumps.

» Be aware of the danger of falling. Icy or slick surfaces can cause extra challenges to people with bodily weakness.

» Provide for an option to jump to the front of the line for confession so that people who cannot stand for long do not miss out on confession due to the length of the line. Another option is to provide a bench for people with mobility challenges to use while they wait for confession. The priest can call people up from the bench rather than having them stand and wait.

» Stand a few steps away from someone using a wheelchair or scooter so that she does not have to crane her neck up. Sitting next to her is even better.

» Treat wheelchairs and mobility devices as part of personal space. Do not touch them without permission, and provide plenty of room for the person using such a device to move freely.

» If no mobility-assisting device is used, a disability may still be present, such as juvenile rheumatoid arthritis. Do not assume that a person without a device can necessarily stand for long periods or work in a volunteer capacity that involves standing or exertion.

» Provide a music stand to hold up service books for people with mobility challenges. This also helps in cases of arm weakness or impairments in balance.

» If a person is unable to move his or her arms or hands with precision, he might make the sign of the cross with the head by nodding once and shaking his head once from side to side.

» If a person uses an eye gaze detector to communicate, ask her about making the sign of the cross using eye gaze. She can make the sign of the cross using her eyes at any time, and a device might be programed to say, "In the Name of the Father and the Son and the Holy Spirit" along with her eye movements.

Welcoming People with Visual Impairments

When you think about how you will welcome someone into your church, think of the sequence of physical acts that bring you from outside the building and into the space of worship. You will need to know which door to enter, how to navigate the door, and what to venerate, as well as be able to greet a friend and perhaps light a candle and find a service book. These activities might be different for someone with an impairment.

For someone who is blind, Braille notation on signs can help with finding an entry. An automatic door or a person to hold the door open (and tell people that the door is open) can help in navigating the doorway, which is especially important when someone has his hands busy using a cane or a guide dog. A friend who speaks first in greeting shows someone who cannot see that he is in a place where he is known.

A carved icon can help someone with low vision or blindness feel the image in order to venerate it. The unpredictability of candle arrangements in the sandbox might make it unsafe for someone who is blind to light a candle on her own. Because painted icons feel the same as flat boards, many blind people will only be comfortable venerating if someone describes the icon and shows them where it is. A Braille copy of the Divine Liturgy can help them follow the service.

SPOTLIGHT
Icons for Orthodox Christians Who Are Blind

I had the privilege of conversing online with Laura (Theodora) Collins, an Orthodox Christian who is blind. Laura is a member of St. John the Theologian Orthodox Church (Antiochian) in Rapid City, South Dakota. She was gracious in sharing her experience of praying with icons as someone who experiences them through senses other than sight. Laura writes:

I have some icons which are embossed, I think you would call it. They are of metal so that I can feel the images. Even though they're small, so I don't detect great detail in the faces to tell who they are, I knew who they were when I bought them. I have one icon I bought when I visited St. Michael's Cathedral in Sitka, Alaska, where the halo, clothing, hands, etc., are tactile, but the face is painted and completely flat to the touch. I don't like that one as much.

Icons that are only painted really have no significance to me. Although others can tell it is an icon, to me it is just a finished, varnished piece of wood, which could be anything—a plaque with a saying, picture of nature, etc. Because I have had ridiculing here and there during my sixty years of life, I am just hesitant to venerate anything like that for fear of being laughed at, etc. In fact, when I visited an Orthodox congregation once, years ago, which was not my home parish, I felt what seemed to me to be an icon on the wall, just inside the door to the temple. It felt beautiful, with many tiny panes of what I thought was probably stained glass. So I venerated it and found out later it was only ornate decoration; no icon at all. I have gotten skittish because of experiences like that. In public, I do not usually venerate icons. In my own church, sometimes members who know me will tell me that a certain icon is out because of a specific feast day and will assist me to it as we are leaving the service.

For Good Friday, one of our members has made "Christ." It is a wooden cutout, the shape of the crucified Body, and it is painted (so it is still completely flat and blank to the touch), but it is in the shape of His Body. That is fastened to a simple cross that the same member made, and I can touch and know exactly where I might be venerating—His hands, feet, face, or the cross itself. The figure is also placed in the bier for the evening Good Friday service, and, again, I can touch and know where I am venerating, as well as feel and make my choices about the bier itself. I greatly appreciate that!

I also have a collection of crosses. Most have the configuration of Orthodox crosses. I especially like the budded cross configuration. I have found ones of stained glass, plastic, wood, ceramic, etc., in various and sundry places. Many come from special places I have visited or have been made by special people out of ribbon or other craft supplies.

About where I keep icons: Just as people who have sight keep them in a special or prominent place in their homes, to be reminded throughout the day or as they pass the icon corner, etc., I keep mine in places where I will pass them tactilely. I have one in my purse, in a specific zipper pocket. In the winter, I keep an embossed icon or one of those lovely rope rosaries in my coat pocket. Others reside in the top drawer of my dresser, where I go on a daily basis for my hairbrush and other such things. This probably sounds sacrilegious to some, but if they were on the wall, that "out of sight, out of mind" cliché would definitely apply.

As Laura's experience demonstrates, icons can be very meaningful for Orthodox Christians who are blind, provided they can be deciphered through touch.

Tips for Welcoming the Blind or Visually Impaired

» Welcoming a guide dog, also sometimes called a "seeing-eye dog," as a prescribed medical aid (not a pet or unregulated animal) necessary to the navigation and safety of the blind church member can be an important way to help him fully participate in church.[72] Persons who have guide dogs to assist them should contact the priest before going to the church, as guide dog acceptance varies across jurisdictions and parishes and is up to the discretion of each priest.

» Tell someone with a vision impairment that you would like to shake her hand before doing so.[73]

» Provide Braille prayer books.[74]

» Tell people who are blind when worshipers are bowing, crossing themselves, or kneeling so that they can participate to the extent possible.[75]

» Some blind people engage more fully in the service by doing all of the motions; for instance, making their cross at every petition of the litany, as this helps them to follow the service and stay engaged.

» For people who are blind, incense can be very meaningful as a way to enter into prayer. Holy myrrh and the oil of holy chrism also provide fragrances that help persons who are blind to engage their senses and attention more fully in worship.

» Bells are also joyful, as they signal proximity to church.

» The Library of Congress National Library Service for the Blind and Physically Handicapped has a few Orthodox titles in their Talking Books collection, including St. John Climacus's *The Ladder of Divine Ascent* and *Facing East* by Khouria Frederica Mathewes-Green.[76] These can be helpful resources to have available for group studies.

» Carved wooden or embossed metal icons allow blind Christians to recognize the holy images and to venerate more knowledgeably.

» At home, whereas someone sighted might place icons where she can see them, someone blind might carry a carved icon in a pocket or keep icons in places where he will pass them tactilely throughout the day.

» The icon of Christ on the Cross that is available for veneration at the end of Holy Week can be very meaningful to people who cannot see, because they can "see" the shape of His Body in that icon.

» Understand that some people who are blind will not venerate painted, flat icons, since they are indistinguishable from wooden surfaces. It can be helpful to announce in the online bulletin which icons will be on the stand.

» Providing a music stand to hold the (rather large) Braille Divine Liturgy book can be helpful so that the person is free to rest her arms and to make the sign of the cross.

» For persons with limited vision, high-contrast icon prints—black ink on neon yellow paper—can make holy images visible. This can be particularly helpful for study groups or Sunday school lessons.

» A sample church bag to help a child with visual impairments might include a Braille version of the Divine Liturgy, a carved fingertip labyrinth necklace or disk, a tactile book such as one from the DK Braille line (www.penguinrandomhouse.com/series/1DK/dk-braille), a prayer rope, a small carved or embossed metal icon, and a small handheld cross.

Welcoming People with Hearing Impairments

Not everyone with a hearing impairment experiences a total loss of hearing, and there is a wide range in types of hearing loss. Some people with hearing impairments communicate through sign language, but many people might be able to hear with the assistance of hearing aids. Use gestures, or touch someone with a hearing impairment lightly on the shoulder or arm in order to get his attention. If you are able to sign, welcome the person with sign and spoken words. Remember that someone with a hearing impairment doesn't have access to all of the sounds of language and movement that you perceive. Watch out for him if there is a lot of movement nearby, and warn him with a gesture or by getting his attention with a light touch if he needs to move. Remember to welcome him with a smile and a kind greeting, even if he cannot hear and you cannot sign. God hears, and the person will feel the warmth of welcome.

Tips for Welcoming People with Hearing Impairments

» Print the gospel and epistle reading in the bulletin.[77]

» Sermon notes or transcripts help people who are deaf or hard of hearing to access the teachings of the sermon.

» Posting videos of sermons on some online platforms allows people to read them with closed captioning.

» Encourage clergy to learn sign language.[78] Consider engaging a sign language interpreter for special feast days.

» If the priest always uses a microphone for the reading of the holy gospel and for the sermon, and the reader always uses a microphone for the epistle, people who are hard of hearing will have an easier time following.

» Note in the bulletin which version of the Divine Liturgy will be served that Sunday.

» Have service books for all services available to use.

» Provide a music stand for service books so that people who speak sign language can have their hands free to respond and say the Creed and the Lord's Prayer in sign while still following the service.

» If you have a sign language interpreter, speak directly to the person, and the interpreter will translate. Look at the person directly rather than the interpreter.

» Consider hosting book studies via online group meeting

chats through text rather than speech.[79]

» A sample church bag for a child who has a hearing impairment might include an age-appropriate book on the Divine Liturgy with photographs (not stylized drawings) to help the child follow the service visually (for example, *What Can I Do at Divine Liturgy* by Kristina Tartara, or *The Divine Liturgy for Children*—available from Ancient Faith Publishing), a quiet prayer rope, and a holy icon book in case the child's view of other icons is blocked.

SUMMARY

» To welcome people with disabilities as "angels unawares" means that we recognize that they are made in the image of God.

» Healing from God is not only or primarily about removing bodily disabilities or ailments, but about knitting each person together as fellow members of the Body of Christ.

» We must focus on kindness, dignity, and respect when we welcome persons with physical impairments.

» When God looks at people with visible differences and disabilities, He sees His image. We must treat people with honor and love.

» Don't seek to satisfy your curiosity about someone's disability, but satisfy the call to love God and your neighbor.

» Tips are laid out for welcoming people with impairments in mobility, sight, and hearing.

REFLECTION QUESTIONS

1. In the Church, "Christ is all, and in all" (Col. 3:11). Does it change how you feel about persons with physical disabilities

when you think of them as in Christ with you as fellow members?

2. The Assembly of Canonical Orthodox Bishops of the United States of America advises that an important expression of welcome is "removing emotional barriers, refusing to consider disability in a patronizing manner either as a test from God or the target of our pity."[80] Have you ever taught or treated someone with a disability as though they were disabled due to a lack of faith?

3. Jesus tells us, "It is written in the prophets, 'And they shall all be taught by God.' Every one who has heard and learned from the Father comes to me" (John 6:45). People with disabilities in our churches come because they are called and taught by God. This helps us to remember to treat people with disabilities with dignity. How might you modify the teaching ministries in your parish to include these people who have come because they are also learning from the Father?

CHAPTER 9

Breaking Invisible Barriers

WELCOMING FAMILIES WITH HIDDEN DISABILITIES

T HOUGH ANY DISABILITY CREATES CHALLENGES for family life and participation in church, the invisible disabilities, especially those that affect social and communication abilities, most often keep families away.[81] This is in part because we do not have experience or scripts for how to welcome these families. Also, parents of children with invisible disabilities might not have a script for parenting in a different way than they thought they would parent. That makes it harder for them to advocate for their families to find a place in church life.

This chapter will focus on two areas: First, we will look at some of the ways to make a beginning of welcome for families with hidden disabilities. I spotlight the need to accommodate with spaces in this section, because invisible disabilities require physical adaptations as much as disabilities that affect mobility. Second, we will make a beginning in addressing some of the needs of parents of children with hidden disabilities. I spotlight accessible book groups in this section, because these parents rarely have a chance to develop their own spiritual formation with church groups.

Welcoming a Family with Invisible Disabilities
There just has to be a spirit that there's not a "right kind"
of person.

—Nicole, mother of an autistic child
in an OCA parish that welcomes her family

Believe Them

If a family shows up at your church with autistic children or
children with other hidden disabilities like ADD/ADHD, sensory processing disorder, developmental delays, or learning
disabilities, the first thing to do is to believe them when they
tell you about their disabilities. Don't minimize or dismiss
them by suggesting that they're overreacting to small behavior
differences, and don't criticize their parenting when behavior
differences are unexpected.

Children with disabilities aren't only going through a
phase. A child who is young will not grow out of being autistic,
whether or not she adapts to regulate some of her behaviors
as she ages. A child who cries because of sensory overwhelm
should not be dismissed as being shy. You might have known
someone once whose neurotypical child did not speak until
he was four, but that does not mean that the child in front
of you will be able to communicate through speech. A child
who wiggles constantly might seem normal to you when you
notice him for five minutes, but he might be experiencing an
inability to know where his limbs are if he stops moving. A
boy who interrupts and stands up constantly in class might be
panicked about not knowing how to participate.

The important thing is to believe the diagnoses that parents or people with disabilities offer. Don't try to second-guess
them or smooth over your own surprise or confusion by

dismissing the diagnosis. A diagnosis is a gift that helps families know how to help their disabled members. It's not embarrassing, and it's not shameful. If you feel embarrassed or ashamed and try to soothe someone by denying a diagnosis, what you will actually communicate is that you aren't listening. You don't see the children all the time, so it's important to take a family's concerns seriously, even if you have not seen all of the needs that they describe.

In the case of children who are unaware of danger and might run away from their parents unexpectedly, doubting someone's diagnosis can even be dangerous. Children might run into the street if they're outside, or they might try to go to off-limits places in the church if they get away during a service.

One of my children has a really hard time staying in church sometimes. He has no sense of danger or what is off-limits, and he is very strong and fast. He's also cute in a cherubic way, which for some reason makes some people think I'm exaggerating about the severity of his autism. Several times he has escaped my grasp and run around the church, and no one has helped me to catch him, even if he has gone to the vigil candles at the front of the church. I have asked people to help, but they seem to think he's only being a cute little child. They don't realize that he will touch the fire. Even after years of therapy, he still doesn't completely understand that he needs to stay with the group. Our least stressful days are those when friends are standing nearby at church and can help catch our son by the hand if he gets away from us.

Ask What Helps, and Help Them

Ask what helps, and welcome the adaptations that the parents offer. One of the kindest things that our churches have done for us is to let us go to Communion at the front of the line right after the choir, even though we cannot sit at the front of the church. Two of our autistic children get confused by lines and start to cry loudly if we delay too long, because they don't understand how time works. They fear that they will not get to go to Communion if they cannot see the priest because of the line.

Remember that even if a child can behave herself quietly, that does not mean that she is paying attention. Parents might ask for an accommodation in class or church that helps their child focus or learn. Some examples of adaptations that can help a person with invisible disabilities regulate herself include wearing sunglasses or noise-canceling earmuffs in church or class, using a bag of quiet activities and/or engaging books in church services, and eating special allergy-safe foods.

Sometimes teachers assume that distracted-seeming children with disabilities need to leave class, but that is not always true. Sometimes a focus activity helps a child engage the lesson and stay in class. If you can find an adaptation that helps someone participate in the sacraments, prayers, and learning in the church, do your best to help the family implement it so that they and the rest of the church can grow in holiness.

Make Space, Not Just Time

Most of all, be willing to make space for families with invisible disabilities. Making time can help a little, but the biggest way to accommodate is through spaces. Sometimes people misinterpret a request for a quiet room—a space—as a need for a time-out, a cooling-off time period. These are not the same thing. In fact, many people with invisible disabilities do not have ordinary understandings of time or the passage of time, so offering them time can seem nonsensical to them. Confusion comes about when a family asks for help with a calming space and is instead offered time in a crowded space, like a typical cry room.

> My daughter doesn't handle crowds and noise well and is always trying to find a quiet place to be during coffee hour. We have been chastised for some of her "hiding" spots, and it is difficult sometimes to bring her to church, not knowing whether she will be able to find a quiet space or if we will need to go home earlier. —*A Serbian Orthodox parent*

A calm space, whether a bride room, an empty classroom, a quiet hallway, a corner of the choir loft, or a broom closet, can help people with overstimulated senses to calm themselves. The primary requirement is that the person can have space around him that is not filled with other people. The movements of other people are not only unpredictable to many people with invisible disabilities, but they are also distracting.

Most autistic people cannot ignore or filter out other people's movements. This can lead to intense overwhelm as their brains try to track the movement of every person in the room around them and to focus on the most important movements of the church service or classroom. A physical accommodation like a focus activity helps cut through the noise of all that input in class. An area clear of close crowds can help in church services. A calm space can help someone regain a sense of balance when the overwhelm is too intense.

SPOTLIGHT
Spaces Help My Family Stay in Church

Tonya is an Orthodox Christian mother to an autistic son, P, and has parented while being part of several Orthodox jurisdictions over the years. I talked with Tonya about what has helped her family most at the different churches they have attended, and a theme emerged. Here is her account of how spaces have helped her family participate in church life.

Space plays a critical role in our ability to participate in Liturgy and the life of the Church. It wasn't as critical until P started getting older. When he was small in that toddler/preschool stage, I could mitigate his sensory issues simply by wearing him during church. He particularly like the ring sling in a hip carry, because it allowed him to be supported, and he could look out as much or as little as he wanted. Sometimes he hid behind the "tail." Other times he watched openly. I think having the fabric of the sling helped mitigate his sensitivity to smell—particularly incense—as well.

We didn't notice that sensory issues bothered him until he was around five or six. He grew too big to be worn or carried for long, but he was unable to sit or stand still for long, either. Since his birth, we've lived in four different cities and attended a number of different churches. The ones that made it easiest for us to attend—the ones that didn't mark us as "that family" with "that kid"—offered space for him both to move around and to retreat from some of the sensory input of the Liturgy.

In our little mission church, we used the basement of another church, which was a big open room with floor-to-ceiling windows along one side. He could wander around, look out the windows, and so on. If the incense got too much for him, we could step outside the doors to a hallway leading to the stairwell. The parent who stepped out with him could still hear what was going on, and our son could get a break.

In another church, we were able to sit in the back pew directly in front of the choir, which allowed my husband to still participate in the choir while we all sat together as a family. This particular church offered activity bags in the narthex that were filled with a clipboard, coloring sheets, an assortment of books from the church library, and some small quiet toys. I appreciated these so much, because it was a very specific statement that children's presence in the Liturgy was valued, that it was important.

The issue we had with one church in particular was largely due to a lack of space. The narthex was small and felt claustrophobic. There was a small area with a few children's books and a couple of chairs, but if more than one family needed to take their children out, there was no room for anyone. The kids were having a particularly restless morning—P, the autistic one, was around seven or eight; J was two or three—and we were moving in and out of church a lot. The choir was very loud because it was miked and didn't really need to be. P was attempting to crawl under the row of chairs (his usual move when the noise/incense are too much). At one point during the eucharistic prayer, we gave up and just went out to sit in the narthex till time for Communion. A woman came bounding after us and proceeded to tell us that we couldn't go back in, and that "no one in the church can pray because of you." There was a much longer lecture involved, and she was quite sanctimonious about it.

After she went back into the church, I looked at my husband and mouthed, "We need to go. Now." We packed up and left.

We agreed that we were both so angry we were no longer pre-pared for Communion.

When we moved to our current parish three years ago, it took us a while to find the right place. The Sunday school kids typically sit together down in the front with the Sunday school teachers. That didn't work for our family, because P was just too restless in that churning sea of kids. We tried me and the boys sitting in the back after my husband joined the choir. That didn't work, either. Inevitably we'd end up in the small children's room at the back of the narthex. The room has a speaker so you can still hear what's going on in church, and there's a glass window that allows you to see into the church. It's not ideal, because I want my children to be *in* church and participating in the Liturgy. But it works better than sitting in other places downstairs.

Somewhere along the way, we started sitting up in the choir loft. The loft runs the width of the church, but the choir only takes up the center third. There are a few pews and a few rows of chairs on either side. P can pace behind the choir if he needs to. He can look out the windows. He can lie down on or under the pews. Occasionally he still asks to go downstairs to the chil-dren's room, but I'm starting to think that this is more to visit the babies and hang out with our priest's daughter, who has Down syndrome. I'm working on delaying his requests for a bit to build up more tolerance for staying in the Liturgy.

After Communion, the kids go down for the second half of Sunday school. Although still a very traditional classroom for-mat, the Sunday school staff has been wonderfully patient and understanding about our autistic son's issues and quirks. An older student has volunteered to be his "para" so that he can be more independent. And they changed the location of his classroom to a larger room to give him some space to pace if needed and to help him not feel so closed in.

We are able to stay and visit with our friends in the parish at coffee hour due in large part to how the social hall is divided up. The original building was added onto in order to provide a larger hall. The space between the church and social hall is often called the "small hall," and it contains the church library and some carpet squares for the kids to sit on, along with a table or two. P often gets his snack and goes out there, where it's quieter. While he's been known to get himself into trouble a time or two (or five), it's mostly a good solution.

In thinking about our interactions with people and space over the years, two factors stand out as being so important: appropriate space and being connected to people who know our situation and are understanding. Our current parish has an autistic member who grew up in the church, and I'm sure P reminds people of this man as he was growing up. It helps so very much when people get it.

Tonya's experience demonstrates the way that emotional welcome and hospitable spaces go together. In speaking to families of children with invisible disabilities, these considerations have been recurring concerns.

Ministering to Parents of Children with Invisible Disabilities

Like Tonya, other parents of children with invisible disabilities are less stressed not only when churches make space, but when the parents have church friends who understand and accept them. One mother described the welcoming culture of her OCA parish as a church where families with disabilities know they have a place because so many church members "are quietly very accepting." Another family described their joy in fellowship with other families with disabilities as a "happy little band of misfits" at coffee hour. Whether your parish culture is quiet or exuberant, there are lots of ways to accept families with hidden disabilities, including the parents.

Parents of children with hidden disabilities are often isolated socially due to the demands of special-needs parenting and the need for them to assist with their children's communication and social interactions. If parents are in Sunday school classes to help with their children, they are not participating in adult Christian formation classes or fellowship. Many churches have sermons at a time when children are in Sunday school, and parents who assist their children in class miss the sermons. The exclusion extends to other ministries for adults, too, because of the high time demands of parenting when they have to help their child with more parts of their routines than neurotypical children would require.

Parents might not have time to read books or get to study groups. They might not be able to disrupt their family's routine in order to attend extra evening church services often. Many parents who spent a lot of time in formal prayer before they had children with invisible disabilities told me that they have a hard time praying in daily life. Their old scripts of how to pray and how to participate in services and even how to parent no longer apply due to their children's needs, and they are left feeling adrift from their connection with God.

Parents of children with invisible disabilities can find help by talking with their priests. If you don't know how to pray in your circumstances, ask your priest to help you find a prayer rule that fits your life now. Consult the chapter on nonverbal prayers for ideas. Ask your godfamily and other special-needs parents about prayer practices that help them. Though people sometimes talk to their priests for confession or to ask for prayers, they don't always think to ask for help with connecting with God in daily prayer. Whether you are a priest or a parent, it might help to bring up the question of how to pray so that the entire family stays connected in prayer.

When it comes to learning and studying, options outside of Sunday mornings might be more adaptable for including parents of children with invisible disabilities. Often book groups meet at church in the evenings, and sometimes they even ask participants to read several hundred pages before a meeting. Neither the location nor the high reading requirement works well for most parents of children with high needs. However, there are ways to adapt book groups so families with invisible disabilities can participate.

If book groups meet at church or a home in the evening, video conferencing tools like Zoom or Skype can help parents participate in discussion even if they cannot be present. Another option is to have smaller groups within larger study groups so that a few people can come to the home of the parents of children with invisible disabilities. For instance, if a larger parenting group meets in person or by Skype/Zoom each week, smaller three- to five-person discussion groups might come to the home of parents of children with hidden disabilities once a month so that they can be included in person. The Lord modeled the wisdom of having a smaller group meet in addition to larger groups with His disciples; smaller groups also help families with disabilities participate better in learning.

Another consideration is the reading load. Books like this one are set up so that groups can pick chapters to discuss, with bullet point summaries to help catch people up who didn't have time to read in full. Take advantage of section and chapter divisions in larger books, and do not read them all at once. Taking your time will help everyone understand and have more ideas for discussion, and the lower reading load will make it possible for parents of high-needs children to participate.

My godson's mother introduced me to another great option for parents with tight schedules: a not-book group.[82] Rather than reading whole books, she and a group of her friends watch videos or read blog posts, articles, or book chapters before they meet for discussion. This method has the advantage of using multiple media in order to meet different learning needs, and it can be adapted even for regular book studies. When an author posts YouTube or live social media video links, they can add another dimension to chapters that the group is interested in discussing.

SUMMARY

» Welcoming families with invisible disabilities requires that you believe the family when they tell you their child's diagnosis and work with them to make adaptations.

» Just as you offer physical spaces and accommodations to help people who need wheelchairs due to their visible disabilities, offer physical accommodations to help people with invisible disabilities participate in church. Accommodate with space, not only time.

» A calm room or area can make a difference in a family's ability to attend church. Tonya shares several examples of how spaces for her autistic son have made a big difference in her family's participation in church life.

» Parents of children with invisible disabilities are often excluded from faith formation because of the demands of high-needs parenting. They often even miss sermons.

» Priests and parents of children with invisible disabilities should talk about how to pray now that family life is different than they had anticipated.

» Accommodate parents with accessible versions of book study groups, including video conference calls, not-book groups, and small groups than meet less often and in parents' homes.

REFLECTION QUESTIONS

1. What are some spaces in your church buildings where families with invisible disabilities might take a calming break from crowds?

2. How do you pray? Are there parts of your life that you don't know how to bring to God in prayer? Mention this to your priest.

3. Do you get to hear the sermons at your church? Are notes, recordings, or transcripts of sermons available for people who cannot hear or who have to tend to their families during sermons?

4. Are you able to attend adult Sunday school classes? Would you be able to participate in a study group that met for an hour on a weeknight? What about thirty minutes over a video conference call? Think of what you can fit into your schedule around your parenting, and bring those ideas to event organizers.

SPOTLIGHT
Special-Needs Liturgy and Community Gathering

For when His Body and Blood become the tissue of our members, we become Christ-bearers and as the blessed Peter said, "partakers of the divine nature."[83]

—St. Cyril of Jerusalem

The Need for Inclusive Liturgy

Many people I have talked with over the three years that I gathered interviews for this book have expressed a desire for regularly scheduled services of the Divine Liturgy that specifically accommodate families with special needs. From families who lament the overstimulation from crowds and the feeling that they are distracting others by attending church, to adults with disabilities whose conditions make the frequent bumping into others in crowded services potentially dangerous, many people who give all they can to attend services would welcome a less crowded, more inclusive and disability-conscious Divine Liturgy. While I was able to find some examples of special-needs ministries that catered to a very specific setting,[84] it was only when I heard about the St. Catherine and St. George Special Needs Liturgy that I found a model of inclusive services that can be replicated in other parishes. One of the biggest challenges that would-be coordinators have expressed to me is that they need a model to present to their churches so that they can adapt it and make plans for a sustainable ministry. Such a model is spreading in the metro area of New York City.

The Archangel Michael Greek Orthodox Church of Port Washington, New York, has carried on a ministry to families with special needs since 1990, and the practice has spread to nine area parishes in Queens and Long Island.[85] *Some of the churches provide transportation to those families who need it. Some of them coordinate parental support groups. All of them have monthly services of the Divine Liturgy that particularly include families with special needs. The Divine Liturgy is celebrated in about forty-five minutes to an hour, and the community gathers for food and fellowship afterwards. I thank God that, through the Koinonia for Exceptional Orthodox Children group on Facebook, I was introduced to Maria Evangelou Christodoulou, the Leader-Coordinator of the St. Catherine and St. George Special Needs Liturgy and Community Gathering in Astoria, New York. With the blessing of her priests, Maria shared with me how her church community formed a monthly Special Needs Liturgy and Community Gathering. I share it here in the hope that this example of welcome will encourage others and perhaps help other communities as they consider similar ministries.*

Our Children Are Allowed to Be Themselves

Three years ago, Archimandrite Fr. Nektarios Papazafiropoulos of St. Demetrios Cathedral, Astoria, as well as St. Catherine and St. George of Astoria, New York, together with Fr. Anastasios Pourakis, asked if it was possible for me to lead, coordinate, and gather our families for the monthly Divine Liturgy, as well as prepare refreshments for gathering together after the service. After the service, the gathering of the community serves as a parental support group, a place to meet, to talk, and to get to know each other. I humbly accepted, and I knew I would love this beautiful ministry for my family as well. My son, Panayiotis, lives with Asperger's syndrome. I was just learning more about Asperger's myself, as he was diagnosed only five years ago.

You Need a Team to Build a Strong Ministry

Our clergy and the special-needs committee of volunteers and supporters, community members, donors, and our amazing families have all helped to make this ministry what it is. You can only build something strong when you have a team. Our community is super amazing: God-fearing, faithful, unbelievably encouraging, and very supportive. I'm humbled to be a voice and blessed to be a mother, a role model, and a leader in my community, because I know very well the feeling of not fitting in or not showing up. It is a struggle for many of us, even as it is easier now to cope than twenty years ago.

The gatherings for our special-needs families service are on the first Saturday of every month unless rescheduled, and we started them in 2015. Our clergy's vision to invite families living with disabilities to the Divine Liturgy service from 9 AM to 10 AM has been a success. The clergy emphasize the importance for all to support any family feeling shy or in doubt because of any outbursts, movement, or crying. The clergy always state, "Our children are allowed to be themselves." With this support and communication, we and any community can move forward. Our children and families with special needs, together with typical families, receive Holy Communion. At 10 AM, a structured gathering is set up and ready to begin in our church's hall.

Benefits of the Monthly Community Gathering

Our beautiful community comes together every month firstly because they have a deep faith. Also, we want to teach our children from a young age about our Orthodoxy and our traditions. No matter the challenges our families face, we must keep moving forward and passing along the Faith. In these gatherings, we support and guide each other and enjoy being together. We offer advice, trade ideas, share recipes, and more. Everything begins from our worship together. Putting God first in our lives starts with lighting our candles and venerating our icons, together.

Gathering Logistics

At our community gathering in the church hall, we share light refreshments like bagels, eggs, juice, fruit, cake, and coffee. I prepare some, and some of our families with special needs, friends, and the community members will donate delicious baked cakes, muffins, and other coffee foods. Definite blessings!

Working together to support each other is what makes this ministry work and last. I believe it takes a unique concern, a certain love. I also believe that we are here for the kids first and foremost. To keep an important event like this going, you need a super structured, quality activity and organization. My concern is to find activities that are appropriate. I consider how an activity will bring us together and how we can help each other with a particular experience, as well as calculate what the interests are for the families with special needs. It's amazing to see the bonds blossoming as well as being built! What blessings! What miracles! Not only the children, but also the adults love the small activities we prepare. For example, two years ago, we made chocolate-covered cookies. Another time, for the Sunday of Orthodoxy, thanks to our clergy and to Fr. Anastasios who collected and donated materials, we were all able to make small icons. They came out beautifully! Another factor is making sure I always bring up the Divine Liturgy service and this event, to connect our worship to the building of community together.

Equally important, I keep up to date on social posts and community announcements. This adds to the growth of the ministry. Inviting and including typical friends and families is a must! I believe firmly that when we get to know each other a bit, we are able to communicate. Even a "hello" in church helps to build our whole community.

Togetherness with Our Angels on Earth

Only togetherness will bring awareness of one another's gifts and the blessings of community. If I had to summarize the traits of someone who will lead a similar program, I would say that the person should be concerned, positive, and supportive to our children and families with special needs. A quality program will include children through young adults and older. Our friends and families with different abilities, difficult or not, will be able to bring awareness in their own unique way. They bring love with easy friendships to all. We treat children with disabilities as our angels on earth! Because of this, we seek God first. We strive to keep in touch and in a constant communion with these families. A great team and a supportive clergy will ensure a sustainable, ongoing event. God bless all our angels on earth and those who carry the cross to carry them!

SUMMARY

» There is a need for Divine Liturgy and community gatherings that cater to families with special needs. One model that is spreading in the New York metro area includes short (forty-five minutes to one hour) services of the Divine Liturgy followed by community gatherings. In these gatherings, parents of children with special needs can support each other, and the community participates in fellowship and structured activities appropriate to the needs of the group.

» Worship together is the basis of the building of community. The clergy remind everyone, "Our children are allowed to be themselves." That regard for one another in the love of Christ helps the community to focus on carrying forward and passing along the Faith in appropriate ways for families living with disabilities.

» A sustainable ministry to families with special needs requires a team of clergy, a volunteer coordinator, community members who help with food and activities and donations, families with special needs, and typical families who join for fellowship. Community grows from togetherness centered on worship. Friendships and kindness blossom when people come together, and this is how we put God first.

REFLECTION QUESTIONS

1. If your church does not have a special-needs ministry, what would it need in order to start one? Are there lessons from this example ministry that you can include in your regular church gatherings?

2. Have you taken time to build friendships with the families with disabilities in your church? How might you start? Remember that even a kind "hello" can build community.

CHAPTER II

The Four Levels of Scripture & Attention

TEACHING PEOPLE OF ALL ABILITIES
ACCORDING TO HUMAN NATURE

P ERSONS WITH DISABILITIES OFTEN STRUGGLE to learn in the typical church school or book study environments that most churches use. This is because the standard for telling people how to participate in a group is usually focused on behavior rather than attention.[86] As a result, people with communication challenges not only have a lesser chance of understanding what is being taught, they also are not likely to get help with focusing on the things they need to learn if their behaviors indicate that they do not understand.

From a teacher's perspective, attempts to maintain classroom order through punishing poor behaviors and rewarding good behaviors do not help students learn. The more students act out because they cannot attend, the more time the teacher focuses on maintaining order. One of three outcomes then occurs: the classroom spirals into chaos, the children whose attention has not been engaged are asked to leave, or the children all behave by the rules (sit down and be quiet). Unfortunately, though, many "well-behaved" children do not pay attention and thus do not learn meaningfully.

Of course, certain behaviors signify attention, such as pointing one's face and body toward the speaker. But telling learners to sit still and listen—focusing on the behavior—doesn't help to bring about the attention (listening) or the behavior (sitting still). What works best for a teacher is to gain and share attention with the students. Once attention is shared, learning can happen.

It is easiest to get attention when we know how our brains prioritize attention. *Every* human—whether they have normal cognition and abilities, learning disabilities and delays, cognitive disabilities, neurodivergences, or distractions due to other disabilities—will process attention in the same order. Understanding that order helps us to know how to approach one another and remove the barriers to learning (or handicaps[87]) that might arise from disabilities. Since this order of paying attention is something everyone experiences, knowing the levels of attention helps us prepare to teach all students and thus give staying power to the teachings of the Faith we want to pass along.

The Four Levels of Attention

Every person will pay attention to feelings first, sight second, and thinking third. Once all of these three preliminary types of attention are in place, the highest level of attention, joint attention, can take place. After we look more closely at these four levels of attention, we will see that they parallel the four levels of reading Scripture that Orthodox Christians have practiced in the Church since the beginning. This parallel shows us how God has made us for His mercy, because the highest level of attention and the highest way of reading

Scripture help us to know the love of God, showing us how to live in God's Kingdom.

Feel First, See Second, Think Third—Joint Attention
Feel First
About thirty years ago, breakthrough research on the brain revealed that our bodies process emotions before we even think.[88] It turns out that we first pay attention to the sensory input that we take in through our eight senses and our emotional feelings. Eight senses? Yes. Sight, hearing, taste, touch, smell, of course, and also balance (vestibular sense), pressure on joints and muscles (proprioception), and what is happening in our bodies (interoception) all impact our emotions before we even think.[89]

For teaching, knowing about the senses and that we all pay attention first to the feelings (both sensations and emotions connected to those sensations) is important for beginning teaching interactions. Are we arranging our spaces and lessons so that sensory and emotional needs are met? Is there a physical reason a child might be unable to settle to learn?

See Second
After our feelings, next we notice visual memory or images. However, these images do not have stories associated with them by default. The images will take on the meaning of the feelings. For example, if a child is afraid because a neurological and sensory-processing difference has made him feel as though he doesn't have hands or feet, or if a child is panicked and cannot breathe well due to an allergy, he will not see the cheerful book or puppets or pictures as cheerful. To him, the images will be part of his nightmarish feelings.

That's why we start first by addressing sensory and emotional needs. Then, when we present a visual aid or an example, it will be in line with the calm, centered feelings of the students. Attention works in a cumulative way: the later levels of attention are affected by the earlier ones. Setting up a space well (which we will address in Chapter 12, "God as a Place: Teaching Through Space," page 128) and providing calming, centering activities to meet sensory needs will thus make our visual teaching more effective.

Since we venerate holy icons, the need to make sure that attention is cultivated toward peace from the beginning is even more important. We want the holy icons to be associated with peace rather than emotional chaos.

Think Third

After we have felt and seen, we are able to pay attention to thoughts. This includes words and language as well as cause and effect and connections between different ideas. Once again, the effect of attention is cumulative. A child who does not have her sensory or emotional needs in balance might be confused, unable to focus on ideas, unable to communicate or participate, or fixated on one word or idea—even if that word or idea is not relevant, or if they misunderstand it.

Joint Attention

This form of attention, also called *triadic* attention, is shared attention between communication partners and an object or subject they are paying attention to together.[90] It's the kind of attention we practice when we hear the prayer, "Let us be attentive." We look at each other's faces, smile, and make sure we are standing or facing the Gospel. Parents might look back and forth from the reading to the child to see how they're understanding and to share their joy. A child might then look to a parent to see what sense to make of the new experience. The back-and-forth attention between the other person and the action they are both attending sets the stage for communication and learning.

The Order of Attention and Teaching

As mentioned earlier, these aspects of attention are cumulative, which means in this case that they build upon each other to create the learning experience. The way the early Fathers read the Scripture mirrors this pattern of attention that modern science is only now discovering. But before we look more closely at the levels of reading Scripture and how they relate, we should look at two helpful surprises in the levels of attention. First, interoception—the eighth sense that has only recently been studied in detail—tells us how sensory experiences translate into gut feelings. Second, joint attention is one of the ways that human nature is created in the image of the Holy Trinity.

Interoception: What's Going on in My Body, and What Should I Do?

We've all had the experience of following our "gut feelings" when we make decisions. Those gut feelings are formed by sensory information that we notice as feelings in our bodies and also as emotions. Interoception is the sense that tells us whether our hearts are racing, whether we're hot or cold, whether we're full or hungry or thirsty, if we need to use the restroom, and whether we're excited or depressed. These feelings form the basis of our decision-making in the short term, and they also make a big difference in how we make decisions long-term. The feeling in our bodies when we enter church or church school (or any other experience) gets stored in our memories as a "somatic marker," a bodily feeling or "gut feeling."[91]

In a church setting, if we can help children feel engaged, calm, and interested, they will process their attention in the present through those feelings. Those feelings will be stored in their memories to make a gut feeling later. This is the science behind the biblical wisdom, "Train up a child in the way he should go, and when he is old he will not depart from it" (Prov. 22:6).

Joint Attention and the Holy Trinity

We need joint attention in order to be social, to express love, and to learn from one another. It's called *triadic* attention because it occurs between two people and a third interest (either another person or an object). Of course, the word for the Trinity in Greek is *Triada*, but the resemblance between joint attention and the Trinity is not just in the sound of the words. Rather, joint (triadic) attention follows the pattern of love.[92] We cannot know love until we love our brother and sister, love God, and also love the act of loving them. Those three elements of love—loving God, neighbor, and oneself—are the parts of the Great Commandment that Jesus gave us: "You shall love the Lord your God with all your heart, and with all your soul, and with all your mind. This is the great and first commandment. And a second is like it, You shall love your neighbor as yourself" (Matt. 22:38, 39).

This pattern of love is one way that God has made humans in His image. It's a built-in way that we can see that God made us for Himself,[93] and the right use of joint attention will lead us naturally toward God. We see the pattern of the Holy Trinity in the threefold attention of love. It reminds us who we are made for and that God has made triadic love as the way to know Him. The purest form of joint attention we experience is the triadic love shared between God, neighbor, and the self.

When we exercise joint attention in teaching and try to build joint attention in our students, we are following the pattern of love. It's vital to teach in the way that fosters attention, because in doing so, we not only engage the most natural way of learning, but by doing so we point our natures toward the love of God.

The next chapters will cover ways to engage these levels of attention in detail, but first let's look at the ways that the Fathers read the Scripture along the same lines as the levels of attention. If we are going to change the way we teach and arrange our spaces, we need to see how those changes are in line with the teachings of the Church and the love of God.

The Four Levels of Scripture

In the early Church, we see from the beginning a pattern of reading the Scriptures on at least two levels: the literal and the spiritual. This way of reading is present in the letters of St. Paul (2 Cor. 3:6), and by the time of St. Irenaeus about a hundred years later, the spiritual meaning of the text was taking on its own layers.[94] When St. Jerome and St. Augustine talked about Scripture at the end of the fourth and beginning of the fifth centuries, they explained the levels of Scripture in more detail, with references to four levels of meaning.

In later centuries in the Western Church tradition, the four meanings were handed down in verses that were easy for students to memorize.[95] Usually, the four meanings were arranged by what the teachers saw as the most basic meaning to the most lofty, from earth to heaven. The four levels that became commonplace[96] were the literal or historical level, the allegorical level that explains the spiritual or Christ-centered meaning, the moral level that explains how to act, and the heavenly (anagogical) level. However, when St. Augustine described the four levels of Scripture, he began with the spiritual level, because Christ is the beginning.[97] We can only read Scripture or know anything through Christ. Thus St. Augustine's levels of meaning in Scripture are as follows: the Christ-centered level, the historical level, the heavenly level, and the virtue level. These levels match his description of what we find in Sacred Scripture:

> In all the sacred books, we should consider the eternal truths that are taught, the facts that are narrated, the future events that are predicted, and the precepts or counsels that are given.[98]

Christ is the first meaning of Scripture, for he is the "eternal Truth." The "facts that are narrated" are the historical meaning of Scripture. Our hope in heaven is related in "the future events that are predicted." The virtues that show us how to walk in the light of Christ and in consideration of our heavenly destiny are "the precepts or counsels that are given."

We can see how these levels unfold in texts such as the beginning of Genesis, where Christ is the beginning. God makes the world from nothing in the beginning, and we believe that the end will be like the beginning in that we will experience a perfect communion of love with God. We know that we must love one another in order to enter the love of God that was in the beginning when He made us, and our love for God will unite us all in heaven.

These four levels of meaning in the Scriptures match up with the four levels of paying attention. As such, they show us that the Church has taught us from the beginning about how we learn.

Feel First: The Christ-Centered Meaning

Christ is not a feeling, but Christ speaks to us through the Scriptures as our Alpha and Omega, the beginning and end. The gut feeling we have at the approach of Christ will draw us toward Him the same way that baby John the Forerunner leapt in his mother's womb at Christ's approach. When we engage attention first by recognizing the Incarnate Christ, for instance, by making our first action together the veneration of a holy icon of the Savior, we draw the senses toward their proper use in experiencing the presence of the Lord with us.

See Second: The Historical Meaning

Children's Bibles and movies follow the historical meaning of the text for a good reason. Once we know that we are seeking Christ, we want to see Him. All actions in a scriptural story unfold in the light of Christ so that we can see what happened in reference to Him. When we teach the literal or historical meaning, we must engage the sense of sight. This might mean acting out stories, showing images, or teaching with a picture-based language system.

Think Third: The Heavenly Meaning

Here is where we make connections between the Lord we're experiencing and the direction God is calling us. Heavenly meanings relate not only to the final resurrection, but also to the presence of God in the Holy Eucharist. Here we might ask about the way that God is and how we are. This is the part of learning where we experience God as a place—heaven—and in communion. (See the next chapter, "God as a Place: Teaching Through Space," page 128, for examples of how thoughtful learning emerges when spaces point us toward God.) We often seek to engage this part of attention through talking or extensive use of language. The heavenly meaning is also the part of the Scripture that we can say the least about, since much of it is a mystery to us.

Joint Attention: The Virtues of Love

When we read the Scriptures in order to learn how we should act toward God and one another—in communion with the Incarnate Lord, in light of God's provision in history, looking to the direction God has given us about heaven and communion with Him—we find good habits that we can imitate. These imitations of God will follow the pattern of joint attention and love for God and our neighbors.

Attention levels and the levels of Scripture both build on one another and circle back to each other. This means that we are using the earlier levels of attention when we engage in joint attention, and we use the other levels of Scripture when we read about how we should act in order to love like God. We need to go back and use those earlier forms of attention and levels of meaning in Scripture in order to advance in ideas or really get the meaning of something. In other words, even when we want to use joint attention to point out how we should act, we should do so while engaging the feelings (senses and emotions) with visual storytelling.

To teach according to the nature by which we learn—as shown in the latest brain science and the sacred tradition of studying the Scriptures—we must avoid simply telling people what to do. We must not treat the revelation of God, who came to us as one of us in order to make us like Him, as a list of dos and don'ts. We must not assume that a well-behaved class is paying attention. We must not neglect the senses, for they produce the feelings that lead to habits, and we must always seek Christ first.

Since we learn this way, we ought to teach to gain the attention of the learner. This is particularly important for persons with the types of disabilities that make joint attention harder to gain. The Divine Liturgy trains our attention, but we need to make sure to complete the triad of joint attention and joint love as we extend community out into the teaching and common life of the Church. To communicate and to love, we need to check in with our brothers and sisters as we go. The following three chapters will address ways to engage attention in the patterns of your teaching and your church.

To teach according to human nature and to reach persons with disabilities, we must shift the focus from trying to gain attention first with spoken words to gaining attention with feeling. We must engage the senses through Christ-centered worship, honoring the Incarnation first even in our classrooms and lecture halls and homes. To do that, we have to change the way we arrange spaces. Rather than an afterthought, the arrangement of space is of vital importance for teaching that imitates the pattern of the Incarnation. We will consider this pattern and how it should shape our classroom spaces in the next chapter.

SUMMARY

» Our brains process attention in a set order, no matter our level of disability or ability. The order is Feel First, See Second, Think Third, and Joint or Triadic Attention, where we pay attention to one another.

» We process feelings in such a way that our sensory and emotional experiences are stored in our memories as gut feelings.

» When we pay attention, the results are cumulative and interactive. We interpret one layer of attention through the earlier ones, and once all levels are achieved, we interpret all the levels through one another.

» Joint, or triadic, attention follows the pattern of love. Both of these functions of human nature reflect the image of God the Holy Trinity.

» The way our attention works reflects the way the Church has understood the meanings of Scripture.

» The levels of meaning of Scripture are the Christ-centered, the historical, the heavenly, and the virtues.

» Since we can see from brain science and the holy tradition how humans learn, we should teach in such a way that every student, including students with disabilities, can learn. The following chapters will go into detail about how to do this.

REFLECTION QUESTIONS

1. What is the first thing a person experiences on entering your church or classroom? What is the focus? What are the feelings they might experience with their senses? What might engage their emotions?

2. Have you taught the Scriptures with both historical and

spiritual meanings before? What about all the levels (literal meaning plus the three levels of spiritual meaning)?

3. What does it mean to you that Christ is the beginning? How does this understanding change how you read Scriptures? How does it change the way you teach? Does it change how you learn?

4. Now that you know that thinking is not the first way people pay attention, do you want to change how much you talk in lessons?

5. Recent statistics have shown us that sixty percent of young people do not return to the Orthodox Church as adults. A priest has suggested that failed models of education contribute to the decline.[99] How might teaching according to human nature reverse that trend? How might persons with disabilities be brought into the Faith if we were to teach in this way?

CHAPTER 12

God as a Place

TEACHING THROUGH SPACE

The location of the saved will be God himself.
—ST. MAXIMUS THE CONFESSOR[100]

Lord, You have been our dwelling place in all generations.
PSALM 90:1 NKJV

Faith is the substance of things hoped for, the evidence of things not seen.
HEBREWS 11:1

Hitherto I have lived in God: I have thought, felt, and subsisted in Him. In future, I shall also live in Him.
—ST. JOHN OF KRONSTADT[101]

NOW, FAITH IS THE SUBSTANCE of things hoped for, the evidence of things unseen" (Heb. 11:1). We might not be able to see faith, but it is substantial. Spiritually, it is a gift of attention to God at all times and in all things. Physically, faith is the received Tradition in prayers, holy teaching, services, and the way we arrange spaces and move together as the Body of Christ.

Though we have heard time and again that we can walk by faith and not by sight and that faith is the substance of things hoped for, and though we have many customs that are part of the holy Tradition along with the holy words we pray and teach, few people remember that we can *touch* faith. Everything around us can shape our senses so that we experience God in this world and in these bodies. God became man that we might become divine, and He knew that we needed to learn through our senses.[102] Sadly, though, much of our teaching has not sought to teach faith as though it is accessible to our bodily senses.

We have tried to get to the intellect, to teach through thinking, without remembering that our bodies are saved along with our minds and souls. In fact, we have to teach to the senses in order to form memories or engage the mind. Since most people's brains work very quickly to assign meanings to their sensory perceptions, it's easy to forget that thoughts come after feelings.

Our thoughts are our attempts to make connections between sensory impressions and spiritual truths, but they cannot be guided correctly without guiding them through those sensory impressions.[103] This is why, for instance, we go through fasting and prayers with our bodies in order to act in accord with the Holy Spirit. We cannot leave out the proper interpretation of sensory experiences, but neither can we teach without them.

We are surrounded by a culture that denies the Incarnation and therefore denies the sacred importance of the body. As a result, because we might have picked up on the disembodied

chatter of our surroundings, we sometimes put more emphasis on what we can understand mentally than on what we
can receive physically. As we saw in the last chapter, talking
about thoughts before engaging attention through the senses
is futile.

Thankfully, faith is not limited to thinking. Faith is a gift
received, whether we understand it rationally or not. But if we
want to teach the Faith or to prepare the way for people to
receive faith as a gift, we have to do so by engaging attention.

Attention, as we've seen in the previous chapter, follows the
same order for all people, and it has as its pattern and aim
the love of God and neighbor. How do we teach according to
nature when our nature requires that we learn by shaping our
gut feelings and drawing our attention through our bodies?

We Learn through Spaces

This is not a strange idea if we consider two things: first, that
our memories are shaped by spaces,[104] and second, that part
of the truth and goal of the Christian life is that God is and
becomes a place for us.[105] For families with disabilities, these
truths are gifts, because they mean that limitations in rational
understanding or differences in learning abilities cannot stop
us from communion with God. It is possible to teach children
with extreme disabilities through the way we interact with
spaces in churches and classrooms and homes. The reasons we
can teach despite limitations is because the building of memories through space reaches out to the pre-thinking part of our
attention and, even more importantly, because God is everywhere present and fills all things.

Places Shape Our Memories

In the time periods when we Christians started building churches in houses and later in dedicated buildings, there was a common practice of memorizing large amounts of information such as scripture, poetry, speeches, and even lists for business and daily life. Writing was expensive, and books were hard to come by. Yet we have many examples of saints who memorized the entirety of Holy Scripture. They did this by walking around familiar places, first in real life and later in memory, while reciting parts of the text. The order of the words became fixed in their memories in the same order as they walked around the spaces. If they needed to know what came next in the text they memorized, they would remember walking to the next part of a building or open place, and the words would come to mind, too. These familiar, remembered spaces that were layered with memories were called "memory palaces." Churches were built and painted with this model in mind.

Using this model helped St. Augustine to see that the story of creation was a microcosm, or "tiny universe," of human nature and salvation history.[106] The word that the Fathers used to talk about the connecting pattern of Church–human nature–salvation history was *microcosm*. Saint Augustine read his own life as a microcosm of the history of God creating and saving humans, because the pattern showed him how God creates and saves us in His love. The layers of meaning were built into memory by interacting with familiar spaces, such as churches.

In fully painted Orthodox churches, you will notice right away that the space is shaping our memories through the iconography and the way the building makes us move together. The story of salvation is painted on the walls and ceilings, a tiny retelling of the universe.[107] We too, as humans, are a tiny retelling[108] of the story of salvation and of the universe God has made. These tiny universes of humans and church buildings and iconography interact with each other and reflect each other so well because God is with us and teaches us according to our nature, drawing us to Him through all of our senses.[109] It's not an accident that humans, the Church, and salvation history fit the same pattern, because God teaches us and has arranged the world for our salvation.

This concurrence of pattern in humans, the Church, and salvation history provides another way that the somatic markers—the bodily feelings of learning in a space—that we talked about in the last chapter can help us learn. First, they help us develop gut feelings that will direct our attention through the other levels. Second, the somatic markers aid our memories in recalling texts. When we read the *Catechetical Lectures* of St. Cyril of Jerusalem, for instance, we see St. Cyril reference the places where the crowds are standing. They learned about the life of Christ in the very places where Christ lived his life.[110] The preaching in those same places was layered with many levels of gracious meaning, which each year the people would remember when they came to those places again. For the Christians walking where Christ walked, memorizing the Creed went along with the tangible evidence of the places where He lived. But this effect takes place for Christians in Orthodox churches all over the world as well, where we can learn the Faith by moving through the memory palaces of our churches.[111]

For Christians living with differences in sensory input, either because they have an impairment affecting sight or hearing or body or because they have a different way of processing sense input, this all-encompassing way of teaching is especially good news. If one sense is impaired, God still teaches through others. Moving in the space of the church will itself help to teach about God. The grace of God that enters the soul when we go to the Divine Liturgy will always be sufficient no matter our disability, because we cannot have only a little bit of God. God is everywhere present and fills all things, and God is simple—always entirely God.

If it's hard to accept that people remember through space despite their disabilities, the following story from my experience might help you to see what I mean. By paying attention to how space shaped this person, we found a way to minister to one another so that we were both filled with profound joy:

For many years, I attended a church with a young man who was born with only a small part of his brain. He was able to walk around but not to speak. His mother brought him to church once or twice a month, but she seemed concerned that he was bothering people. I watched him over many months and saw that he was not walking randomly around the building. He would stand up as soon as the choir began a song, and he would walk toward it. Or he would head toward the baptismal font. He would otherwise not go anywhere. In that church, the tradition was that everyone would gather around the font and sing together when someone was baptized. I was in the choir, and I noticed that the boy walked toward me either when I was in the choir or when I was by the font singing. I realized that he loved music and knew that the music was always in one of the two places he walked toward. I found him after a service once, standing by the font. I sang to him, but I slowed down and held the pitch for a long time. He tried to sing with me, just a loud sound. He had no control over his voice, but I could control mine. I harmonized with him, and together, we were singing. After that day, we sang together near the baptismal font whenever he came to church.

Church buildings have been designed as ideal memory palaces, both in their shape and the way that we move through them. As St. John of Kronstadt tells us, "the whole temple appears to me to be sacred history in action, a wonderful scripture of the works of God, accomplished in the human race."[112] Church buildings are microcosms of salvation history, where space is arranged so that we can know ourselves as having a place in the mercy of God. Like our churches, our classrooms and teaching patterns can reflect the pattern of God as a place where God's mercy makes us at home. This sense of church as home is open to families with disabilities, too, because God in His mercy became human so that we all might know Him through all of our senses.

Teaching When God Is Our Place

We believe in God. If you are not used to the concrete thinking that many people with neurodivergences or cognitive disabilities experience, you might have read that first sentence abstractly. Maybe, if you think about it for a moment, you might say that you believe in God in the way you might say you trust in God. That's one of the meanings of that phrase. But another, perhaps hidden in plain sight, is that we believe in God as a place, the way that fish swim in water or we breathe in air.[113] This is true now and will be even truer in heaven, for, as St. Gregory and St. Macrina tell us about the resurrection, "God becomes a place to those who are worthy and a home."[114]

When you start to think of faith as believing in God as a

place, several possibilities arise in how to approach teaching, and these possibilities open the way for teaching children and families with disabilities. If we believe in God as a place, why do we teach by seating people at tables, with coloring sheets and very little engagement with the senses? If we believe in God the way fish swim in water, why do we only teach by talking about thoughts?

If we believe in God as a place, why do we not arrange classrooms so that the prayer corner is the primary focal point? If we believe in God as a place, why do we often teach children to pray in sanitized, private ways such as folding hands and closing their eyes, which blocks out their ability to pray with the help of the sacred space around them? If we believe in God as a place, why do we often fail to teach children how to move in holy ways, such as bringing candles or flowers into their classroom prayer areas?

If we believe in God as a place, why do so many people still question whether it is good for children and families with disabilities to be fully included in the services and community life of the Church, where God is especially present to us?

In teaching children with autism, ADHD, Down syndrome, and learning disabilities, I have found that not only do they think outside the box—that is, differently than typically abled people—but they think outside their heads, using the room to process their learning. Thankfully, the Church has a long history of teaching through spaces, and I can apply the truths that God is a place, and that places teach, in order to help those students to learn, too.

This insight has led me to create learning centers that allow the children to touch the Faith in concrete ways. We have dress-up stations alongside golden circles fastened to the walls so that the children can act out their calling as living icons. Rather than telling them about victory crowns of martyrs, they dress up in pretend laurels as they look at an icon of a martyr saint. They know even if they cannot read well or talk well or do math that they are like the martyrs who help them.

When the children bring flowers to their prayer corner after I hand them a flower at the classroom door, they know that they can honor God by giving what they have been given. These children, some of whom might never be able to make a rational argument that we give to God from His own gifts, nevertheless give to God from His own, and they live the faith that they receive.

God is present to us as a place in the holy spaces where we gather as the Church. God teaches us through our senses, and churches teach us to understand our place in God's mercy through our senses. God is also present to us in our teaching spaces. In order to teach as though God is a place, we have to reach all of the senses. The following three chapters will help you evaluate the ways that you can teach with space and engage the senses in order to help all people, with and without disabilities, to pay attention to the God who is with us.

SUMMARY

» We can touch faith. That is, because of the way God made us, and because of the Incarnation, we can experience God through our senses. This means that we can teach and learn about God by engaging the first level of attention— feelings—that we saw in the last chapter. We don't skip straight to thinking about God, because even God doesn't teach us that way.

» We cannot teach people to think correctly without first

training their attention toward God through their senses.

» We learn through spaces because places shape our memories, and God is in fact a place for us.

» Church spaces reflect human nature and salvation history, because God made us to dwell in Him. Through those spaces, we can know God through our senses.

» The way we learn in classroom spaces, both by their arrangement and by moving through them, should also reflect the truth that God is a place for us. We can arrange our learning spaces so that they teach us about God even if we don't have the language and communication abilities to think or speak about Him easily.

» We should look at how we currently teach and see if we are following the model of Christ, who became human in order that we might know Him through our senses. The following chapters will show us some places to begin.

Reflection Questions

1. Think of your feeling when the priest comes out with the Holy Gifts and sings, "Remember us all in your Kingdom." What is your gut feeling? Can you remember what he sounds like as he sings? Can you remember what it's like to walk the path down the center of the church to go to Communion? How does the space and song shape your memory?

2. Imagine your church space as a pop-up book of the Faith. Which stories are told on the walls, the layout, the icon stands, and the places people gather?

3. How do people move through your church building, hallways, and social hall? If you were looking at your church floorplan from above in the same way a traffic map shows

roads, where would the paths of movement be? Where would a traffic app flag an area of the room as a high-traffic or traffic slowdown area? Are those places, where people are forced to pause, the places where they learn? Would a slight rearrangement of furniture allow the movement of people to flow so that pauses happen near places worthy of attention instead?

4. Read aloud this passage from St. John of Kronstadt: "If we were to draw the Lord's image on every possible space, we would not be doing too much, because the Lord is truly and completely present in every smallest and largest space. If we saw the Lord everywhere, there would be nothing better, we would only be acting properly, for God is always at our right hand, wherever we may be."[115] Where does your church (classroom? home?) place icons? How does their placement shape you to know that God is with you there?

5. Try teaching in a tent when you discuss God as a dwelling place. When I have taught lessons in a tent, I have found that the sense of shelter and vulnerability from interacting with the space differently has led to insights about God's protection and love for us.

CHAPTER 13

Imitating God by Teaching to the Senses

He became Himself an object for the senses, so that those
who were seeking God in sensible things might apprehend
the Father through the works which He, the Word of God,
did in the body.

—St. Athanasius[116]

WE CAN TEACH PEOPLE ACCORDING to nature by engaging the senses in order to draw attention to God. In doing this, we are not innovating but are imitating God, who became human to meet us where we are. In this chapter, we will look at the different areas of sensory need and how your church's learning environment meets those sensory needs. This will help you see ways to engage attention for all learners, including those with disabilities.

Don't hesitate to ask for help adapting lessons and interventions for church. Professionals such as speech and occupational therapists and special education teachers might not know everything about our Faith, but they can help strategize so that the patients in their care can participate in church life.

In special-needs education, there is a term for the activities that meet our needs to balance and learn through all of our senses: a sensory diet.[117] Sensory diets usually concentrate on balancing whole-body needs by making sure to provide sensory input in a few key areas. Sensory diets as used in therapy have to be tailored to each person specifically, but the checklist below will help you to see how activities at church can contribute to a sensory diet.

Even if you do not have a family member who is using a sensory diet, reading through this list will help you to see how different parts of ordinary church life engage the senses. When you start to examine the habits and patterns of the life of the church from this perspective, you can think about how to engage the available senses of persons with disabilities as you teach, pray, and fellowship with them.

A Beginning Sensory Diet Checklist for Your Church

The following list covers several of the areas of a typical sensory diet with ways that church activities fit into those areas. Where appropriate, I have added the therapeutic terms in parentheses to make it easier to consult with professionals if you have that opportunity. The top three categories—heavy work, tactile, and movement—are the most important for helping people to regulate (which means "controlling one's behavior, emotions, and thoughts in the pursuit of long-term goals"[118]). But I have included other categories as well to help you think more broadly about engaging the senses in teaching at church.

Heavy Muscle Work or Deep Pressure (Proprioceptive Input)
» Carrying a church bag filled with books and quiet items
» Pushing/pulling open the church door or classroom door

» Weighted lap pad to use in the service or in classrooms
» Big bear hugs with godfamily and special, trusted church friends
» Pushing on the ground while kneeling
» Altar boys carrying lanterns or fans
» Carrying heavy toy/activity in Sunday school
» Lifting heavy service books/placing books in or out of pew holder
» Climbing stairs into balcony

Touch (Tactile)
» Sunday school lessons with sensory bin elements like kinetic sand, flowers, beads
» Prayer rope, prayer bracelet, or prayer ring
» Dress-up (Bible and saint character clothes for classroom skits, fleece costumes for pageant)
» Fleece and faux fur for lessons dealing with biblical animals (sheep)
» Soft, all-cotton clothes for those with strong sensitivities, with less formal attire explained to priest ahead of time as needed
» Sequined or velvet pouch for offering/candle money or small prayer book
» Silk or cotton headscarf
» Textured blocks in Sunday school lessons
» Flannel and felt teaching aids
» Reversible sequined book covers or lap pad covers (also provides visual input)
» Church bag items: squishies, velvet pouches, mermaid sequined notebooks, silicone spiky slap bracelets

Movement (Vestibular)
» Making the sign of the cross over oneself
» Prostrations
» Metanias (bowing and touching the floor during some prayers or before icons)
» Standing on tiptoes and leaning for veneration of icons
» Carrying up vigil candles
» Moving while carrying sacred items when serving as an altar boy
» Swaying while holding a child/being held or swaying gently to the chanting
» Sunday school lessons that have children act out big movements such as small and tall/reaching to sky

Working the Mouth (Oral Motor)
» Crunch snack in Sunday school class (fresh fruit and allergy-friendly crunchy snacks)
» Water in a quiet sippy bottle in church (with priest's permission)
» Kissing holy icons
» Singing the responses or singing in the choir

Moving Hands or Feet to the Other Side of the Body (Crossing the Midline)
» Making the sign of the cross at each petition during the litany
» Turning pages in a prayer or service book
» Giving self a hug to calm down
» Crossing arms over chest when going up to Communion
» Coloring pictures or painting icons

Visual

» Looking at the holy icons
» Watching the movement of the priests and deacons
» Looking at a beautiful prayer book
» Watching the candles in the narthex or near icon stands
» Bright colors for teaching
» Liturgical color changes and contrasts
» Sunlight pouring through a window through a cloud of incense
» Sunday school rooms with a lighted tree for lessons on trees and bushes in the Bible
» Using a visual schedule (a series of captioned pictures arranged in order they are accomplished) to track sequence of events

Temperature and Light Changes (Alerting)

» Warmth from crowded rooms
» Going outside in cooler weather for processions
» Jumping into cold water to retrieve the cross
» Being blessed with water or rose water
» Drinking holy water
» Drinking a cold beverage in Sunday school or coffee hour
» Lighting changes at Vespers and Pascha
» Turning Sunday school lights on and off
» Using lights in lessons
» Faster-tempo service music and hymns

SUMMARY

» Ask therapists who work with family members to help you modify and adapt interventions to help your family thrive in church. For instance, if your child uses a visual schedule in school or for morning routines, you can find out how to use a visual schedule for church services or church school.

» Sensory diets are activities that engage senses in order to help people with disabilities stay self-regulated. They always cover the areas of heavy muscle work/deep pressure, touch, and movement, and this list also includes additional sensory diet categories of working the mouth, moving hands and feet to the other side of the body, visual input and processing, and temperature and lighting changes.

» When you look at the way we teach in the church through the lens of a sensory diet, you can better see the richness of possibilities for teaching to the available senses of persons with disabilities.

REFLECTION QUESTIONS

1. What is your favorite sensory experience in church?

2. What calms you down in your daily life? What calms down your loved one who has a disability? Can you find a parallel in church life that you can include in your church routine?

3. If you observe a children's Sunday school class, which sensory options are used in that class? If you're an adult, do you feel engaged in any of these sensory areas in church or adult lesson times?

4. Sometimes we think that the outward, sensory experiences in church are not as important as the spiritual experiences. But the truth is that we cannot have one without the other. Think about a time you felt close to God. What were you doing? What were you looking at (if you are able to see)? What did you touch? Where were you in space? Now think of how you might share a truth about God. Which senses will you engage to help your disabled loved one know that truth?

CHAPTER 14

Prepared to Praise

ACCESSIBLE PRAYER CORNERS

*But when the chief priests and the scribes saw the amazing
things that he did, and heard the children crying out in
the temple, "Hosanna to the Son of David," they became
angry and said to him, "Do you hear what these are saying?" Jesus said to them, "Yes; have you never read,
  'Out of the mouths of infants and nursing babies
  you have prepared praise for yourself'?"*

—MATTHEW 21:15–16

W HEN JESUS THREW THE MONEYCHANGERS out of the
women's (and children's) court in the Temple on Palm
Sunday, he gave the children back their place to pray. Whether
we are preparing for children with disabilities or for adults
with disabilities, we should follow the example of preparing
accessible places to pray. Thankfully we do not have to throw
moneychangers out, but we might need to rearrange spaces
in order to make prayer corners accessible for all children. An
accessible prayer corner will be open to everyone, but it will
especially welcome children with all types of disabilities into

the experience of praying and praising God. When we change our learning spaces so that they focus on making the love of God accessible to people with disabilities, the focused space teaches everyone who enters about the grace of God in the Church.

I developed an accessible prayer corner after years of teaching special-needs children in church groups and by learning how my own autistic and other special-needs children were able to interact with God. I have shared the different prayer areas of my previous Sunday school class and my homes with people online, and I have seen other Orthodox parents of special-needs children adapt and expand on the concepts. What I learned is that anyone can do this. This chapter is a practical look at best practices for accessible prayer corners based on my teaching experience, my training as a parent interventionist in teaching my nonverbal children, my own memories of praying as an autistic child, and the feedback of friends with different disabilities and impairments.

The specific elements of an accessible prayer corner come later in the chapter after a review of the ways that prayer corners allow teaching to the senses in imitation of Christ. Many people have most of the elements in place already and will only need to make small changes to make their prayer corners accessible. Those small changes can make a big difference in how learning happens in a space, and I encourage you to make them. But before we get into the particulars, let me tell you a story about the first accessible Sunday school classroom I set up.

The first Lent after I had set up an accessible prayer corner in my preschool Sunday school classroom, our church hosted the Pan-Orthodox Vespers for the Sunday of Orthodoxy in our area. I opened my classroom so that children could play there after the service. The room was arranged so that the focal point was the prayer corner.

If you looked into the room, you felt drawn into it—not just inside the door, but all the way to the prayer corner on the far wall. A large icon of Christ the Savior graced the wall, and below it, icon prints were mounted at child level for them to venerate. For the very young or children who couldn't lean over to venerate icons on the wall, portable diptychs were available for the children to kiss. For those who could not speak, a picture version of the Lord's Prayer was mounted to the wall above a hook for toy censers and prayer ropes. Flowers filled a basket under the Theotokos, offerings of that morning's Sunday school students, who carried them joyfully from the door of the classroom into the prayer corner. Little felt candles, placed by the children, dotted the sand in the box under the icons. Children's Bibles sat on the shelves under the small table that held the sandbox, along with a bin filled with lavender flowers, whose fragrance filled the area. The lavender bin hid tiny holy icons of the church's patron saint. The children who found them would venerate and carry them around during class time.

I knew from experience that children of all ages were drawn to the prayer corner, as older Sunday school students often dropped by before or after class to put in flowers or swing the toy censers. But at that Vespers, the adults visiting from other churches were also drawn right in! About thirty minutes into the fellowship time after the service, several of the visiting clergy were even in the classroom, along with various families with small children. By setting up the space so that the prayer corner invited people in and gave them a physical way to pray, I had laid out a welcome mat for children with disabilities and—to my surprise!—for people of all ages and abilities. It was that moment and that little prayer corner, in fact, that prompted me to talk to my priest about my earliest ideas for this book. He gave me a blessing and also helped me to develop many of the concepts so that the practical and theological merged together seamlessly. That's what this prayer corner does: it makes the practice of prayer possible for all people in their learning spaces. Prayer with God is the theology we all do, even the weakest and smallest of us.

Teaching through Space

The most effective and lasting way to teach is through the ways we arrange and prioritize spaces.[119] The ancients knew this well, and they learned vast amounts of stories, scriptures, and sermons by associating ideas with places that were familiar to them. In daily life, our movements around our homes, classrooms, workspaces, and churches teach us just as much as the lessons we might study in those places.

An accessible prayer corner for homes and classrooms will tap into this human way of learning in three dimensions. Such a prayer corner is a wonderful asset for sharing the Faith with children with disabilities, impairments, and neurodivergence. Unlike the speech or reading or heavily language-based ways of teaching that fail to engage attention or enable children with disabilities to interact, it is a meaningful way to build the practice of hoping in God.

An accessible prayer corner or wall teaches with space. Some of its welcoming aspects are:

» It is obstacle-free.
» It gives children specific actions to do to enter into prayer.

» Icons are placed so that children with disabilities can venerate them.
» It engages all the senses.

Obstacle-Free

The prayer corner invites everyone because it is unobstructed visually or physically, it engages through several senses, and it is appropriate for use by people with limited verbal abilities and limited mobility. The prayer wall is the primary focal point of the room. When you enter the room, you can see it on the far side. It is large and beautiful, tactile, and—this is very important—obstacle free.

Other parts of the room might be tucked into nooks or around tables, but children can reach this prayer area by going in a straight, unobstructed line from the door. Prayer shouldn't be tucked off to the side of life if we want to form kids around it. Just as the altar area is the focal point in a church, the prayer area should be the focal point in a Christian teaching space. If you have a small prayer corner in your current classroom, watch the children to see if they go to it first. If they do not, perhaps it's time to rearrange a little so that it is the central focus of the room.

Praying Through Actions

The prayer area gives children several things to do to pray and offer their love. They can make their cross. They can add a little bouquet or stem of silk flowers to the basket. They can put a felt candle into the sandbox mounted under the icons. They can kiss the icons. They can kiss or hold a little wooden cross. They can read a picture version of the Lord's Prayer. If you have a blind student and offer a Braille version of the Lord's Prayer, the student can read along. Children with limited speech and abilities can hold up a "help" hand to the icons. (See section on "The 'Help' Hand" in the next chapter.)

Those without words or with difficulty speaking can press a prayer button so that a speech-output button says, "Lord, have mercy. Lord, have mercy. Lord, have mercy," or recites the Lord's Prayer. If you add a small hand bell or a toy censer or empty hand censer, children can imitate the ways of praying that go with those items. An offering of sturdy prayer ropes helps children touch the ongoing and unending life of prayer in the circle of beads or knots. Children can flip through picture Bibles to see illustrations of the stories of faith. They can smell lavender or rose petals in a nearby sensory bin.[120] If you start and end lessons at the prayer corner, they will move their bodies around the room in the rhythm of prayer, which teaches them that God is both behind and before them and with them (Ps. 139:5).

Icons Within Reach

To make veneration accessible, an icon or two mounted on swing arms can be helpful. The swing-arm icon mount allows children to venerate even if they're using a wheelchair or scooter or if they have difficulty reaching over the candle box because of their height. In an accessible prayer corner, every part of the prayer routine is available to children, with or without disabilities.

Icons that are especially meaningful for the children, such as St. Nicholas and the Theotokos, should be mounted or placed at a level where the children can kiss them or touch them without help. Some prayer corners include a large variety of icons, but having a few at child height, either on the wall, on a shelf, in portable diptychs, or mounted with swing arms, allows children to engage in veneration regardless of their height or mobility restrictions.

For children with visual impairments or who learn especially well through touch, a carved or relief icon or two will allow them to see with their hands. Carved wooden iconography is a growing practice in Russia and Ukraine as well as other parts of the Orthodox world, and holy icons made with canonical patterns in carved wood have recently become widely available through online sources. Sometimes resin icons based on carvings are also available, but resin is more fragile than wood. Resin icons do not hold up well with people who suffer coordination challenges.

An alternative to wooden icons is metal relief icons. However, according to Orthodox Christians who are blind, it's best to avoid flat-faced icons if you use pressed-metal versions, as they don't give any information for the blind person who wants to venerate.

Another way to make the prayer area more engaging for children with impaired vision is to mount a carved or resin relief icon to a swing arm, or place it on a low shelf rather than flat on the wall. The felt candles in kinetic sand and the small silk flower bouquets can be navigated easily and safely by touch, unlike lighted candles, which can be dangerous for children and people with limited vision or dexterity.

Engaging All the Senses

Children are encouraged to use all of their senses to engage in prayer when they approach an accessible prayer corner. This prayer area meets several types of sensory needs and encourages children to pray with their eyes and hands open to the beauty and presence of God. If you add a bin of lavender or rose petals with travel-sized icons hidden in the flowers, the beautiful aroma also engages those who pray.

Here are the items you'll need to set up an accessible prayer area in your home or classroom:

» **Holy icons**. You can usually purchase holy icons in church bookstores. If you have particularly uncoordinated children and worry about the icons being damaged, laminated prints are also acceptable for sighted students. Make sure that some of the icons are low enough for the children to reach on their own for veneration. Provide a metal relief icon or carved wooden icon for students with visual impairments. If you hang icons on the wall for a children's area, consider using adhesive picture-hanging strips so that the icons are less likely to fall or to pull nails or tacks from the wall onto the children.

Larger, handwritten icons on heavy wood might not be suitable. In our home we have a separate area for them. They sit on ledges rather than hanging from the wall, and they are out of reach of younger children. However, our accessible prayer corner contains many reproduction icons on smaller wooden backings, and they are mounted with picture-hanging strips to help the children venerate them safely.

» **Swing-arm icon mount.** I have had success using an articulating tablet mount with a few modifications to hold a 6" by 9" icon. For larger icons, you might consider a swing-arm television mount. If you have more advanced carpentry skills, you can build an articulating mount from scratch. The key is to allow children with mobility devices like wheelchairs, walkers, and scooters to be able to reach and venerate the icon. The swing arms also help provide access to shorter children who have trouble bending over the sandbox and flower basket to reach the icons.

» **Flowers and a wall-mounted flower basket.** You can find wall-mounted flower baskets and silk flowers at your local craft or home-decorating stores or online. Make sure the basket is easy for all the children to reach. The reason I recommend a wall-mounted flower basket instead of a vase is that vases tip over easily, which frustrates children. A basket that is mounted to the wall well can hold more flowers and is less likely to be damaged or to fall. Bringing a flower to the basket is a wonderful way to enter the learning space and to begin interactions prayerfully.

» **Wall-mounted half-moon planter, felt candles, and kinetic sand.** You could also set a sandbox on a small table, but a wall-mounted planter allows clear floor space so that children in wheelchairs can roll up to it more easily. A half-moon-shaped, hanging planter box mirrors the shape of many candle boxes for lit candles in churches. It will hold two or three kilograms of kinetic sand, which can be divided and partly removed for use in lessons or for a calming sensory break, then replaced as needed. You can use felt candles[121] that tuck over a small stick for mounting in the sand, or you can follow the adaptation from Annalisa Boyd, author of *The Ascetic Lives of Mothers, Hear Me,* and *Special Agents of Christ* (available from Ancient Faith Publishing). Her family made pretend candles from low-cost popsicle sticks with felt flames glued on. Felt candles can be stored in a box or a short bud vase to be brought out for the children when they are gathering to learn and pray.

» **Laminated visual prayer aids.** You can laminate prayers from an icon coloring book, draw your own steps for prayer, or stop by my Special Needs Resources tab at www.summerkinard.com and print out some of the free resources that work best for your classroom or home. Laminate the pages, punch a hole in the corner, and hang them on the wall to use when you pray together. You can also print out the Flexible Orthodox Liturgy Visual Schedule cards onto cardstock, cut them out, number the backs, and mount them in order onto a binder ring to hang in your prayer area or toss in your church bag.

» **Speaking prayer buttons.** Recordable answer buttons come with the capacity to record different lengths of sounds. The less expensive buttons record about eight seconds of sound. In my most recent update to my family's homeschool prayer corner, I used an eight-second recordable answer buzzer to record, "Lord, have mercy. Lord, have mercy. Lord, have mercy." Because my children like to press the small red "record" button, which erases messages, I also sealed the red button with melted beeswax once I had recorded the prayer. I mounted the button to the wall with removable picture-hanging strips so that I can change out the batteries in a couple of years. I also have a more expensive recordable button that the children can push to hear the Lord's Prayer. If you are shopping for recordable buttons, keep in mind that the Kyrie Eleison/Lord, Have Mercy (three times) prayer is about seven seconds long, the Lord's Prayer is about twenty seconds long, and the prayer before meals is about eight to ten seconds long.

Teaching is not only imparting knowledge and habits. It's preparing the way of the Lord. An accessible prayer corner prepares the children God has called into your home or classroom.

When you use the prayer corner regularly, establish a routine of bringing flowers and adding a candle to the sandbox first. In my church school class, I stood at the door holding flowers to hand to the children as they entered. They would then proceed directly to the other side of the room, where they offered their flowers to honor the Theotokos. My co-teacher then held out the felt candles so that each child could choose one to place in the sandbox under the icons. The children kissed the icons before they moved to play or sit, and in this way, each child entered the room in prayer.

Growing with Prayer

Once you have lived with an accessible prayer corner for a while, you will notice that patterns develop in your thought. When you are sad or anxious or need help, you will go to the prayer corner to offer those feelings and prayers to God. That is because when we form the habit of bringing a beautiful gift to God, we gain courage to bring our struggles to God as well.

Whether you are teacher or student, living around the focal point of an accessible prayer corner will change you. You will start to feel greater freedom from your worries, because you have a place to leave them. You will start to notice your joys, because you have a place to gather them. Your daily life and memories will begin to take on the shape of prayer, because you have given prime space in your class and your home to praying. This is why making an accessible prayer corner is a best practice. It welcomes those with disabilities and strengthens everyone who draws near.

REFLECTION QUESTIONS

1. Are icons the focal point in any part of your classroom or home? Have you made their importance clear by clearing the path to them? What do you do to interact with your prayer corner? What are some actions you might do to make prayer a habit of movement through your spaces and in your body? (See chapter 15 on nonverbal prayer (page 157) for more ideas.)

2. Do you have a place in your classroom or home where you always gather to sing? What about a place where you bring your happy photos or acknowledge the hard parts of your life? For some families, the kitchen is where they sing, and the refrigerator is where they gather the physical reminders of joys and concerns. What if you put these things near your prayer corner?

3. If you're not used to praying with space, gather some sticky notes, a roll of office tape, and a pen near your icon wall or prayer corner. Tape up photos or reminders of people or events when you thank God for them or commend them to God. Write down the things that really bother you, and stick them next to or behind the holy images so you can see that they're being looked after.

CHAPTER 15

Nonverbal Prayer and the Logos of God

He who possesses the word of Jesus is truly able to hear even His very silence.

—St. Ignatius of Antioch[122]

IT MAY SEEM TO BE a paradox to say that we can love and follow the Word of God without words. Yet, for many people, prayer must often or always be without speech. As we approach this subject, it is helpful to remember that our Lord Jesus Christ, the Incarnate Word of God, was born an infant who, like other infants, did not speak. Yet He was fully God and fully human even then. This God who speaks mercy even in His silence is with each Orthodox Christian when we pray. Even those persons who are not able to understand the logic of holy revelation in their minds can still receive the grace of the Logos. They can still enter into the communion of love of God and neighbor in the Church. It is with this understanding that we turn to look at ways to pray without words.

Since the faith is one and the same, he who can say much about it does not add to it, nor does he who says little diminish it. —St. Irenaeus of Lyons[123]

157

Let us also remember that even people who can ordinarily speak might sometimes be rendered speechless by exhaustion, grief, confusion, excitement, or illness. Some disabilities make communication challenging at times of strong emotion. Other disabilities make speech impossible but allow for the expression of prayer in other forms of language such as signs, pictures, or writing. As you go through this chapter, if you need resources on nonverbal prayer for a specific person, be aware that some of these ways to pray will work better for some people than for others. They are offered here as tried-and-tested means of praying that have helped other Orthodox Christians, in confidence that God has provided ways for every one of us to pray. As always with spiritual practices, ask your priest for guidance in helping you to grow in prayer, including these nonverbal prayers.

Popping the Sensory Bubble

Because many people struggle with sensory-processing differences due to their disabilities, I have included some practical prayers based on my experience both in teaching autistic and neurodivergent children and in praying as an autistic Orthodox Christian. People with disabilities affecting their sensory processing and language can experience a sensation of their senses freezing or overloading. This can lead to an inability to speak rationally, which may show in behaviors such as silence, yelling, crying, acting silly, repeating themselves, or mimicking others. When this pattern occurs, to get back on track, the person needs to reintegrate his senses with the rest of his brain processes. The shorthand I use to describe this is "popping the sensory bubble." That's because the frozen/looped state of overwhelm feels like an isolating bubble, but some types of actions can break through the bubble and help the person self-regulate again.

Prayers for Overwhelm

Several times a week, one of my children gets stuck in a sensory feedback loop. She begins to scream and cry but cannot tell where the sound is coming from. She shouts, "Too much!" and is overwhelmed even by looking at our calm faces. What helps her the most is a form of nonverbal prayer that I share first because it will help everyone, with or without disability.

The prayer is simple. When everything is loud to you and when faces are frightening to you, when you cannot predict or decipher the world—in short, when the world is "too much"—look at the holy icons. When my daughter has her moments, we point her to a holy icon or bring one to her quickly. "Look at the icons," we say calmly. "Their faces are still. They're quiet." It's the stillness of the holy icons that can reach her and give her a place to focus in those moments when everything else is moving and loud to her. This prayer, of silently gazing at the holy icons, draws us into the peace of Christ.

When I am overwhelmed, I pop the sensory bubble in a different way. I pray with my hands, using a sensory tool called a stretchy string (also called a sensory string or silicone stretchy). It's a thick, rubbery silicone string about thirty centimeters long that I tie in knots and untie. While I do this, I remember St. Irenaeus's teaching that the Virgin Mary untied the knot of Eve's sin.[124] I ask the Lord to also untie any knots of sin in my heart and to untangle my path and make His way of salvation clear and straight to me. For groups, this same idea can help people ask the Theotokos for help in another nonverbal way. They can hold a branch or cloth in front of an icon of the

Holy Theotokos, with strings to tie on it, understanding that she will help to untie the knots with her prayers.

The "Help" Hand

Abba Macarius was asked, "How should one pray?"
The old man said, "There is no need at all to make long
discourses; it is enough to stretch out one's hands and say,
'Lord, as you will, and as you know, have mercy.' And if
the conflict grows fiercer, say, 'Lord, help!' He knows very
well what we need, and he shews us his mercy."[125]

Another way to talk about overwhelm is to speak of it in terms of spiritual struggle. Though not all sensory struggles are due to spiritual issues, the aid of the Holy Spirit helps with all kinds of struggle, whether physical, sensory, or other. Abba Macarius's teachings on prayer and the spiritual struggle led me to teach my nonverbal children to pray to God with the use of a small, hand-shaped paper with the word *help* written on it, which I cut out and laminated for them.

The practice of using picture symbols to communicate is a proven, evidence-based practice for people with speech and communication challenges.[126] The practice of saying "Lord, help!" as our sincere prayer when we are overwhelmed is a practice from St. Macarius the Great. We can bring those two together by making a "help" hand and touching it to our holy icons in order to pray.

If you are able to speak but are teaching someone nonverbal how to pray, model the "help" hand's use for prayer when you go to the icons to pray. If you are not able to speak when you are upset, also pray with the "help" hand when you cannot say "Lord, help!" aloud. In that way, you will remember your prayer better and be more present when you go without words in your distress to ask for help.

This practice assists autistic people in another way, because one of the effects of autism is not knowing that they can ask for help. Autistic people do not usually ask for help unless they have practiced doing so and also practiced thinking of asking for help as a good option. For this reason, it does not often occur to them to ask the saints for help, either. Having a "help" hand as a nonverbal prayer aid provides a visual reminder to ask for help.

The Sign of the Cross

We can make the sign of the cross even if we cannot say God's name while doing so. Not only is the sign of the cross a nonverbal way to pray that is accessible to people with many types of disabilities, but it is also a powerful weapon in spiritual war. When children are taught to make their cross not only because they are told to do so, but with the understanding from great teachers like St. Anthony the Great[127] and St. John Chrysostom[128] that making the cross is a weapon against evil, they tend to cling to the practice more.

It is one thing to tell a child to make his cross because he is supposed to do so. It is quite another to tell him that when he makes his cross, demons run away like cowards and spiritual brightness like lightning shines forth from his face to frighten away evil. Yet this is the truth that our Holy Tradition has handed down to us. We make the sign of the cross to repel evil and to shine forth the light of God, who conquered death by death, reminding ourselves and every spiritual entity that Christ is risen and has conquered evil.

A child with disabilities might not be able to sing the Paschal hymn with everyone, but he might be able to make the sign of the cross by himself or with assistance. Teach him what it means, and it will become a prayer with great meaning for him. Even if he does not understand, the prayer is still powerful.

Prayer in Pictures

For people who cannot speak easily or for whom communication is a challenge, praying in pictures is a good option. Several methods support this type of prayer beyond the "help" hand or looking at holy icons. Pictorial languages (such as Min-Speak or the symbols in BoardMaker) can be used to make picture representations of the Lord's Prayer or other simple prayers.[129] These can be printed out fully formed or fastened onto a blank page in sequence with hook-and-eye fasteners.

Another way to pray without words is to use picture symbols on puzzle pieces to fasten together. Some teachers use large, foam-floor puzzle pieces to represent parts of a prayer so that students can move from one square to the next as they put the prayer together.

Matching pictures to words or to the same pictures also teaches prayers. In addition, matching helps people who cannot keep track of the passage of time due to their disability. A visual schedule for the Divine Liturgy helps to track prayers, for instance, and a matching sequence for a prayer by itself helps track the parts of the prayer. Even if a person has low working-memory capacity due to disability, she can still see from the picture what the next word or phrase is and place the same picture on top of its match. This works well not only with longer prayers like the Lord's Prayer or the Prayer Before Meals, but also with the Trisagion, the Jesus Prayer,[130] and "Lord, have mercy."

Praying with Your Hands

When the desert Fathers prayed, they made ropes and baskets with their hands. Building on this tradition, we can pray with our hands as we knit or crochet or do other handicrafts, such as knotting or beading prayer ropes. Sometimes when I crochet, I match the rhythm of the stitches to the Jesus Prayer. Many people intentionally pray for the people who will receive the finished blanket when they sew, knit, or crochet. It's not an unusual idea that God meets us in prayers when we make things with our hands, since in the Bible God even blessed the craftsmen who built the tabernacle with spiritual ability to work with their hands (Ex. 35:31).

SPOTLIGHT
An Autistic Christian Connects with God

Monica Spoor is an autistic Orthodox Christian writer who is part of the Moscow Patriarchate. In her book, Spirituality on the Spectrum, *she recounts some of the practices that have helped her to connect with God through prayer with her different brain and without words:*[131]

It is important to realize that autism is a *brain* difference, not a mind difference. Since the mind is very closely connected to the brain, it manifests itself more prominently there, but the heart also uses the brain. We process things differently, and that applies to both heart and mind.

The pitfall here is thinking that the heart itself, while unaffected by autism—our potential to connect to God is *not* affected by autism—can without exception be reached in the same way as everyone else. The "how" of reaching the heart may be different as well, since again, it also uses the brain.

It bears repetition and further exploration because it is a very important point:

Autism is a **brain** *difference, not a mind difference.*

However, our mind is not the same as our brains, and autism is a brain difference.

The goal—whether the road we travel is that of hesychasm or any other—is only one: to connect to God, to attain unity with Him. That is where all of us ultimately belong. Autism affects how we connect to God. Not *that* we can connect to God—that is something that nothing in the world can ever take away—but *how*.

A while ago I started an experiment. I decided, for one week, to try and pray entirely without words, only using actions. Cleaning the icon corner, decorating with flowers, making and lighting candles, using a bowl of small white stones and transferring them between bowls as intercessory prayer.

As Monica demonstrated in her book, excerpted above, many devotional acts that support prayer can be a form of prayer themselves.

Making and Lighting Candles

We light candles to offer ourselves and our prayers to God. For many people such as Monica and other autistic Christians who struggle with communication, lighting candles serves as a way to connect with God without using words. If you cannot make your own candles by dipping, molding, or rolling, another way to pray with candles is to decorate them. Godparents often decorate baptismal candles or Paschal candles for their godchildren. Families with disabilities might enjoy praying by decorating candles for Pascha or other vigils.

In our family, every Nativity fast or Lent we cut out and

shape gold-tinted beeswax from sheets and make cross and Chi-Ro patterns that we press onto small beeswax candles. Those small, decorated candles go on our name day cakes for the rest of the year. If you try decorating with patterns shaped from colorful beeswax sheets, there is so much flexibility that even people with low dexterity from apraxia or dyspraxia can often participate. Other families we know roll beeswax candles to light on each Sunday of the Nativity fast. For persons who cannot move easily or see, working with beeswax still engages the senses of smell and touch.

Intercessory Prayer

Monica's method of intercessory prayer involves transferring white stones from one bowl to another to mark intercessions. To build on Monica's method, you can also add words or pictures or Braille words (with fabric paint) to the stones so that the person praying can focus on a person or idea. In our family, praying with stones and bowls is not an option because of the divergent abilities of some of the children, who might break things with heavy stones and drop the bowls. We use smooth pieces of polished wood instead, and we use small hanging planters attached securely to our prayer wall instead of bowls. Another way to use this method is to lift up, kiss, and move travel-sized icons as a way to ask for the intercession of the saints.

We also practice nonverbal intercession with maps.[132] In my family, we sometimes spread out a map on the table and allow the children to place very small holy icon prints on different areas of the map as a way to commend those places and the people who live there to God. A more active way to do this is to hang a map on the wall and toss a sticky ball at it, praying for the people represented by the place where it lands. For people with disabilities that give them a great deal of physical energy that needs to be directed, this sort of very active prayer actually quiets their minds and focuses them on prayer.

Let My Prayers Arise[133]

Children with high needs for physical activity are also easily engaged in praying as a group around a prayer silk. Take a large silk shawl, scarf, or play silk and place it in the middle of the group. Each person can hold a part of the silk or have the silk temporarily connected to their arm or mobility device with a stretchy hair fastener if they have mobility challenges. An adult or volunteer can lead prayers, such as the Our Father or the Trisagion prayers, and the people gathered around lift up the silk as they pray to show that they are letting their prayers rise.

Silks will puff up and wave in beautiful ways when they are moved by a group of even two people, and the feel or sight of the movement reinforces the act of offering prayer. Another way to use prayer silks is to go around the circle and give participants the opportunity to mention people they're praying for or simply to be quiet at their turns. The group leader sings or says "Lord, have mercy" after each prayer as the group lifts the silk again.

Worth Searching For

The Kingdom of God is like a pearl of great price, and like a coin, and like a lost sheep. In all of those parables, the Kingdom is worth looking for and rejoicing over when found. To teach that lesson, I often pray with my children and students using "pretty boxes." Pretty boxes are bins that I fill with lavender or rose petals. I add to them small travel icons, prayer candles, and tiny crosses. The children enjoy the sensory input of moving the petals through their hands and smelling the flower scent, and they delight in trying to find all the treasures in the box. When they find all of the items, we venerate the icons and crosses before setting the bin aside.

SPOTLIGHT
Theotokos Gardens

Julianna (Lisa) Wuertz is an Orthodox Christian layperson who is part of the Joy of All Who Sorrow Orthodox Church (OCA) in Culver City, California. I met Julianna online through her Liturgical Living blog and sites, and I have used some of her resources in my accessible Sunday school class and in creating accessible prayer gardens for my autistic children. I invited Julianna to share her experience with Theotokos gardens[134] because her community's practice gives people with and without disabilities a way to pray with or without words. Importantly, her story of exchanging seedlings on the Feast of the Annunciation provides a wonderful model for a community practice that can easily be adapted to include families with disabilities.

I first learned about Theotokos prayer gardens when I was a catechumen in 2013. Annunciation fell on a weekday that year, and some fellow moms of littles were all getting together for a Liturgy. We had our kids bring white lilies to put in front of the icon of the Theotokos on the iconostasis, and then after Liturgy we went to the park, bringing a flat of flowers to exchange with each other. This way each family got a few of several different kinds of plants.

The ladies had a list of medieval plant names[135] and brought tongue-depressor wooden sticks to label each plant with the medieval prayer-garden name. Like the typical catechumen full of a million questions, I wanted to know why and all the things about it, but I was still accepting of it and thought it was a very beautiful thing to participate in.

As far as how I put my garden together, I do like to try and find some blue flowers on the list if I can. But my gardens each year are usually built more around whether or not we do a flower exchange on Annunciation and what we end up with, or it is based on what I think will actually stay alive in my clay soil with triple-digit summers, my lack of a green thumb, and kids/dog that can be pretty rough on our backyard. I'd love to be pious enough to put more spiritual thought into it, but usually the spiritual part for us comes in after we've picked the plants and then look up their names on the list.

I think the tangibility is great for all kids, and getting dirty in the garden and digging and keeping it up instills some responsibility, compassion, and gets some wiggles out. I have two kids with polar-opposite sensory issues, and at least for my sensory seeker, being outside, doing hard work, and getting all that input really helps us all live together much more peaceably! It was also sweet when they were much younger to see them just go up to the icon and venerate all on their own, since it was right at their perfect height to do so. They love making their garden area around the icon shrine beautiful for the Theotokos.

Prayer Gardens

In our family garden, we grow a lot of herbs. Each feast day of the Elevation of the Cross, we bring out a large resin Celtic cross statue and have the children paint it in bright colors. Though all of my children are emerging in verbal skills now, for many years two of the children were totally nonverbal. Yet they were able to participate in this feast by painting the cross with the rest of our guests and family.

After the cross dries, we set it in the herb garden near the basil to reinforce the story that basil grew at the foot of the Life-Giving Cross. In other parts of the year, the children help to care for the herbs and plants in our garden. We have a family member with a chronic condition who introduced the children to growing tomatoes a few years ago, and the children pray for him every time a tomato ripens. In this way our garden is a place of prayer that connects to the Church year and the particular needs of my family.

SUMMARY

» The Logos of God is with us even when we cannot speak due to disabilities or exhaustion. This chapter offers many options for nonverbal prayer to help families with disabilities pray. They can be adapted for church-group use as well. Consult your priest about how you can incorporate nonverbal prayers into your daily life.

» The chapter explains many ways to pray without words that engage Tradition and the senses. They can be prayed alone or in community.

REFLECTION QUESTIONS

1. Do you ever have a hard time praying? Have you considered nonverbal prayers?

2. Sometimes reading prayers from the prayer books is impossible either because of disabilities or circumstances arising from caring for loved ones with disabilities. Even listening to recorded prayers or reading silently with our eyes or by

Braille can sometimes be unfeasible. We must remember in those times that God looks on the heart and will receive our prayers without words, too.

3. Is it hard for you to remember to ask the saints for help? Which types of nonverbal prayer might help you remember the saints?

CHAPTER 16

Spiritual Care of Persons with Disabilities

Even if a man be lame, or his eyes have been torn out, or
he be disabled in body, or has fallen into the most extreme
weakness, none of these things prevents grace from coming
into the soul. For grace seeks out only the soul which is
eager to receive it, and ignores all these external things.[136]
—St. John Chrysostom

A s the Tradition bears witness, there is nothing to stop grace entering the soul. Yet people grow best in grace when they are attended by faithful priests and spiritual elders to guide them. For persons with disabilities, sometimes spiritual care needs to be adapted to specific needs. Commonly, we see priests care for people with mobility challenges by bringing Holy Communion to the person unable to walk up during the Divine Liturgy, and there are many other ways that priests adapt spiritual care in light of disabilities. For instance, if a priest is not able to speak sign language, a deaf or hard-of-hearing parishioner might have to use written communication or even text messages as part of spiritual counsel. Because there are so many variations on disabilities and their attendant needs, it's helpful to consider a general approach to spiritual care. In this chapter, we will hear from a priest who shares an overview of his approach to the spiritual care of families with disabilities.

SPOTLIGHT
Direction, Not Distance: A Priest's Perspective

Over and over again, as I heard from families living with disabilities in the Orthodox Church, the number-one aid people cited in helping them grow in the Faith was having a priest who tries to understand their needs, including those specific to their disabilities. Unfortunately, the opposite was also true but thankfully much rarer. I asked several priests whose parishioners with disabilities had identified them as helping them grow in the Faith to share their wisdom about the spiritual care of families with disabilities. To so many of these faithful priests, the idea of abandoning any of their parishioners to fend for themselves was so strange that they couldn't fathom that they were doing anything unusual by meeting church members with disabilities where they were.

Though these fathers were kindly disposed and prayed for me in my writing, I was not able to gather additional, longer stories from those conversations to share as spotlights on their own. (Some of their advice shows up in examples in other places in the book.) At last, I was put in contact with the Reverend Father Martin Watt (Fr. Marty), priest in charge at Holy Transfiguration Orthodox Church (OCA) in Ames, Iowa, who kindly and humbly shared the following insights from his approach to pastoral care for families with disabilities. It is my hope that these insights will encourage other laypersons to talk with their priests, that seminarians will be able to gain wisdom to prepare them for their future service, and that priests reading this book with their parishioners will be able to use this reflection as a starting point to talk with the people in their care.

Meet Them Where They Are

I begin with a certain underlying premise, and that is that everyone, whether disabled or not in their person, has to be met where they are, and nowhere else. It may seem intuitive, and yet this principle seems to me to be greatly ignored in some circles. Christ certainly met people where they were. He had to—because they didn't know they needed to be somewhere else. Where we, as pastors, run into problems sometimes is that we expect to proclaim the truth and expect it to be instantly accepted as truth by the person to whom we are speaking.

But in fact, that isn't the model we see in the Gospels at all. The process of acceptance was not instantaneous, except in the places where people sought out Christ. Rather, the woman at the well (Photini or Svetlana) went through a process of trying to understand what she was being told. Even then, her acceptance seemingly was not unconditional. She only knew she had to know more. She didn't know what perfection was or sophisticated theological terms and processes. The remainder of her life was following, learning, and growing.

Ongoing Relationship Aids Healing

A good physician tries to incorporate her own knowledge of the human being and target a course to healing. Many times, perhaps most times, the person being treated doesn't know what "healed" looks or feels like. As pastors we have to stand with people, walking with them on their journey, not simply making a diagnosis and offering a prescription and then being considered "done." We need a relationship with our healers—be they physical, mental, or spiritual—so they can take the necessary time to know us, what works, what doesn't.

In my own case, I am a type 2 diabetic, and I've struggled to keep my diabetes under good control. My physician tries things. Some work, some don't, but without the long-term relationship, no progress would be made at all. It all starts over should I change physicians.

The same is true for priests and spiritual guides in the Christian Faith. We must be spending time. We cannot simply look at a manual and copy and paste. Rather, each prescription has to be tailored to the needs of our patient.

Recognize Limits Without Restricting Possibilities

In the context of those living with disabilities, I tend to place primacy on the thoughts and observations of caregivers closest to the situation, without violating the confidences and trusts of the person. Young children, especially, are best left with one set of rules—that of their parenting caregivers. I always defer to their judgment about what the person with a disability is capable of doing.

As people become more and more independent, it is still important to recognize the limitations without restricting the possibilities. Regardless of the person's presence on this spectrum or that spectrum, they must understand that they are loved. In some respects, dealing with those who have cognitive or neurological differences is easier, because the expectations are generally low.

Service Is Prayer

The toughest counseling and advice is for parents. It takes an awful lot of discussion before they understand that God desires self-sacrifice through the ascetical disciplines, and the ultimate self-sacrifice in any case is parenthood. Marriage is a close second. More than reading from a prayer book or fasting or almsgiving, the discipline involved in being a spouse and especially a parent is really sufficient for spiritual growth. It is prayer. Not just "instead of" prayer—but that service becomes prayer.

In persons with cognitive or neurological differences—with which I have had precious little experience, by the way—the objective is to start with where they are and then look for small changes. Can they begin to identify areas where they are being selfish? Can they begin to identify when relationships are damaged? And then, can they begin to reconcile those damages through asking forgiveness? For those with emotional challenges this can be particularly difficult, and yet critically important.

Direction, Not Distance

The other aspect, though, is that there is a goal—but not a goal that we expect to reach. Sounds counterintuitive. God will perfect us through union with Him. In the parable of the talents, there is no minimum return to get in the graces of the master— the one who made two talents is received the same as the one with five. But to the one who made no effort at all, the Kingdom is denied. We see the same in the wages given the laborers in the vineyard. The effort expended was different for all the workers—and the wage was the same. But one had to go to the vineyard in order to get wages.

Progress Is a Function of Direction

In other words, we can draw a target (Christ), but it isn't our proximity that determines our salvation—rather, it's our direction. If we are moving toward the center of the target, regardless of our current proximity or location, then God will (in my belief and understanding) honor the trajectory with salvation and complete the endless journey into His depths. The recognition of this allows us to be less concerned with our momentary state and more concerned with our direction. Am I giving more? Am I sharing more (which is an area we don't often consider as spiritual progress)?

Our Faith is one of healing, not juridical punishment, and for those who function fully in society, and those with limitations as well, the practice for the priest is the same: to meet you where you are and focus on the trajectory of your life.

REFLECTION QUESTIONS

1. Saint Gregory of Nyssa tells us that humility is a characteristic natural to both God and humans and that "if, therefore, you imitate God in what is possible to your nature, you will yourself have put on the blessed form."[137] This is good news for families with disabilities, because God comes to us where we are. How does this fit with what Fr. Marty said about recognizing limits without restricting possibilities?

2. If you are part of a family with disabilities, have you thought of your service to one another as prayer? How would this idea change your attitude? How would it change your sense of God's presence?

3. The Scripture tells us, "Draw near to God, and He will draw near to you" (James 4:8), and St. Gregory of Nyssa tells us that God repays our efforts according to the largesse of His nature, not the smallness of our nature.[138] What are some small ways that we can turn toward God in life with disabilities?

PART THREE

Kenosis

CHAPTER 17

Self-Emptying Disables the Disability

Knowledge of their Maker is for men the only really happy and blessed life.

—St. Athanasius[139]

So if there is any encouragement in Christ, any incentive of love, any participation in the Spirit, any affection and sympathy, complete my joy by being of the same mind, having the same love, being in full accord and of one mind. Do nothing from selfishness or conceit, but in humility count others better than yourselves. Let each of you look not only to his own interests, but also to the interests of others. Have this mind among yourselves, which is yours in Christ Jesus, who, though he was in the form of God, did not count equality with God a thing to be grasped, but emptied himself, taking the form of a servant, being born in the likeness of men. And being found in human form he humbled himself and became obedient unto death, even death on a cross.

—Philippians 2:1–8

Virtues

ONE OF THE WAYS WE become like God is by exercising virtues,[140] the patterns of obedience and self-control guided by the love of Christ that enable us to imitate Him. Virtue is an embodied, community experience, and it is guided by mutual humility and love between members of the community of the Body of Christ. We serve our fellow Christians with disabilities, and they serve us. In the sacraments, God acts. In prayers, we meet and commune with God. In virtues, we follow God. This imitation of Christ requires that we believe and that we exercise our free will, because virtues train our wills to seek God.

Yet disabilities affect our ability to do as we please. In fact, some people are not able to communicate enough to tell us if they are even able to believe. Before we look at the path of virtue for people with disabilities, we must first examine how free will applies to persons with disabilities. Afterward, in this chapter, we will look at the shape of virtue guided by humility and love in Christ. We imitate Christ's humility and love in both giving and receiving help.

To demonstrate that humility and love in growing, lifelong virtues, we will examine some of the ways that patterns and practice can help us teach with an aim of forming habits, and we will learn a way to make simple prayers habitual. We will conclude this section on kenosis with examples of how children with disabilities give of themselves to the Church.

Holy Limits and the Freedom of the Will

He has fitted us for the practice of virtue. If we be willing, there is nothing to stop us, even if we be poor, weak in body, outcasts, nameless, or slaves. For neither poverty, nor

*weakness, nor bodily disability, nor slavery, nor any other
such thing could be a hindrance to virtue.*

—St. John Chrysostom[141]

Our bodies are given to us by God for our salvation, yet not all bodies are the same. We see this most obviously in the fact that God made us from the beginning male and female. There are limits to our bodily existence that go along with bodily sex, and these limits are given for our salvation. The Lord's Incarnation as a male was a sign that He was truly human, because having a bodily sex is part of being fully human.[142] Though Christ is all in all (Col. 3:11), this new life in Christ is given to people in their bodily characteristics of sex, tribe, language, nationality, and abilities.

Putting on Christ does not change people's country of origin, sex, language, or status; rather, it transcends every limit, gathering up every human no matter their distinctions, so that we become members of one Body. Fully human bodies are always limited.[143] But these limits give us particular means of exercising virtues and imitating God in these given bodies and in communion with one another as members of the Body of Christ. This is important, because like other bodily limits, disabilities do not stop our ability to become like Christ through imitation.[144]

To see how these personal limits do not hinder communion with God, it's helpful to compare reasoning about disabilities with reasoning about bodily sex, because both are bodily characteristics given to us at birth or, in the case of some disabilities, due to circumstances beyond our control. In this way, the patristic reasoning about the holiness of bodies as both male and female gives us insight into how the providential gifts of disabilities also do not hinder bodily holiness. The different sexes of human bodies provide opportunities for holiness, because both males and females are made in the image of God and called to know and commune with God (see Gen. 1:27; Joel 2:28; Acts 2:17; Gal. 3:28). The standard for what is human is not one sex or the other, but God, who made each in His image. There was a time when the surrounding culture asked the Church if women were defective men who either could not become holy or who would have to be resurrected in male bodies in order to become holy,[145] and the Church answered no.[146] Women, like men, are made in the image of God to imitate God and become like God.

Today, we live in a culture that asks whether persons with disabled bodies are defective abled persons[147] who either cannot become holy or who will have to be resurrected with no trace of their disabilities in order to become holy, and we the Church must answer no. Persons with disabilities are made in the image of God to imitate God and know God and become like Him. Just as men and women have different embodied experiences and different opportunities for holiness according to the limits that God has given them, so people with disabilities have different embodied experiences from their counterparts without disabilities and will have some opportunities for holiness specific to their bodily existence. The prerequisite for holiness is not bodily sex or bodily ability, but being made in God's image and being restored in God's image through baptism and the whole life of faith as members of Christ's Body.

For instance, men can be fathers and women, mothers, but both are called to holiness in their particular God-given persons. So also a person who can speak and a person who cannot speak are both called to holiness, though they will use the means given them to praise God. Bodily limits such as disability or biological sex do not exclude anyone from the holy calling we receive in baptism.[148] Rather, like the banks of a river, these bodily limits constrain us in the love of Christ, giving direction to each person's path of holiness within the Body of Christ, of which we all, male and female, with and without disabilities, are members.

It is important to understand the gift of limitedness, because we imitate Christ with what God has given us. The limits we are given in disabled bodies do not limit our ability to become holy or to believe.[149] Even if someone has a disability that makes him unable to profess faith on his own, the faith of others will help him.[150] Everyone baptized as an infant relies on this faith of others already, and that faith is no less shared when someone grows up without being able to understand or communicate faith on her own. Every type of faithful struggle brings holiness. We see this clearly in the example of the Holy Innocents, who were killed for Christ's sake while they were still infants.[151] Yet they suffered for His sake without sin, and they are worthily remembered as martyrs.

Free will is part of the image of God shared by all humans, and it is a trait shared by persons with all sorts of disabilities. When we encounter someone whose disabilities constrain their bodies or reasoning or social movements, we must see that person as still having free will. Though they might not be able to make certain choices, given their bodily limits, yet they are free to choose the good in every situation they encounter.[152]

For instance, my will is limited in that I cannot will myself to be cured of my dyslexia or autism or severe food allergies or arthritis. My blind friends cannot cause their eyes to see by an act of will. But we are free to choose God. My friends can choose to walk by faith and know God as He reveals Himself, even without eyesight. I can choose to love God with all my strength even when my strength is weakness (2 Cor 12:10).

It is the ability to cling to God in love that makes a will free, and we are given that ability in baptism, when we enter the Body of Christ, who suffered for us out of love for us. In His love for us, Christ made for each of us a way to choose good and choose to turn in the direction of the love of Him in our particular struggles. Bodily limits do not limit the love of Christ, who humbled Himself for our sake. Rather, following Christ's example, we Christians with disabilities can choose to pour out the love of Christ through the graced limits of our given abilities.

Virtues: Humbly Imitating Christ Within the Constraints of Love

For the love of Christ constrains us; because we thus judge, that if one died for all, then were all dead: And that he died for all, that they who live should no longer live unto them- selves, but unto him who died for them, and rose again. Therefore from now on know we no man after the flesh: yea, though we have known Christ after the flesh, yet from now on know we him no more. Therefore if any man be in Christ, he is a new creation: old things are passed away; behold, all things are become new.

—2 CORINTHIANS 5:14–17

We who are members of the Body of Christ through baptism have entered into His death and share the freedom of His Res- urrection.[153] Though our bodies are limited, these limits have become boundaries that guide us in the love of Christ rather than shackles that keep us from doing good. In Christ, what is truly good is revealed to us, and we are free to choose Him. We know this because of the great humility of the Son of God, who became human and emptied Himself for our sake. It is His humility and self-emptying that we are called to imitate, whether we have disabilities or not. We can all imitate Him and have the same mind in us that was in Christ Jesus, for the mind of Christ is shown not in displays of wisdom or bodily power or brilliant intellect or popularity or charm, but in His humility (1 Cor. 1:17–25, particularly 22–25).

Humility is the virtue that our human nature shares with God's nature.[154] That's why we strive for it first. God is love, and we must love one another in order to know God. We love one another for the sake of God, who made us, and love frees us from every inequality by teaching us to humbly honor our fellow members of Christ's Body as greater than ourselves.[155] When we talk about virtue for families with disabilities, humility is our starting place, and love is our goal. The other virtues, such as practicing moderation and bravery, and seeking wisdom and justice, help us to suit our efforts to what is needed in our circumstances and modeled in Christ, the Head of the Body whose members we are.

Virtues beautify not only the soul, but also the body, including our bodies with disabilities. Our bodies, whether disabled or not, whether or not we look "beautiful" to people who only value appearances, are truly beautiful only when we act beautifully by imitating Christ.[156] This kind of beauty doesn't diminish with age or even death. The beauty of virtues is even with us in the resurrection,[157] because the goal of virtues is to be like Christ, and we shall all be like Him when He appears (1 John 3:2).

Humility and Love in Giving and Receiving

There is a need for humility when we give of ourselves and when we receive from others. It is only when we have humility that we act in love, and only love makes any good action truly good. If I wish to serve a fellow member of the Body of Christ, I must do so with both love and humility, for as the Apostle Paul says, if I "have not love, I gain nothing" (1 Cor. 13:3). This is important to remember when we want to offer help to people with disabilities. We only act lovingly if we have the same humility that Christ showed for us and our salvation.

If a family with disabilities is in crisis and needs meals delivered, I am not loving if I show up with food but also haughtily judge or shame them for the untidiness or disarray of their household. If a family with disabilities needs help finding space to stand by a wheelchair in a church service, I am not loving if I act put out when I move my things aside. If a student with a disability comes to my classroom, I am not loving if I set her in a corner to entertain herself instead of trying to reach her. Humility is not lowering oneself to another's level, because none of us is above another. Humility is coming alongside a fellow member of Christ's Body, equally graced with the love and gifts and freedom of God, to show her love right where she is.

The need for humility and love is also necessary when we receive help from others. If we are all to share the mind that was in Christ Jesus, the Head of the Body of which we are members, we must give and receive love with humility. The Lord humbly received His Incarnation, humbly received His manger, humbly received the instruction of His parents, humbly received baptism, humbly received the perfume poured out on His feet, and humbly received the repentance of sinners.

We who need help from our fellow members of His Body must strive to receive it in love and humility, too.

In her book *The Scent of Holiness*, Presbytera Constantina Palmer tells the story of Sister Markella, a Great Schema nun who was disabled and relied on others to care for her. Though she often asked for help from those around her, she was never embarrassed or ashamed. Sister Markella is a good example of someone who practiced the virtues of humility and love in receiving. As Presbytera Constantina writes:

> It seems to me, recognizing that we need help and being able to accept it when it's offered is the first step to acquiring humble-mindedness. If we can't receive the help of our neighbor, whom we see, how will we be able to trust and accept the help of God, whom we do not see?[158]

This reversal of the question in 1 John 4:20, "for he who does not love his brother whom he has seen, how can he love God whom he has not seen?" serves to highlight the dual roles of love and humility that Sister Markella demonstrated by receiving help and that her community demonstrated by offering it.

As we saw in the chapter on nonverbal prayer, many people with disabilities have an especially difficult time asking for help, because their disabilities inhibit the social processing that is required to remember to ask for assistance. Another difficulty arises on the part of the broader church community that might not know how to ask for the leadership or participation of families with disabilities, fearing awkwardness if the request is inappropriate due to a misunderstanding of the disabilities. It is also sometimes hard for people with disabilities to know if their gifts would be welcome if they offered them to serve the Church, and people without disabilities often do not know how to offer help. Members of the Body of Christ must learn to communicate needs and offers of service in order to enable one another to give of themselves humbly and in the love of Christ.

A Step Toward Communication: Practice

Virtues develop over time, through repetition and practice. This is true of love and humility and also in the development of communication. In my family, I have three children who spent some or most of their lives unable to speak or to communicate. In fact, one of my children was assessed at the beginning of his diagnosis as having less than the first percentile of communication and language abilities. Yet, by God's grace and with lots of hard work and help, we have been able to help all of the children to communicate and speak. Though some of their skills are still emerging, we have put habits into place which allow us to build their skills over time. From this experience, I have learned some lessons about building communication from scratch. These lessons can also help us in the Church to make a beginning of the good habits of humbly and lovingly asking for and receiving help.

Asking for and Receiving Help: Beginnings
Communication is always a partnership.
It starts with sharing joint attention. If you don't have someone's attention, you are not communicating. If no method is given for the person to respond, you are not communicating.

Meet each other in a place that is accessible and safe.
If you want to talk with someone who is autistic, a loud, crowded room is not a great option. If you want to meet with someone who has a mobility impairment, don't pick a room that requires traversing stairs.

Use a variety of media to enable communication.
Online forms and bulletins, mailed letters, phone calls, live videos, posters, and face-to-face conversations, text messages, and online meeting technology can reach different people with different abilities to communicate. In addition to these media, use picture sequences to tell stories without relying on words.

Provide a way to respond and continue the conversation.
Give contact information for the person in charge of organizing a particular ministry.

If a ministry is closely related to another ministry, provide contact information for both. For instance, if someone with a disability sends in a prayer request indicating an illness or flare-up of a chronic condition, he might also appreciate being able to get in touch with a meal coordinator.

If no contact information is supplied, sometimes people think they have communicated a need or a desire to serve when they have not. Make the contact person and procedure for volunteering or asking for help very obvious in all places where you mention a ministry.

Communication takes time to catch on.
People learning any kind of language, whether it is sign, speech, or an alternative form of communication, will require

about two years to develop an ability to use the language fully. The key is to be consistent every day, rather than giving up when progress is not visible.

For churches, it's very important not to give up on trying to communicate if progress is not apparent for many months. It takes time for people to know whom to contact, how to contact them, and which sort of needs and gifts can be addressed where.

Repetition is vital.
If you make an announcement about a need for volunteers one week, few people will notice it. If you make an announcement in one format only, many people will miss it. Repeating announcements on a regular basis and through several media will allow members of the Church to get the message.

If you need help with an issue related to a disability, be prepared to communicate with several people over time in order to receive help. For instance, if you want to help set up a quiet room for your child, you will likely have to explain the need and how you can help several times, even if space is available, and even if you donate materials and labor yourself. Build repetition and a longer timeframe into your expectations when you ask for help. The process of gaining consensus does not mean that people are ignoring you.

Modeling teaches everyone.
Clergy, teachers, staff members, and ushers can model communication by providing information to members and volunteer coordinators. This information should be available in the media that best suit the persons with disabilities' means of communicating. For example, an usher who pauses and

introduces another speaker in a conversation to someone who is blind and then describes aloud gestures like reaching for a handshake will teach bystanders how to relate to a blind parishioner.

Family members can model the appropriate form of communicating with the person with a disability, too.

Generalize the skill in order to keep it going.

The communication of needs and offers to serve might start small, with checkboxes to volunteer on a stewardship form, cards in an offering plate stating that a meal train would help a family in crisis this week, and an email address and phone number (that definitely will be answered) for pastoral or educational needs. The habit of communicating and connecting people with disabilities with the fullness of the community will grow from there.

Sometimes churches spend a great deal of attention communicating with charming, popular, or wealthy parishioners, because these people either tend to be more visible and entertaining or more likely to donate large sums to church buildings and programs. If you think that your church communicates well with everyone already, make sure that you have truly generalized communication skills beyond the popular, charming, and wealthy parishioners.

Self-emptying requires communication about needs and resources. Thankfully, communication is based on skills that families and ministry leaders can learn together. Love will perfect these habitual attempts to communicate, for it is love that transforms the "sounding brass and clanging cymbal" into the language of humans and angels (1 Cor. 13:1).

Summary

» Disabilities do not stop us from practicing virtues, which are actions that help us imitate Christ.

» Disabilities do not keep us from choosing God in love, which is the truest freedom of the will. Even if disability makes communication difficult for members of Christ's Body, they still have faith, virtue, and free will.

» Bodily limits, including disabilities, are part of the way of our salvation, not limits to free will.

» Just as humans, male and female, are made in God's image and can be holy, so people without and with disabilities are made in God's image and can be holy. People with disabilities are not defective able-bodied people. The standard of holiness is God, who made us all in His image and who is not limited from making us holy by our limitations.

» Both God's nature and human nature share the virtues of humility and love. These two virtues are the beginning and end of virtue. We begin with Christ's humility and aim to imitate His love.

» We need humility and love in order to offer ourselves in ministry and to receive help. It takes love and humility to ask for help and humility and love to offer it.

» For families with disabilities and their church communities, one of the biggest challenges to self-offering and receiving help is learning to communicate needs and resources.

» Good communication helps prevent misunderstanding so that we can communicate not only with humility but also with love, which keeps us from being "sounding brass and clanging cymbals," in other words, nonsensical and unhelpful, to each other.

» The pattern of learning to communicate for people also applies to churches.

REFLECTION QUESTIONS

1. The Fathers often talk about virtues as the paints used in making art. This metaphor helps people understand how virtues help to restore the image and likeness of God in us. As a church, we might not all be able to exercise all of the virtues due to our bodily limits from disabilities, but all members together still make up the Body of Christ, the full image of God. Does your disability (or your loved one's disability) particularly suit you to certain virtues, such as humility? Kindness? Self-control? Generosity? Faith? Peacefulness?

2. You have probably heard people in public discourse use disabilities as reasons for treating some people as less human than fully abled people, unworthy of life or inclusion. The Church, however, says otherwise. Every person, including those with any kind of disability, is made in the image of God. Have you treated people with disabilities as though they were less human than people without disabilities? What would be different if you saw each person with disabilities as though he or she were not a mistake?

3. When water flows through narrow gorges, it becomes deeper and faster. Our bodily limits direct love toward God and our neighbors much the same way that gorges direct water. How does accepting our limits with humility help us to love more powerfully?

4. Communication is a habit that requires love and humility as well as consistency, clarity, repetition, patience, and application to everyone. Have you ever tried to ask for help but felt you were not noticed? Have you ever had a gift to offer but did not know how?

CHAPTER 18

Habit-Forming Lessons

Hear, O Israel: The LORD our God is one LORD; and you shall love the LORD your God with all your heart, and with all your soul, and with all your might. And these words which I command you this day shall be upon your heart; and you shall teach them diligently to your children, and shall talk of them when you sit in your house, and when you walk by the way, and when you lie down, and when you rise.

—DEUTERONOMY 6:4–7

WE ORTHODOX CHRISTIANS ARE USED to the idea that it's good to repeat the same prayers every day and every week and every year as part of our practice and training in faith. When we repeat prayers, we build layers of meaning so that even the simplest prayer can help transform our whole lives. Our cycle of Scripture readings and celebrations of feasts and saints repeats every year, as well, so that one year's feast day recalls years past and sets up patterns to carry forward. Teaching lessons about the Bible and traditions should also focus on repetition.

Most of the time Sunday school curricula cover a new passage from Scripture each week. This practice has the goal of introducing students to a great deal of Scripture, but the effect is often that depth is sacrificed. By switching to a new story every week, teachers and curricula are leaving behind students with disabilities who need to learn in a variety of ways and more than once in order to grasp a lesson well. To help these students learn best, we should repeat topics and lessons at least a few weeks in a row, building meanings each week. In this way the story becomes familiar enough for the students to see layers of meanings. The good news is that practices that help students with disabilities are also best practices for students without disabilities. Everyone learns better when lessons seek to form a habit of learning deeply rather than give a passing impression of a story.

Best Practices for Lessons that Form Habits
Prayer Corner Entry Routine
As we have seen, we learn as whole persons, with our thoughts and feelings anchored around bodily experiences. Because of this, lessons that form habits should begin with a physical prayer routine, such as the example in the chapter on accessible prayer corners. Entering the same way with physical acts of prayer every time you meet will help to calm and center a student with disabilities, making him ready to learn.

Lessons That Build on Each Other
When you pick a scripture to teach to a class that includes students with disabilities, plan to teach it over the course of three to five weeks, building a new level each time. The pattern is as follows:

» introduce the lesson and add a tactile element to help children touch the story,

» focus on a part of the lesson in more detail, and

» connect the lesson to Orthodox practices (such as venerating holy icons, lighting candles, fasting, almsgiving, making the sign of the cross, and so on).

Some lessons can be extended by teaching part of the lesson in several tactile ways. For instance, I once taught the parable of the sower for five weeks by using different tactile sensory anchors for the "seeds" in the story. I brought beads in dough with fake floral-decoration birds to eat the seeds, *lots* of pompoms to show that the seeds grow when we take care of them, and even a ball pit where the seeds were the balls. We poured them in a little at a time, puppet birds stole the seeds, and we finally poured the balls on the children when they told us some age-appropriate practices that help them grow in faith (like praying, making their cross, being kind, and coming to church) in order to represent the good soil.

Most lessons can be expanded over three weeks so that students have a chance to learn, remember, and make connections. Even though I am giving examples for children's Sunday school, this pattern can be adapted to teaching all ages. People remember better when they are taught deeply and over time.

The first week will introduce the story with a visual sequence to help students with disabilities follow along. This can be a sequence printed out with symbol cards to match in order, or it can be small objects that represent the parts of the story. After the story is told, the first lesson's time period will have a brief review where the students can set the story pieces in order. Then the first lesson will give students a way to act out the story.

The remainder of the first lesson time can be spent playing with the tools for acting out the story or with other play learning activities in the classroom. For instance, for the Good Samaritan story, a printed sequence of six cards with matching pictures can tell the story: A man goes on a journey to Jericho; he gets hurt by robbers; a temple priest passes by without helping; a Levite passes by without helping; a Samaritan stops to help; the Samaritan takes care of the man who got hurt. The tools for acting out the lesson can be rolls of gauze. Students can make bandages on each other's arms, their own arms, or on dolls.

The second week will repeat the story and the visual representation from the first week. For most of the students, this will be review. For those who were not present the first week, this will catch them up. This week will focus on an important part of the first lesson. A simpler three- or four-card sequence can explain the deeper look at part of the lesson. For instance, in the Good Samaritan story, week two would look more closely at how to take care of someone who is hurt. After the main lesson has been reviewed, the teacher would add a brief lesson modeling what we do if someone is hurt. Cards in this sequence could be laid out on paper, reading, "When Someone Gets Hurt, I:" followed by space for the following cards: Pray for them, Help clean them up, Offer a bandage or ice pack.

The children could practice these steps, volunteering to pretend to be injured and to be the helper. Everyone can practice saying "Lord, have mercy" together. Then children can have adhesive bandages and ice packs to try out for the remaining lesson time. The sequence is left out for the students to review.

The third week will apply the scriptural lesson to part of our Orthodox Faith in particular. After reviewing the sequences of the first two weeks, the teacher will connect those ideas to an Orthodox practice. For instance, in our Good Samaritan lesson, the third week would review the first two lessons and introduce icons of the Holy Unmercenary Physicians, such as St. Panteleimon. The children would be taught that we can ask the saints to pray for us and help us when we're sick or hurt. The class can sing or read the hymns for the saints' days. Everyone can venerate the icons. Then the children can have access to the icons for veneration in their prayer corner and the bandages, gauze, dolls, and sequences in their lesson area, so they can continue to play out the lesson to understand it.

Sensory Anchors to Lessons

As the examples above illustrate, students learn best when there is a sensory anchor to the lesson. This can be play items in the case of children, but even adults remember better when they can act out or touch a story. Sensory anchors can be reused between lessons, and some types of sensory anchors even help to highlight the patterns of objects and meanings that build throughout Scripture. I say more on this below.

Students Act Out the Story

The Church is not built upon spectacle[159] but on participation. When all students act out lessons, they follow the pattern of participating in learning that mirrors participating in God in our worship. For students with limited mobility, careful planning can still allow them to be part of acting out lessons, whether they hold or represent a still part of the story, have something brought to them, or the children simply gather around them so that they are part of the group. People with disabilities learn best through imitating and acting out lessons, because everyone learns best this way. In classes with youth and adults, this participatory element can come through making a drawing, calling out answers that are collected onto a board, repeating a phrase or script, or moving around to apply a lesson in the moment. With children, acting out stories is a major component of learning and can involve a great deal more movement and props.

Focus on What's Worthy

In Philippians 4:8, the Apostle Paul tells us, "Whatever is true, whatever is honorable, whatever is just, whatever is pure, whatever is lovely, whatever is gracious, if there is any excellence, if there is anything worthy of praise, think about these things." Lessons should follow this advice and teach toward the good goal of imitating Christ, rather than telling people what *not* to do. For instance, children will understand and act on the direction to pray for someone who's hurt far more easily than the demand not to ignore someone who is hurt.

For people with disabilities, this pattern is particularly important, because there is no way to act on a negative. While someone with a language, attention, or social communication challenge can do things positively, she will usually become stuck or confused or dwell a long time on trying to solve the puzzle of how to act on a negative instruction—how *not* to do something.

If you focus on teaching what is good, the path for imitation becomes clear.[160] This is an important consideration for people with disabilities who must especially rely on following rules as a way of processing the world. After all, why cause people to think on something you do not wish them to do? That's counterproductive. We see this same truth reflected in the words of St. Porphyrios: "You won't become saints by hounding after evil. Ignore evil. Look towards Christ, and He will save you,"[161] and "Do not choose negative methods to correct yourselves."[162]

Patterns That Teach

Because God made the world and made us to know Him, certain patterns in the natural world teach us about our Creator. For instance, as many of the Lord's parables and also His miracles show us, God repays us according to the abundance of His nature.[163] We see this in the parable of the mustard seed, which produces hundreds of seeds each season from one plant, and in the way that the small offerings of a few loaves and fishes fed so many thousands of people when the Lord blessed them. There are many patterns in Scripture and the Holy Tradition which can teach us about God. Those patterns relate to each other and build on each other to give a fuller vision of salvation history and the grace of God.

When we base lessons around these patterns, we can move easily between stories that contain similar elements to help us understand the way God's mercy reaches through every story. This is how the Apostle Paul was reading Scripture when, in 1 Corinthians 10:1–5, he tells the story of the supernatural rock that followed Moses in the wilderness and concludes, "and the Rock was Christ." We read the prophets in the same way when we call the Holy Theotokos "the uncut mountain" in our festal hymns. As we saw in Chapter 11, "The Four Levels of Scripture and Attention," we read the Scriptures through Christ, in order to see Him.

Though this is not an exhaustive list, here are ten patterns to notice in Scripture that connect with other stories: Trees,

Water, Food, Journeys, Deserts, Reversal, Light, Sheep, Gardens, and Mountains. At first you might think that these patterns are strange, especially since some of them are so concrete. Why is a tree or a desert or food important to our knowledge of God? But when you look at the places where the pattern markers show up, you will see that they signify important stories.

Take trees, for instance. Without even naming them all, we quickly see the Tree of Life, the trees under which Abraham sat to receive the holy angels, the Burning Bush, the tree of Jesse, the tree of Zacchaeus, the palm trees, the fig tree, the Tree of Life which is the Cross, the trees that grow along the river of God whose leaves are for the healing of the nations. Those scriptural patterns carry over into our prayers, hymns, and spiritual songs, and they are present in the lives of the saints as well. Thus the Theotokos is also hymned in *Agni Parthene* as the "wood and tree of life" and depicted in holy icons in the style called "the Burning Bush." Because those patterns in the Scriptures, the prayers, and the saints have already trained us to do so, when we look for God in the stories of our own lives, we will easily recognize that God is with us around those same patterns!

These patterns are also simple ways to engage the attention and form deep habits in our students with disabilities. Many persons with disabilities are what we might call "concrete thinkers." That is, they tend to focus on the meaning of things that corresponds to real, lived experience. Though, as we saw in the earlier chapters on attention, everyone actually learns best with concrete anchors and ideas, teaching with concrete, tangible, or demonstrable examples is especially important to concrete thinkers.

Studies have shown, for instance, that without learning about the truths of the Faith through concrete examples, most "high-functioning" autistic people become atheists.[164] We need not lose members from the Body, however, because in the Incarnation the Lord has come to teach us so that we can meet Him through our senses.[165] Teaching to these patterns is helpful to a person whose disability keeps him from understanding metaphors. Such a person can understand the spiritual meaning of texts, prayers, tradition, and his own life through the habit of engaging senses. The Incarnation of Christ gives all people, including people with disabilities, access to spiritual truths through bodily habits.

In order to build habits, these patterns can be represented with sensory anchors. This can mean teaching youth groups on location—under trees, in gardens or deserts, in kitchens, on pilgrimages or hikes, by the water, in the mountains, and so on—or bringing some representative elements into the learning space. For younger students, lessons can be centered around sensory bins filled with sand, seeds, water, clay, rocks, and other representative objects. For Sunday school and youth group gatherings, sensory bins provide a nonverbal, inclusive, social, hands-on way to touch lessons and learn with full attention.

If you use these sensory anchors consistently when a lesson features its accompanying pattern (garden::seed, sand::deserts, trees or leaves::trees, waterside or water bin::water, lights::light), you will engage attention, connecting lessons across Scripture and Tradition through the means of the concrete experience of items. For each lesson, touching the objects or gathering in places that illustrate the pattern will help all students form memories and connections between stories. In this way, even children who have difficulty in seeing metaphors will be able to learn the spiritual meaning of Scripture and Tradition through their senses.

Summary

» Repetition at regular intervals is the key to forming habits, which allow us to understand the lessons that help us practice virtues.

» We are used to the idea of repeating prayers and cycles of readings. We also should shift our teaching so that we repeat lessons three to five times in order to engage attention and build up layers of meaning.

» Best practices for teaching lessons that form habits include these elements: consistent prayer corner entry routine, three to five lessons that build on each other for each story, sensory anchors to the lessons, having students act out the story, and a focus on what is worthy rather than teaching through negatives. Tell people what to do, not what *not* to do.

» Several patterns are woven throughout salvation history in Scripture, prayers, and Tradition. Focusing on these and providing the same sensory anchor when these patterns show up allows people to make connections and build spiritual meanings through their senses. Some of these patterns are Trees, Water, Food, Journeys, Deserts, Reversal, Light, Sheep, Gardens, and Mountains.

» Because of the Incarnation, we are able to learn spiritual truths through our bodily senses. If we teach through repetition, pattern, and with the aid of a sensory anchor that goes with the repeated patterns, people with disabilities that hinder abstract thinking can also learn spiritual truths.

Reflection Questions

1. Pick one of the ten patterns that teach (Trees, Water, Food, Journeys, Deserts, Reversal, Light, Sheep, Gardens, and Mountains). Can you think of a story in the Bible that contains such a pattern? What about a hymn or a prayer that mentions that pattern? Are there any stories from a saint's life that come to mind that involve that pattern marker? What about in your life?

2. Have you ever noticed that people tend to have the best conversations when they're doing something together—knitting, eating, cooking, shelling peas, walking, sports? Learning alongside one another is one of the earliest skills in human development, and it is often unaffected by disabilities. Think of the pattern in the first reflection question. Which sensory anchors reminded you of that pattern? Which sensory anchors might you use to teach a child with a disability about that pattern? How about an older young person? An adult? If you know people with disabilities, think of sensory anchors that they can access, keeping their disabilities in mind. For instance, if someone has a mobility challenge, passing around a piece of granite rock might be more appropriate than going up a mountain.

CHAPTER 19

Praying the Tradition

*It is above all by means of prayer that man unites himself
with God, opens himself to the grace that God ceaselessly
bestows, and receives from him every aid, strength, and
blessing.*[166]

—JEAN-CLAUDE LARCHET, *The Theology of Illness*

ONE OF THE WAYS WE can live faithfully with disabilities
is to pray with passages of Scripture and the Holy Tradition to help us grow in hope and faith. This custom helps
us to live as though we are not alone, as if there is help for us
from others who understand, and as though there is consolation even in our struggle. When we start to have a habit of
praying the Tradition in regard to our disabilities or the disabilities of the persons we love in our family or church community, we find that we really aren't alone. There is help for us
from others who understand. There is consolation even in our
struggle.

Our spiritual elders and priests might also offer us very
short prayers to help us pray through our disabilities. In her
book *The Sweetness of Grace*, Presbytera Constantina Palmer

relates how her grandmother helped her to pray when she struggled as a child with a learning disability. She recalls her grandmother telling her, "Now, Con, every morning when you wake up you should say, 'Holy Spirit, enlighten my mind,' just five simple words."[167] After many years of praying that five-word prayer many times a day, Pres. Constantina felt the prayer come to fruition in her ability to understand her studies, but she also struggled hard to learn. This story shows how a short and sweet prayer, repeated many times a day, can help us find holiness in our disabilities by helping us recognize God with us as we struggle.

How to Find Passages

Not everyone who loves God and is faithful has a working knowledge of Holy Tradition or all of the Holy Scriptures. Whether you're familiar with the Bible and Tradition or not, remember that you are not alone. Go to your priest and ask him if there are scriptures that he believes will encourage you. Go to trusted elders and friends who have cultivated kindness and mercy through their study of the stories of faith. Ask them the same. Ask God to remind you of good words you have heard but might have forgotten. Listen for passages from the Divine Liturgy's prayers, songs, and readings that stand out to you as something you have been longing to hear.

In the meantime, I have gathered a few passages here that might help you get started in praying for yourself or your family or community member with a disability. Sometimes it's easier to pray these prayers at quieter times, such as when everything is silent at night. When praying for a child, especially a child whose needs take up all of your attention during the day, it is often easier to start a new prayer while they are asleep. But you can pray them whenever you think of them, whether you're in a moment of calm or overwhelm, crisis or peace. Eventually, the prayers will help you remember that God, who loves us, is with you. You will get used to God being there, and then you'll feel bolder in asking Him and the saints for help even more.

Praying a quotation is different than reading a prayer. This kind of prayer is more like repeating something in gratitude, the way the woman at the well (St. Photini) ran through her town repeating that Jesus had told her everything she had ever done. I like to add these sorts of prayers after the Lord's Prayer. It can help when you first begin to pray like this to say, "Thank you, Father, that . . ." before praying the quotation. Pray with the intention that the prayer be true. When we say "amen," that's a way of showing that we intend the prayer to be true. Therefore, it's okay to end a quotation prayer with "Amen" as you make your cross as usual.

Excerpts From the Tradition to Help Pray for Different Needs

The Value and Meaning in All Human Life

» For whatever the Holy Spirit touches is hallowed and changed. —St. Cyril of Jerusalem[168]

» It is impossible that the creation of any man would be superfluous in a universe where not even the creation of a single leaf of a tree is superfluous. —St. Augustine[169]

» For the glory of God is the living man, and the life of man is the vision of God. —St. Irenaeus of Lyons[170]

Breathing

» Let Christ be as the breath you breathe; in him put your trust. —St. Anthony[171]

» How near is our Lord to him who believes! He is like the air, like the breath of our lungs, like the beating of our heart. —St. John of Kronstadt[172]

Silence and Inability to Speak

» Since the faith is one and the same, he who can say much about it does not add to it nor does he who says little diminish it. —St. Irenaeus of Lyons[173]

» The Holy Spirit indwells the soul and the mind as the producer of speech, wisdom, and knowledge. —St. Didymus the Blind[174]

Struggle to Move

» My grace is sufficient for you, for my power is made perfect in weakness. —2 Corinthians 12:9

» Thou dost beset me behind and before, and layest thy hand upon me. —Psalm 139:4

Overwhelming Emotions

» I feel bright, warm, and calm when I turn with my whole soul to the spiritual sun, the sun of righteousness, Christ my God. —St. John of Kronstadt[175]

» God Himself comforts the souls of believers as a mother comforts her child. —St. John of Kronstadt[176]

Sight

» Who indeed sees better than the man who sees Christ? —St. Ambrose[177]

» Let not the loss of your bodily eyes trouble you; for the eyes that are failing you are only such as flies and gnats also can see with. But rejoice that you have the eyes wherewith angels see, by which God is seen, and his light is received. —St. Anthony the Great[178]

» Blessed are those who have not seen, and yet have come to believe. —John 20:29

Hearing

» Morning by morning he wakens, he wakens my ear to hear as those who are taught. —Isaiah 50:4b

Fear

» Perfect love casts out fear. —1 John 4:18

» Nothing will be able to separate us from the love of God in Christ Jesus our Lord. —Romans 8:39[179]

SUMMARY

» We can find help in praying for ourselves or loved ones living with disabilities by using quotations from Scripture and the Holy Tradition as prayers.

» These prayers are short enough to memorize so that we can pray them frequently.

REFLECTION QUESTIONS

1. Asking spiritual fathers and mothers for a word is a beautiful custom. Yet we often forget to ask for this kind of help to address the disabilities we live with in our families and churches. Have you ever asked for a word of counsel? Have you asked for help praying for the needs arising from disability in your life?

2. What are some of the things that trouble or worry you about your disability or the disabilities that your loved ones live with? Is it a surprise to you that God is close by and cares about those struggles?

CHAPTER 20

Altar Boys and Myrrh-Bearers

CHILDREN WITH SPECIAL NEEDS SERVE THE CHURCH

Do we work to dispel misunderstandings and make all aspects of parish life accessible to persons with disabilities? Do we see people with disabilities as givers and not always—or only—as receivers?[180]

—FR. JOHN CHRYSSAVGIS

IN THE INTRODUCTION TO THIS book, I mentioned that one of my autistic daughters was almost totally nonverbal for over a year due to sensory-processing challenges.[181] Though she had learned language early, she went through a period of time when she was not able to formulate words or carry on conversations. She would stare silently for long minutes and have frequent meltdowns, including during the middle of the Nativity pageant.

During this time period when we were working to help her, my daughter found her older brother's copy of the parish Pascha play. She began to read it every night before she went to sleep. Eventually, she came to us and asked us, slowly and carefully, if she could play Mary Magdalene in the Pascha play the following year. We were stunned, because she almost never spoke in public and had left the Nativity pageant in tears after microphone feedback overwhelmed her. Nonetheless, it was clear to us that our daughter had memorized the entire play, loved the story of Mary Magdalene meeting the Risen Lord, and very much wanted to be a part of it.

I went to our Christian education director and told her about my daughter's request. I was nervous, because of course she had been present for some of my daughter's meltdowns and had noticed her silence. To my surprise, she listened to what we told her about our daughter and said, "Yes. Absolutely. She can play Mary Magdalene."

The director made sure that her daughters greeted my daughter at rehearsals and spoke gently and kindly to her. The kindness set the tone of inclusion, and everyone involved was welcoming and supportive of her and all of the other participants. After a couple of months of rehearsals, our daughter began to blossom. She was still quiet in crowds, but she talked more often and worked hard on strategies to help herself focus.

On the night of the Pascha play, my daughter, who had spent so much of the previous year and a half in silence, rose on her tiptoes and flapped her hands in excitement. She called out so that everyone could hear, "I have seen the Lord!"

That joyful experience of humble service on the part of our Christian education director and the humble self-offering of our daughter comes to mind when I read in the question at the opening of this chapter, "Do we see people with disabilities as givers and not always—or only—as receivers?" Because we had a Christian education director who saw that my daughter had something to give to God and to the Church, she not only had a chance to imitate her favorite myrrh-bearer, but the peace and confidence she gained by being accepted helped her grow in her abilities to communicate across her whole life. This flourishing happens for people of all ages, with and without disabilities, when we imitate Christ by offering our gifts to one another.

Every Sunday, this same humble self-giving happens in Orthodox churches around the world when children with disabilities serve in altars and bring vigil candles to the front of the church. Girls who live with disabilities often participate as myrrh-bearers in Holy Friday services. Many churches assign girls—including girls with disabilities—to bring vigil candles up to the solea each Sunday, too, as a way to remember the myrrh-bearing women, who were the first to share the light of the Resurrection. Boys with autism or learning disabilities serve as altar boys, carrying that light back into the church each week.

These are not the only ways that children with disabilities can offer their gifts to the Church. They participate in oratorical programs, children's choirs, service projects, and welcoming others into the church with kindness. Their prayers, whether shown in lighting candles, making their crosses, and venerating icons, or through silence and presence, benefit the entire Church. These children are like the children waving palms who first greeted Jesus, asking Him to save us. Like those first children, they are heard.

Welcoming children with disabilities as full members of the Body of Christ means that we will encourage them to know that their self-offering for Christ's sake is a great gift they can share. This is particularly true in the case of children with hidden struggles, such as learning disabilities and autism, where mutual self-giving in serving the Church can overcome the social isolation they so often face.

Stories of welcome have a powerful effect in encouraging us in the Church, because they help us to see how we might recognize the Lord's presence and His work in our lives, too. As the bishops remind us, "to feel truly welcome in our parishes, persons with disabilities must not be excluded from leadership roles."[182] The remainder of this chapter shares the experiences of a mother and a priest in church services that fully welcome the gifts of these children.

SPOTLIGHT
The Doors of the Church Were Not Closed to Him

Monica Klepac, an Orthodox Christian (Antiochian) mother, shared with me her experience of witnessing the way that her son's service in the altar each week not only helped the community, but also gave him a gift in the midst of his struggles to learn.

My son has dyslexia. A few years ago, we were in the midst of a major struggle, figuring out what help to get him. There was so much pressure to get him reading and so much emotional upheaval for him and me as he struggled. I was at the St. Emmelia Homeschool Conference, and we prayed the Akathist to the Mother of God, Nurturer of Children.[183] My son was standing by Bishop Thomas, serving as an altar boy. Often, I felt like huge parts of life were locked up, and my son just didn't have the key. Books, signs, subtitles, directions—these were all things that he needed other people to unlock for him so that he could fully participate in the world.

But looking at the icons, singing the hymns, and seeing my

son fully involved and serving in the Liturgy, I realized that the doors of the Church were not closed to him just because he couldn't read. The Church, in Her wisdom, gives us a full-body experience with lots of repetition of song and images and all these things that don't depend on strengths with text-based information and stories. I wept with thankfulness that this beautiful place is his home.

A few weeks ago, my son was sitting with me in church. This was the first time in years, maybe, that he was sitting with me, because he is usually an altar server. He is still not a fluent reader, though he is getting better every day. But through the *whole* Liturgy he whispered all the words. Everything that was said by the priest, deacon, laity, choir—even the stuff that is only said quietly at the altar. The boy who struggles to memorize even the shortest sight words had the whole Liturgy deep in his heart because he was there in the middle of it every week.

It warmed my heart that wherever he goes in life, that gift will be in him. It reinforced the revelation I had that the Church was not locked to him just because he can't read well. Through the wisdom of a Divine Liturgy that is multi-sensory and repetitive, the truths of the Liturgy are rooted in his heart.

This story powerfully illustrates that the Holy Spirit in the Church guides every person, including those with disabilities, and He empowers them to participate in faith and ministry.

SPOTLIGHT
Be Christ to Them and Receive Christ Through Them

I was introduced to the Reverend Father Christopher Foley, priest of Holy Cross Orthodox Church (OCA) in High Point, North Carolina, by the family of the autistic altar server he mentions in his reflection. Those family members are friends of mine, and we often have discussed together the special welcome that members of Holy Cross Orthodox Church offered to families with disabilities. In particular, their parish caught my attention because, though in general, families with autistic members have a difficult time participating fully in church life, several autistic members attended the parish from several families. They were not only welcomed, but they were invited to share their gifts of service to the community. Like my home parish at the time, where our priest and Christian education director and ushers had set a tone of welcome, this parish fully recognized people with disabilities as full members of Christ's Body. Father Christopher graciously shared his experience and approach to welcoming autistic people, as well as people with other disabilities, as full members of the Church.

We are truly blessed at our parish to have had a number of kids on the spectrum as members and one as an altar server. My son is twenty years old and is diagnosed with very low-functioning autism, amongst other things. He is not only a tremendous blessing to our family but our parish as well. Many parishioners speak of him as angelic and a joy to have at church. He loves being in church. At times he gets excited and verbalizes this excitement with "holy noise." Many remark that they feel like he sees much more of what is going on at church than the rest of us. I certainly see that. The degree that he is unable to fully engage and connect with the world around him is the degree in which he is unaffected by the sorrow and sin in this world. The eyes of his heart are clear, and he "sees" the world in its beauty and simplicity.

We also have a young autistic altar server who is pretty high functioning. He is also a great joy to have in church. He has been serving now for a number of years. Serving in the altar has really helped him to be able to engage the service more, because it gives him something to focus on. I think our services really help those on the spectrum to worship God, because it is predictable and does not change. Recently, this boy has had a hard time staying focused for the long Lenten services, and I was able to speak with him and give him a blessing to serve as long as he wanted. He could get a blessing to unvest when he felt like he needed to stop. Also, because we have two server teams, and because he focuses better when he is serving, I have told him that he can serve every week. We try to accommodate everyone and make it possible to serve in ways that work for them.

I also tell all parents who are struggling being in church with children, not just those with special-needs children, that there is a blessing to come late if need be. Some kids are just not able to come and be focused for that amount of time, and parents need to know that there is some space to navigate without feeling like they have to be superheroes. It is a stage and usually not a permanent situation.

Even as special-needs kids grow, I have found that they are able to adapt and learn to be present in our services. Also, if the parents feel like the community is supporting them and not scowling at them, this is a healthy place for these stressed-out parents to come with their families.

Before I went to seminary and while at seminary it was very difficult for our family with a young son on the spectrum. Our son was also very late in walking, so we had to bring a wheelchair with us everywhere we went. We were blessed to be a part of a few parishes and a seminary community where our son was welcomed and received with love, and we were supported greatly by these communities. I can't imagine what it would have been like if the opposite were true—and I have heard of this happening at some churches.

I recall a time when we were at church and the bishop was visiting. While the bishop was preaching, our son was quietly playing with a small Matchbox car. The bishop had been preaching for a while when all of a sudden, our son threw the car across the floor, and it slid into the shoe of the bishop. We were aghast and shocked! The bishop kindly stopped, looked at our son with a big smile, crossed himself, and said, "Now I know when I've been going on too long," and finished the sermon. Everyone laughed. It was very sweet. When we came up to venerate the Cross, the bishop leaned down and blessed him, saying, "Thanks for letting me know I was going on too long," and smiled.

It is my position that we need to show hospitality to everyone who comes through the doors of the Church and not only be Christ to them but also to receive Christ through them. A parish community is not fulfilling the mandate to serve others if it cannot welcome and find a place for those whose abilities may be different than our own. We rob ourselves of the blessing we receive from them.

Summary

» Children with disabilities are givers of God's love, not only receivers. This chapter highlights three examples of children with disabilities offering their service to the Church. In each case, the mutual self-giving of the community and the child leads to healing and growth for all.

REFLECTION QUESTIONS

1. Father Christopher said, "If the parents feel like the community is supporting them and not scowling at them, this is a healthy place for these stressed-out parents to come with their families." What are some ways that you can support and welcome families with disabilities? If you are part of a family living with disabilities, what stresses you the most, particularly about church?

2. In the case of my daughter and Monica's son, having an opportunity to serve the community opened up new possibilities that helped them grow, despite their disabilities. What are some ways that you might offer your gifts to the community of the Church? Are you part of ministries where children and youth with disabilities might be included?

PART FOUR

Koinonia

CHAPTER 21

The Iconic Community

*Thou hast said, "Seek ye my face." My heart says to thee,
"Thy face, LORD, do I seek."*

—PSALM 27:8

*By this all men will know that you are my disciples, if you
have love one for another.*

—JOHN 13:35

*He is the image of the invisible God, the first-born of all
creation; for in him all things were created, in heaven and
on earth, visible and invisible, whether thrones or domin-
ions or principalities or authorities—all things were created
through him and for him. He is before all things, and in
him all things hold together. He is the head of the body, the
church; he is the beginning, the first-born from the dead,
that in everything he might be pre-eminent. For in him all
the fulness of God was pleased to dwell, and through him
to reconcile to himself all things whether on earth or in
heaven, making peace by the blood of his cross.*

—COLOSSIANS 1:15–20

In our pursuit, then of a model response to disability concerns, we affirm a God of love and hospitality, in the manner of Abraham and Sarah welcoming the three angels (Gen. 18) reflecting the unity of the Trinitarian God. In this respect, the Church, too, is called to become the image of the Trinity, a unity of persons in communion, a place where everyone is welcomed.

—"Disability and Communion," Assembly of
Canonical Orthodox Bishops of the U.S.A.

Entering the Icon

IN THE ICON CALLED "The Holy Trinity" or "The Hospitality of Abraham," we observe the three angels who visited Abraham around a table laid for four. The person viewing the icon is at the fourth side of the table, invited to join the three holy guests. The angels remind us also of the Holy Trinity, for two of the angels bow toward the third to remind us that the Son is the only-begotten of the Father and that the Holy Spirit proceeds from the Father.

A tree grows behind the angel representing the Son of God to remind us at once of the Cross of Christ and the oaks at Mamre, where the meeting of the three angels took place with Abraham. The angels are dressed in colors that mean power and heaven and humility and royalty and life-giving, all characteristics of God and evoking the language in the Creed about the three Persons of God, who is One. It is an icon of grandeur and love, of humility and invitation to enter into fellowship with God. It reminds us that hospitality is a key element of the Church, which is an icon of the love of God in Christ.

When I think of hospitality, two memories spring to mind.

The first was in college, when a professor emeritus joined a lunch gathering of community members and students. Before he walked into the room, we were an awkward bunch, not knowing where to sit or with whom to speak. This retired professor was one of the most gracious persons I have ever met. He assumed the duties of host, and within minutes each of us had settled in our places around the tables. We were each smiling at the joy of being given a place, and, though I no longer remember why I was at that luncheon, I have never forgotten the feeling that it was an honor to be there. That's what hospitality does: it gives each of us a place, a purpose, and shows to us the gift of each other's presence.

My other strongest memory of hospitality took place in our home, gathered under an icon of the Hospitality of Abraham/ The Holy Trinity on our wall. We were hosting a series of discussions about theology in our daily lives. My husband and I had set up two tables to make one large table in the center of our largest room and had gathered chairs all around. We had covered the table with paper and left pens at every space so people could scribble and write notes. We had cooked and prepared and invited. The feast was ready.

When the people arrived, we seated everyone, ate, and talked about knowing God. But there was a surprise waiting for me in that gathering. I looked around the table at two blind friends, an autistic friend, a friend born with only one arm, and other friends with no apparent disabilities. I was surprised by an unspeakable joy. We had laid the table for friends, and I met God there among us.

The Church is an iconic community because we look like God when we love one another and humbly make room for all members of the Body in our worship, learning, service, and fellowship. As we imitate Christ in love and humility, we are "being changed into His likeness from one degree of glory to another" (2 Cor. 3:18), and this likeness applies to every member. When every member is included, the Body of Christ starts to look like God.

We are also an iconic community because we are a part of the icon of God's hospitality. We sit or stand at the fourth side of the table, being fed with Christ Himself even as He eats with us and our fellow members. Not only in our actions, but in God's welcome of us all, we show a glimpse of God's love. When we, like the angels in the holy icon, humbly regard our fellow members of the Church as greater than ourselves, we take on the stature of Christ, of servants.

If someone sees us bowing in love to welcome a person with a disability, they will wonder why we bend so reverently. If someone sees us lean toward a person with a communication challenge to help her be heard, they will wonder what love inspires such devotion. If they follow our actions of welcome the way that we follow the humble posture of love between the angels, they will look through us to see God.

What starts in our worship of God carries out to transform our community.[184] It is our community with one another and our ability to look like God that is broken when we do not include persons with disabilities fully in the life of the Church. As the Assembly of Canonical Orthodox Bishops of the United States tells us, "We are not a full community without one another."[185] The inclusion of families with disabilities in the fellowship of the Church is no less important than their inclusion in sacraments, prayer, teaching, service, and leadership, for "disability is principally a social issue, while healing is the removal of social barriers."[186] The healing of relationships between members of Christ's Body comes not only through the other parts of our life together, but also through fellowship and friendship.

Hospitality That Heals

Saints are examples of people who have become like God through participating in the sacraments, through prayers, and through lives of virtue. Many saints showed their closeness to God by the way they exercised hospitality to others. Saint Macrina is an example of someone who had purified her life until her monastic sisters saw her reflecting the Word of God, for she was to them "the lamp of [their] life" and "the light that directed the path of [their] souls."[187] After her death, a soldier related a story of St. Macrina welcoming his family with such hospitality when they came to visit her that the hospitality itself was part of a miracle of healing that took place in his daughter.[188] Macrina's example of hospitality that heals is our aim in the iconic community. Though God alone does wonders, and we might not see miracles the way that St. Macrina's guests did, yet we can imitate His love and remove handicaps to participating in community fellowship for our members with disabilities.

Healing the Loneliness of Life with Disabilities

Loneliness and isolation are a large part of the burdens of life with disabilities. Suffering with disabilities leads to a great deal of loneliness, and the Church has often done little to assuage it or to acknowledge the physical and emotional burdens. Suffering is a major challenge for everyone, but especially for persons and families with disabilities. Disabilities are very hard to live with, and often they cause long-term pain in the bodies and minds of people living with them.[189] The suffering can be physically and emotionally painful, financially difficult, exhausting, resource-draining, and isolating.

Isolation makes suffering worse in four ways:

» Being alone makes life harder for families who cope with the physical, emotional, and mental burdens of living with disabilities, because they do not have help with the burdens.

» There is no way to improve or learn better ways to cope if no others are around to teach.

» People aren't meant to be alone, and they will experience an ordinary level of sadness and loneliness that is compounded by the extra burdens of isolation.

» We know the love of God by loving our neighbors, so without our neighbors' love, we lose sight of the fullness of the love of God and even of the gifts of our lives, for "we need one another in order for our gifts to be revealed."[190]

Removing isolation leads to the healing of the community. This is why we must make an active effort to include members of Christ's Body who are living with disabilities. If we want our community to look like God, we have to please God, and God is pleased when we include every member of the Body in our gatherings and friendship. As St. John Chrysostom tells us in his Second Baptismal Instruction, "Nothing gladdens Him so much as our fellow feeling for those who are members of the same Body, our manifestation of abundant affection for our brothers, and our great preoccupation with the salvation of our neighbors."[191] In other words, we as a Church please God most when we do the hard work of having compassion on our fellow Christians and act with kind thoughtfulness to help them along in their salvation.

This advice applies especially when our fellow Christians are members of families living with disabilities, and it applies to our fellowship, not only our attendance at religious services. Saint John Chrysostom tells people who hold gatherings to regard the need to include people whom God loves, and not only people whose power in society will benefit them:

> If you ever wish to associate with someone, make sure that you do not give your attention to those who enjoy health and wealth and fame as the world sees it, but take care of those in affliction, those in critical circumstances, those in prison, those who are utterly deserted and enjoy no consolation. Put a high value on associating with these; for from them you shall receive much profit, you will be a better lover of the true wisdom, and you will do all for the glory of God.[192]

By welcoming those whom God has told us to welcome instead of the ones who can give us power or prestige in the world, we seek God's glory instead of our own. This welcome turns all feasts and fellowship into opportunities for all present, with and without disabilities, to experience the love of God. As St. John of Kronstadt tells us, "If you have Christian love for your neighbor, then all heaven will love you."[193] Inclusion of persons and families with disabilities thus is vital also to the salvation of the healthy and strong.

Our welcome of families with disabilities is an extension of the hospitality of God, who has drawn near to us in Christ. Our community that includes everyone grows from our communion with the Holy Trinity. We must include everyone in our gatherings if we wish to experience the surprise of meeting God around a table.

Offering What We Have in Fellowship
So That God Will Give the Increase

Even if all that we have to offer is our presence and friendship, this gift will not be in vain. We each offer what we have when we come together for fellowship, like the little boy whose loaves and fishes became the means of Christ's miracle of feeding thousands. Unlike the feeding of the five thousand, our gatherings are usually planned in advance. Because of that, we can take one another's needs into consideration as we plan to gather. We can make a good beginning with these five guidelines:

» **Make room for smaller groups within large gatherings**. Many persons with disabilities require extra space and quieter rooms in order to participate in meals and conversations.

» **Spread out small-group meetings across the geographical reach of the parish**. If many of your parishioners must travel more than twenty minutes to get to the church, consider having coffee meetups, meals, and book clubs at cafes or homes on different sides of town. This will help families with disabilities, who often have heavily restricted social schedules, to be able to participate. Some of these families, with enough planning, might even be able to host small group gatherings in their homes.

» **Make sure meeting places are accessible**. An accessible meeting place will have full wheelchair access to doors, tables, and restroom facilities. It will also have a lower volume so that people who are hard of hearing or have sensory challenges around loud noises can focus. It will have several seating options and room for everyone to be together.

» **Everyone eats safely**. If a gathering does not include foods and drinks that are safe for everyone to eat or drink, it's not hospitable. Read more about allergy-safe practices in the Spotlight on Treating Food Allergy Sufferers Like Christ (page 241).

» **Media can aid accessibility**. Sometimes meeting in person is not feasible for families with disabilities. Online gatherings through media such as Slack, Zoom, Zencastr, Skype, YouTube live videos, or Facebook group chats and videos can help people connect to book studies, discussion groups, planning groups, and fellowship times. These media have different strengths and weaknesses, such as text instead of sound, auto-captioning of videos, and the ability to describe something verbally for someone who has low vision, but they can be helpful in removing isolation and including families with disabilities.

SUMMARY

» We are an iconic community when we extend the hospitality of God to include all of the members of Christ's Body in our fellowship.

» Hospitality that includes everyone opens us to the surprise of meeting God at our table.

» Hospitality is part of the healing of the community of the Church. It removes the barriers of disabilities that arise through isolation.

» We have to make an effort to seek out families with disabilities to include them in our gatherings. Following the five guidelines above can help make a way for these families to be truly welcomed into fellowship.

Reflection Questions

1. When was a time that you felt truly welcomed at a social gathering with people from church? What are two things you remember best about that gathering? Can you help make those things available for others?

2. Sometimes we forget that broadcasting the announcement of a meeting is not the same as making sure the meeting is accessible. Often when I ask people if their gatherings are accessible, they say, "Yes," when they really mean, "We have not uninvited anyone." A real invitation to families with disabilities will provide accommodations to everyone's needs and a personal welcome so that isolated people know they are wanted. Have you held a gathering for a meal, coffee, tea, or a book study? What have you done to make it accessible? How have you told people with disabilities that the meeting is accessible?

3. Perhaps it shouldn't be surprising that the Bread of Life shows Himself to us so often at meals, but His mercies "are new every morning" (Lam. 3: 22–23). What are some ways that you welcome Christ into gatherings? Are you welcoming all of His members?

CHAPTER 22

Extending Grace in the Church Services

N OWHERE DO WE HAVE MORE opportunity to act like the beloved community of God in Christ than in our prayer services and the Divine Liturgy. The patterns of prayer and movement through the service train our attention to God through our senses, and the presence of God in the Divine Liturgy is available to all, including those with disabilities. Yet the length of services, the intense sensory input, and the differing developmental ages of the communicants can make it hard for all people to lend their attention to God and their neighbor in a loving way.

We have already overcome many challenges with the good beginning of treating all distractions as prayer requests. But there are further ways to make room for one another in the mercy of God. This chapter will address two of the most common challenges that sometimes lead our attention astray or that have tended to lead to misunderstandings or exclusion of persons with disabilities.

On Shushing

The only person who ought to be shushed in an Orthodox Church is the devil when we breathe on him at the beginning of the service of Holy Baptism. Don't let the serpent hiss out through you when you come to Communion. The head of the snake is being crushed, and God is feeding his children from the Tree of Life. Crush your prideful need to control. Crush your unkindness toward your weaker brothers and sisters. Crush the serpent's head. Do not hiss with the serpent and frighten the little ones whom Christ has called.

There is nothing more repugnant to God than the ill-timed rebuke of children who are coming to Him. Do not do it. Put shushing out of your toolbox of human interactions. If you see a family with disabilities approaching the Communion line, and a child is making some noise, your shush could undo the careful work of days to help the child come for the grace of Holy Communion. Rather, if your attention is caught by a sound, redouble your prayers that God will have mercy on the child, the family, and yourself. That way, when you all commune, it will be in the proper love of Christ rather than the false righteousness of someone who places the need to enforce decorum over the need of God's children to come to Him.

The habit of shushing others is far more disruptive than any noise a distressed person might make. The sound of distress inspires the desire to help. The sound of shushing inspires anger or shame or irritation. It has no place in a church service. If you find it difficult to pray when you're around children or older persons who have disabilities that cause them to be louder than you would like, then humbly, and without making a show of it, move to a different place. Next, pray for the person whose presence distracted you. If you are able to bring yourself to do so, ask the family with disabilities to pray for you, too. This humility on your part will increase love for you from others and will increase your own love for the people around you, including the families that you find distracting.

On Scents and Incense

Incense is one of the joys of church life for many people, even many people with disabilities. For people with impairments to other senses, incense can signal entering the atmosphere of church. Singing, "Let my prayer arise like incense" communicates such a concrete and teachable beauty while incense burns in the altar and rises through the church.

But incense and other strong fragrances can be a point of contention, too, when people who love incense misunderstand those who are not able to be around it. These misunderstandings, and the failure to accommodate people with incense-related handicaps, can lead to a break in community. Thankfully, as many people have written me to testify, the trouble with fragrances and incense is not insurmountable, especially when we understand each other's needs.

Strong fragrances present a challenge to many people. Those with breathing machines or lung impairments can be put into physical danger by an overwhelming fragrance. Those with sensory integration challenges, stemming from developmental delays or other neurological differences, can become overwhelmed, frightened, and unable to understand the rest of their sensory input when they are particularly sensitive to fragrances. An easy thing we can do to help these fellow Christians is to limit the scents we wear on days when we go to church.

Some people with a need to avoid strong scents can find refuge by standing near the choir, which is often set apart from the rest of the congregation—sometimes even in a choir loft above the main room. Singers tend to avoid wearing fragrances so as not to impede one another's vocal production, and there is not usually as much incense in the choir area as in the center of the church. For people with strong aversions to scents due to sensory-processing differences, fewer conflicting fragrances can be helpful. If they smell only incense, they might be able to become desensitized to it after a little while, provided they do not encounter other strong perfumes.

Several other options, besides standing near the choir, might help people with sensory-disability–related incense aversion:

» For many autistic people who are overwhelmed by incense, spending time each day running their hands through lavender or coffee beans can sometimes help them become desensitized to smells.

» If you have a family member with a sensory aversion to incense, talk to your priest about it. He might be able to provide you with a few grains of the incense he uses in the altar. If you introduce the smell of the unlit incense into everyday routines such as kissing your home icons, the fragrance of the burning incense might be less overwhelming in church. Your priest can also help your family prepare for days when he blesses with rosewater or aromatic herbs, such as basil or rosemary or bay.

» Another option is to burn a beeswax candle each day and ask your family member to blow it out at the end of prayer time. That will help normalize the smells of beeswax and smoke that make up the atmosphere of church life.

» For some people, carrying a small piece of beeswax can help. They can work it with their hands as a fidget in church and also smell it when the scent of incense becomes overwhelming.

» You might also borrow a trick from fragrance salespersons in stores: keep a little cloth bag of coffee beans with you in church to clear your sense of smell from the other fragrances that overwhelm it.

For people whose disability is due to a physical lung impairment, the challenges of incense can be even greater. One woman was eventually enabled to stay in services by her priest, who has asthma and understood how to help her. She shared the immensity of her challenge at first:

There is so much potential for people with incense-related symptoms to be misunderstood. Or for people to develop resentment because they feel like their presence is more important than the incense. I can't speak for people who have allergies only, which I thought was all I had at first, but I have a restrictive lung disease with a moderate reduction in lung capacity while looking and feeling like a normal, healthy person, except when I'm exposed to incense. And I can't improve my situation by eating differently, losing weight, sitting in the back, narthex, or balcony, holding a tissue over my face, taking allergy meds, using cough drops continuously, leaving the service briefly a few times, or wearing a mask unless it was a respirator, which would look bizarre. And I have never smoked a single cigarette. As the pulmonologist explained to me, respiratory symptoms (and lung damage) are like sunburn in that you can't tell it's happening until it's too late. I can't necessarily tell when I've had too much exposure during any particular service, but with even mild exposure the coughing persists during the rest of the week. And adult-onset asthma is to be taken seriously.

People with a need to avoid fragrances or even incense due to asthma or other lung and breathing conditions should consult with their priest, asking him about their options on best places to stand and how they might participate in light of their conditions. The priest of the woman in the example above was able to help her by changing the type and amount of incense he used in the services, for instance. Another priest told me that he accommodates both people suffering from breathing trouble and from sensory overload by censing without bells and with only one small piece of frankincense at a time. Others have seen to the provision of separate spaces with HEPA filters and speakers or a closed-circuit TV streaming the service. This practice allows people with an inability to be around incense for long to participate.

Whatever physical accommodations a priest might offer, he can also offer spiritual help to people who suffer from disabilities of breathing. Learning to pray simply is a vital practice that can help, along with taking care of physical and medical needs when one is experiencing discomfort or distress due to a disability. Your priest will be a great help in finding ways to pray if you have breathing trouble.

Some general actions can help people with disabilities that make being around strong scents difficult. These include:

» Keep the rooms cool so as to reduce sensory overload and lower the effect of scents.

» If the choir area is located away from the incense, provide the option of sitting or standing near the choir to people who cannot be around strong fragrances.

» If you are able to provide ventilation by opening doors or windows, this can also help.

» Do not allow tobacco smoking on your church campus.

» Consider an away space with an air filter for people with serious breathing impairments.
» Encourage a desensitizing routine or routines for people with sensory aversions to scents.
» Ask your priest for help if you or your family member has trouble with incense due to a disability.

Have compassion on people who are unable to tolerate incense, and find ways to help them be part of the services and church community.

SUMMARY

» To live as the beloved community, we have to humbly help one another participate in church services. This chapter addresses shushing and incense/fragrances, two issues that often cause confusion, misunderstandings, and a break in community.

» Shushing is meant for the devil, not for disabled children. Don't do it. It doesn't help, and it turns away the children whom the Father has called to Himself.

» Incense and strong fragrances present challenges to people with disabilities, affecting sensory processing and breathing.

» Several strategies are offered for people with sensory-processing challenges. People with breathing challenges should consult their priests. Strategies are offered to help parishes accommodate people with disabilities exacerbated by incense.

REFLECTION QUESTIONS

1. Have you ever been distracted in church by a family with disabilities? What was your response? Did you pray for them?

2. Asking for help when we need it is part of the virtue of
   humility. Have you stayed out of church services due to
   fear of shushing or inability to be around incense? Ask your
   priest for help. What do you wish your fellow members of
   Christ's Body to know about your needs so that they can
   help you?

CHAPTER 23

SPOTLIGHT
Treating Food Allergy Sufferers Like Christ

The following essay is by Victoria Marckx, church school director at St. Demetrios Orthodox Church, Winnipeg, Manitoba.[194] Read her thoughtful application of the call to treat everyone as we treat Christ. Reflection questions and additional tips follow at the end of the chapter.

The phone rings Saturday night. Your pastor is on the phone. "Great news! Christ is coming to *our* parish this Sunday! Oh, and He needs gluten-free, dairy-free food, without nuts." Do you say, "No problem!" and bring out your best? Or does your heart sink because Christ, like so many visitors, will not find anything He can eat after Divine Liturgy?

"Well," you say, "it's not a big deal if people can only drink a cup of coffee. I mean, the important thing is the fellowship, after all!"

Let's look at that for a moment. For many Orthodox Christians, both cradle and convert, this fellowship hour is one of the most important in their week. For cradles, it is often their only contact with same-ethnicity friends, the people who share the rich cultural traditions they grew up with. My own parish is more than fifty percent first-generation Greek. It matters to them. For converts, it is often their only real-life contact with Orthodox Christians at all. They are trying to build the richness of a Christ-centered home without the foundation of family memories to help them make their homes a "little church." Contact with others who share their goals, faith, and celebrations is vital. It matters to them.

"So, why can't they just have coffee and chat? No one is asking them to leave!"

No, but you are not asking them to stay, either. What does that extra hour mean? To some, especially in regions of the USA and Canada where churches are few and far between, this is what it often means: a fast from midnight until Holy Communion, made harder by the fact that when you drive more than two hours to your parish, you have to get up very early and wrangle your children into their Sunday best and out the door. You then have a two-hour drive *back*. All this before you can start cooking a meal.

So, let's say they have family and friends near the parish, or can go to a restaurant, or the parish serves some form of solid, actual lunch food. Life just got that much easier. Eat at church and hope the children nap on the two-hour drive home, and thank goodness no one has to start cooking immediately, because you already ate.

Now consider how it looks to the family who has food allergies. Same time frame, same hungry kids . . . and no options.

Family and friends often do not accommodate food allergies or don't know enough to do so, so they seldom go to Sunday dinner. Restaurants that are gluten-free, dairy-free, nut-free? Even when some restaurants have gluten-free options, the risk of cross-contamination is real, and often servers are not knowledgeable enough to give proper information. Nothing at coffee hour, the kids are melting down, parents are starting to get that hunger headache, and they are faced with a two-hour drive home. Is it any wonder they skip out early, despite the need for fellowship? Or don't come at all, because it's not safe for their children? Or get yet more sleep-deprived by having to pack a picnic lunch for themselves every Sunday morning?

Think of it like inviting people over for dinner at your home, especially on feast days, and telling them they have to bring all their own food and drinks. And plates, cups, and flatware. Essentially, that's what we are doing. You'd never do that in your own home! How is it acceptable to do this in our parishes?

> Then the King will say to those at his right hand, "Come, O blessed of my Father, inherit the kingdom prepared for you from the foundation of the world; for I was hungry and you gave me food, I was thirsty and you gave me drink, I was a stranger and you welcomed me, I was naked and you clothed me, I was sick and you visited me, I was in prison and you came to me." Then the righteous will answer him, "Lord, when did we see thee hungry and feed thee, or thirsty and give thee drink? And when did we see thee a stranger and welcome thee, or naked and clothe thee? And when did we see thee sick or in prison and visit thee?" And the King will answer them, "Truly, I say to you, as you did it to one of the least of these my brethren, you did it to me."
> —Matthew 25:34–40

Matthew 25 is very clear on some things—like feeding the hungry, giving drink to the thirsty, and welcoming strangers. *Do* people feel welcome in your parish? Would you have a table for Christ? When we make sure that the table is richly laden for all, we *are* feeding Christ, and not turning Him away at the door to the hall.

What can we do to fix that?

The good news is that coffee hour has never been easier to navigate. First and foremost, *educate yourself.* The Celiac Association website is a great place to read. Invite a guest speaker from your local chapter if you need to, to talk about how to make your kitchen safe. Talk to the people in your parish that have food allergies, and ask what they need and how you can include them.

Learn the hidden pitfalls:

Soy sauce: yep, it has gluten. Oatmeal: it may not be gluten free. Buy specifically labeled gluten-free oats. Vanilla? The alcohol could be grain alcohol—check, because you never know. That open jar of gluten-free jam or sunbutter? Does it have crumbs in it from previous sandwich making? Did you just put that gluten-free bagel into the same toaster with all the wheat bread crumbs? That word *spices*? It can mean MSG.

It's work—but so is all love.

How St. Demetrios Parish Handles Food Allergies

I'd like to share with you some things that can be done to welcome others to your coffee hour and parish events, and even make it possible for children to go to Church School. While far from perfect, our parish tries to be as inclusive as possible.

Know the allergies.

I am the church school director at my parish. The classrooms are all peanut free, because there are allergies. The church school shares classroom space with our Greek school, and children there have allergies. As a matter of long-standing policy, we take pictures of those children with food allergies and other allergies, and they are updated yearly and kept on the wall in the school office. On them is the child's name, allergies, and whether the child carries an EpiPen.

The parish has sponsored classes for all the teachers on how to do basic first aid and CPR, use the EpiPens, care for someone having a seizure, and use the defibrillator hanging on the wall in the classroom building. All registration forms ask if there are allergies and if the child carries an EpiPen or an inhaler. Newcomers visiting the parish are invited to bring their children to class and are always asked if there are any allergies.

Keep it comparable.

I am personally determined that the children with allergies should have a snack as comparable as possible to the one everyone else is having. It is absolutely no fun for any child, especially one too young to properly understand, to watch everyone else eating cupcakes and be handed an apple. It makes a small, sinking feeling every time, and the child does not feel properly wanted in the place that should be most loving and welcoming—his church.

So, what does this mean? In practice, it means I, as director, make sure I know a few days in advance what parents are bringing for snacks. So: Bringing meatballs and fruit? Great snack! I pull out my dedicated GF crockpot and make meatballs at home, because I trust only myself to do this—unless one of the gluten-free people is making the snack. Bringing cereal cups and milk? Sure. I'll buy a new box of gluten-free cereal and non-dairy milk.

It's never been easier to buy gluten-free. Not a problem.

Often it can get a bit tricky—one lovely lady brought wagon wheels. I went out, bought GF/DF graham crackers, chocolate, and marshmallows, making sure the items were all GF/DF/nut free—and manufactured. Well, they were not wheels but wagon sides. My GF/DF families loved them. Pizza bites? Haven't found a gluten-free, dairy-free substitute, so those days, the kids get gluten-free, dairy-free pizza. Honestly, they don't mind.

We have two tables set up, and one is labeled "gluten-free and dairy-free." The helpers know which children need it. And have you ever seen the look on a three-year-old's face when told that, yes, he can eat *these* muffins? The light from the smile is blinding. Ditto when they learn about gluten-free, dairy-free pierogi. And sausage with no gluten.

Find solutions for the greater coffee hour.

Some solutions to have on hand: Gluten-free, dairy-free sausages can be found at Costco and other large store chains, and egg omelets with various fillings can be made in new muffin cups from the dollar store. Disposable baking trays from the dollar store can be used to make gluten-free bagels all toasty warm. Boiled eggs are gluten free. It's easy to make a bowl of eggs (keep their shells on) and set it on the table.

Keep a separate table and clean it—really clean it—with something like a Lysol wipe or Clorox Clean-Ups. Do not use the same rag and bucket of water you use for the other tables. Put a separate set of plates, cutlery, etc., there to minimize cross-contamination. Label it. Instruct other people not to randomly come by and put things on it. Ask a person who knows those tiny people who need special allergen-free foods to steer them toward "their table."

Provide goodie bags at special events.
When we hand out goodie bags at church school or at Lenten retreats, or any other special event, those goodie bags are allergen free for all the allergies we know about (nuts, peanuts, gluten, dairy, strawberries, raspberries, etc.). We make certain that all the children receive the same items. This means reading labels. We love our little people, though, and so we do this.

Consider options for special events for the greater parish.
Parish-wide events are harder, but ensuring there are several dishes that work for those who need them is not that complicated. Again, when a parish has a potluck, coordinating with the people who have allergies can be key. It may be necessary to assign "main dish," "dessert," "salad," etc., to the people who can handle allergen-free cooking. When I am feeling pressed for time, I often just call a gluten-free bakery and pick up what I need. Our last event had people looking with a bit of envy at the gluten-free table's desserts.

Be careful.
Be constantly aware of pitfalls that may include commercial companies changing recipes and suddenly including allergens. Did you know that some herbal teas contain gluten, and hibiscus tea is often contaminated with peanuts? Cross-contamination can result from many sources, so if possible, dedicate pans or buy disposable ones from Dollar Tree or a similar store.

Educate yourself.
Subscribe to Facebook groups and internet forums that discuss these issues. Read the stories people with food allergies tell: how they describe being at parties and "pretending to eat

something all evening while starving hungry in the middle of people feasting." Feel what they feel, cry, wipe your tears, and determine to learn, learn, learn, and remember that no matter what, we are all members of the Body of Christ, and as such should not let one of our family members leave hungry.

Spiritual hunger is fed by love, and we can show our love by making certain that physical needs are addressed with as much love as possible, so that when Christ comes to *your* coffee hour, He will remember, and on that final Day of Judgment, will say, "I was hungry, and you gave me food."

Some Common Food Allergens Decoded

Victoria's recommendations are wonderful, and they form a good foundation for addressing the needs of parishioners with food allergies. In the course of writing this book, I heard from dozens of Orthodox Christians who suffer from severe food allergies. They shared additional tips that will help your parish keep everyone safe. I have included them in a list below.

But first, let's look at the most common food allergens and some of the ways they might appear in food or on food labels. Some people might be allergic to other foods in addition to these, but we can do a lot to help each other if we learn to spot the top eight most common food allergens.[195] Below are the eight foods that cause the most allergic reactions in people with food allergies, because most people who suffer from food allergies are allergic to one or more of these foods. Though these foods are common and in lots of other foods, they are still dangerous to the people who are allergic to them.

In a food-allergic reaction, the food causes the body to have a strong immune response (which might include hives, vomiting, choking, diarrhea, cramping, fever, numbness, confusion, exhaustion, swelling, heart issues, trouble breathing) that can be very dangerous to the allergic person, even resulting in death if the reaction cannot be controlled. The only way to keep a person with food allergies safe is for them not to eat or breathe the food that can harm them. They cannot have a little bit of it safely, since immune reactions are not predictable. The best policy is to help people avoid the foods.

Another thing to note with all food allergens is that the method of preparing foods does not lessen their potential to cause an allergic reaction. Cooking does not get rid of the allergy-causing part of the food.

This guide is presented to help churches notice some common food allergies, but the list is not exhaustive. Ask your church members about their needs, and follow medical advice for helping them if they have been exposed to an allergen. This list is not medical advice, but it is an accurate and handy guide for teaching church members about some of the most common food allergens that might be present in foods at church gatherings.

» **Milk**: This ingredient is in whole milk, low-fat milk, non-fat milk, chocolate milk, whipped cream, cream, half and half, butter, cheese, buttercream, and buttermilk. It might show up in other product labels as milk, cream, butter, whey, nonfat milk, milk protein, buttermilk, cheese powder, casein, and other ingredients. Sometimes foods will include a warning that says, "Contains Milk," because milk allergy is one of the top eight, most common food allergies. If you're not sure if something contains milk, save the label to display alongside the food.

» **Eggs**: This ingredient is in all forms of eggs (scrambled, yolks, egg whites, egg wash, quiche, boiled, poached), most mayonnaises, custard, meringue, flan, caramel, in many baked goods as a binder and/or glaze, royal icing, eggnog, and in many cake mixes as powdered egg. It might appear on labels as powdered egg, albumen/albumin, yolk, egg whites, meringue, mayonnaise, Ovalbumin, Surimi, or Lysozyme. Since eggs are one of the top eight food allergens, the package might have a warning that says, "Contains Eggs." If you're not sure if a product contains eggs, save the labels of ingredients to display alongside the food.

» **Wheat**: This ingredient is in all forms of bread (except gluten-free), including sprouted seed breads, organic breads, sourdough breads, and rye or barley breads, as well as wheat berries, koliva, all pastas that are not gluten-free, halva, baklava, spanakopita, cookies, prosphora, cakes, stews, sauces, cereals, baked pasta dishes, breadcrumbs, croutons, couscous, tabbouleh, graham crackers, malt, malt extract in sweets or drinks, most beers, many grain alcohols, many nonstick sprays, traditional and common commercial play doughs, many glues, and many types of sidewalk chalk. It might also appear on labels as flour, farina, einkorn, kamut, bulgur, cereal extract, Fu, spelt, semolina, seitan, wheat/vital gluten, triticale, Triticum, glucose syrup, and matzo. Wheat is one of the top eight most common food allergens, so many foods will also have a label reading, "Contains Wheat." If you are not sure if a food contains wheat, save the label to display alongside foods.

» **Tree Nuts:** Tree nuts include almonds, pecans, pistachios, walnuts, hazelnuts, cashews, pine/pignolia/piñon nuts, Brazil nuts, macadamia nuts, chestnuts, and shea nuts.

Tree nuts also include a very long list of rarer nuts, and some people with tree-nut allergies are also allergic to coconuts. They might be served whole, ground into meal and baked into cake or bread, as an ingredient in granola or snack bars, as part of a nougat or praline, in a stew, used as a fasting or vegan milk or cheese or butter substitute, in a cookie or cake, part of a sweet dessert or candy, as an artificial flavoring or extract, part of a chocolate, part of a brittle or candy bark, mixed into fillings, or incorporated as pastes or spreads. They are still nuts, no matter the form. Many labels warn about tree nuts by saying "Contains Tree Nuts," because tree nuts are one of the eight most common food allergens. If you are not sure if a food contains tree nuts, bring the label to display alongside the foods.

» **Shellfish**: There are two types of shellfish—crustacea and mollusks. People with allergies usually have to avoid both sets. The crustacea shellfish are barnacle, crab, crawfish (crawdads, crayfish), krill, lobster (langouste, langoustine, Moreton Bay bugs, scampi, tomalley), prawns, and shrimp (crevette, scampi). These might appear in soups, patties, sandwiches; they might be fried, on salads, in sauces, or served as cocktail foods or spreads. The mollusk shellfish and shellfish-allergy triggers include oysters, abalone, clams (cherrystone, geoduck, littleneck, pismo, quahog), scallops, cockle, cuttlefish, limpet (lapas, opihi), mussels, octopus, periwinkle, sea cucumber, sea urchin, snails (escargot), squid (calamari), whelk (turban shell), and conch. These foods might appear raw or cooked in various ways (fried, stewed, seared, poached). They might be part of sushi, fried seafood, seafood mixes, sauces, clam sauce, chowders, paella, and other dishes. Since shellfish are one of the eight most common causes of food allergies, some labels will have the warning, "Contains Shellfish." If you are not sure if a food contains shellfish, display any labels alongside the prepared foods.

» **Soy**: Soy, or soya, is found in soybeans (edamame), tofu, tempeh, soy sauce, miso, tamari, textured vegetable protein (TVP), natto, sobee, and in protein supplements such as hydrolyzed/concentrate/isolate soy protein. It might also show up in foods as soybean oil, soy grits, soy lecithin, or soy flour. Some foods that frequently contain soy are protein and snack bars, commercially baked bread and other baked goods, chocolate, fried snack foods, packaged meal kits (such as ramen noodles or flavored rice or pasta kits), baby formulas and foods, and even canned fish. It might also appear on an ingredient label saying, "Contains Soy," since it is one of the top eight food allergens. If you are not sure if a food contains soy, display any labels alongside the prepared foods.

» **Peanuts**: Peanuts are often served shelled or in their shells, as beer nuts or boiled peanuts, dry roasted, in crushed toppings, or as peanut butter. They also commonly appear in mixed nuts, peanut butter and chocolate candies and spreads, other types of candy made on the same equipment, peanut butter cookies, peanut butter baking chips, and peanut oil used for frying a variety of foods (including frozen foods and some fast foods or restaurant foods). They are used in some potato chips; arachic oil; nougats; some chili; some snack and protein bars; in graham cracker crusts, pies, and other baked goods; in some flavorings, many eggrolls, and several types of ethnic foods where peanut oil and peanuts are used in cooking. Some but not all people with peanut allergies also react to similar legumes such as buckwheat, fenugreek, or peas. Peanut allergies are one of the eight most common food allergies, and many foods that contain them are labeled, "Contains Peanuts." If you are unsure if a food contains peanuts, bring labels of the food ingredients to display alongside the prepared food.

» **Fish**: Fish usually refers to finned fish and can appear in cooked, raw, and canned or preserved forms, including sushi; in baked, fried, broiled, stewed, breaded, and patty preparations; and in other forms of prepared fish such as tuna, anchovies, bass, perch, trout, tilapia, mahi mahi, halibut, herring, flounder, grouper, swordfish, pollock, cod, salmon, haddock, catfish, and many other varieties of fish. Pickled fish, canned fish, and smoked fish (like smoked salmon) cause allergic reactions as much as raw or heat-cooked fish. Some less obvious sources of fish include seafood stews such as paella, gumbo, bouillabaisse, and jambalaya; fish sauce in ethnic foods; canned chowders; pizza toppings that contain anchovies; Caesar salad and dressing; fish oil (including capsules and supplements); fish gelatin (in some marshmallows); some barbeque sauces; artificial or imitation fish or shellfish (such as imitation crab or sea sticks); caponata; and some ethnic cuisines where most foods are cooked in fish sauce and cross-contamination is likely in the cooking environment. Because fish is one of the eight most common food allergens, many labels will warn, "Contains Fish." If you are not sure if a food contains fish, save ingredients labels to display alongside prepared foods.

When dealing with any of the top eight food allergens, it's better to be safe than sorry. If you don't know what is in a food you serve at a gathering, say so or mark your allergen checklist "unsure."

Additional Tips to Keep Food Allergy Sufferers Safe at Church

Orthodox Church parishes come in a wide range of sizes, and many churches will not have the resources to afford a Christian education director or youth minister or kitchen manager or other staff person to oversee events and foods. However, there are many practices in addition to those that Victoria shared above that can help churches keep food-allergy sufferers safe.

» **Label nametags.** If your Sunday school program has reusable nametags, you can add a sticker that says, "no wheat," "no tree nuts," "no peanuts," and so on to a nametag for a child with food allergies. If you print sticker nametags with a computer or by hand, you can also write allergies on the nametags of people with allergies who cannot advocate for themselves due to their age or disabilities. This will help the people looking after the group to protect the allergy sufferers from the foods that are unsafe.

» **Provide an allergy checklist for social gatherings.** You can print your own or use the one available for free on my website (www.summerkinard.com/special-needs-resources/). Some churches might even have color-coded stickers for potlucks, but that can get complicated in larger groups. A checklist helps people label foods quickly and easily.

» **Gluten is in products that contain wheat.** People with celiac disease cannot eat gluten in any form without experiencing damage to their digestive systems, even if the symptoms do not show up immediately. While celiac disease is not an allergy, it is often misunderstood. That's in part because an ingredient called gluten can be intentionally added to breads during baking, and some people mistakenly think that gluten only comes in that form. However, gluten is in any food that contains barley, rye, MSG, brewer's yeast, malt (including malted milk and malt vinegar), and in any food listed above in the description of the wheat food allergen. It's also in some off-brand glues and toy slimes, which might be an issue for people with allergies who also put non-food items in their mouths due to age or disabilities. People with celiac disease should consult their priest to talk about Holy Communion. They usually do not partake of antidoron at church due to their medical condition, because antidoron contains gluten. However, this is not the result of lack of devotion.

» **Check craft supplies.** For children in Sunday school or other church groups, food is not the only source of exposure. Common brands of play doughs contain wheat, for instance, and some discount brands of sidewalk chalk contain wheat. However, in the United States, Silly Putty does not contain gluten or wheat, and the Crayola and Colorations brands of sidewalk chalk are wheat- and gluten-free. The United States brand Elmer's glue is also gluten- and wheat-free. You can look up major brands online to find out ingredients, or search the product along with the type of allergen to check that craft items are safe to use for church students with allergies. Since some children with disabilities put non-food items in their mouths, this is an important thing to check so that they can stay safe in the learning environment at church.

» **Stock a few safe foods.** In the United States, a brand that makes foods safe for many allergies is Enjoy Life. It can help to have a box or two of their snacks on hand to provide for families with food allergies. Apples, grapes, and fresh vegetables like carrots and broccoli are also low-allergen foods. If you provide these items, make sure to follow Victoria's good advice and keep them on a separate table so that they are less likely to be mixed with allergy-causing foods.

» **Provide fellowship opportunities that don't revolve around food.** Some options include arranging the flowers for the church, painting icons, creating an onsite prayer garden, visiting monasteries, gathering to knit or crochet, singing together, taking a field trip to an accessible playground or play gym, going on group hikes, providing a room with sensory bins for children to play together away from food during coffee hour, and gathering to color while listening to liturgical music. If you have a classroom that is free during coffee hour, consider making it a food-free fellowship zone so that families can mingle without having to worry about a child being exposed to an allergen.

Summary

» When Jesus describes the last judgment in Matthew 25, He says that feeding the hungry is like feeding Him. We should apply that lesson to the way we welcome families with food allergies, too.

» Church gatherings that include food should be inclusive in order to honor the dignity of the image of God in every person present. Practical tips are laid out.

» Not everyone knows what the top eight most common food allergens are or which foods contain them. Detailed above are some ways to spot the eight foods that most often cause allergic reactions: milk, eggs, wheat, tree nuts, shellfish, soy, peanuts, and fish. Knowing what is in foods is important for keeping fellow Orthodox Christians safe at gatherings.

» Other tips that make it easier for families with food allergies to participate include labeling name tags, understanding gluten, checking craft supplies for allergens, stocking a few safe foods, and providing options for fellowship without food.

REFLECTION QUESTIONS

1. In her essay that begins this chapter, Victoria Marckx asks us to treat our fellow Christians who suffer from food allergies the way that we would treat Christ. Does that change the way that you think about people with food allergies?

2. Sometimes food allergies are portrayed in the media as a joke, a character flaw, or pretend. In fact, they are serious medical conditions that can be life threatening, and they arise through no one's fault. When you pray the Lord's Prayer, think of food allergy sufferers when you say, "Give us this day our daily bread," because eating is more complicated for them.

3. If you suffer from food allergies, you might draw courage knowing that humans don't live by bread alone, but by every word of God. How does a limited diet help you be more aware of God? Have you considered your food allergy as a type of fasting?

Conclusion

And we all, with unveiled face, beholding the glory of the Lord, are being changed into his likeness from one degree of glory to another; for this comes from the Lord who is the Spirit.

—2 CORINTHIANS 3:18

Piety versus Devotion

ONE OF THE CHIEF SOURCES of misunderstandings and stereotypes of persons and families with disabilities is the confusion of piety and devotion. Often when parishes encounter someone with a disability that affects their communication and social graces, they get offended on the basis that the person or family with disabilities is not following standards of piety. Some well-meaning people in the parish might even insist that families must attend more church services, fast more, be still and quiet in a crowd, and act like everyone else in order to show that they are serious about being part of the Church and loving God.

Yet, a hardening of piety is not a sign of the love of God. It's a sign of a misunderstanding of mercy. Some people think that mercy means abandoning rules or standards or promoting laxity or laziness. In fact, mercy means making space and saving a place for those who need help or extra room to join the Body.

What is piety? Piety is the way we behave to express our common Faith. It's a social trait. In pagan Roman times, *pietas*—or piety—involved honoring Roman idols and even emperors with greetings, sacrifices, and incense. Social life revolved around that piety, because the common faith was seen as the cause of Roman prosperity and power. The Christians were persecuted for not being pious in the way the Romans saw as appropriate. The Christian religion was seen as a threat to the Empire because the Christians didn't observe the social customs that most Romans saw as the key to making their deities happy. Unhappy deities meant that Roman society would crumble. To us, this might seem like magical thinking, but it was a powerful common belief.

It's easy for us to see that piety in the Church is not a magical key to win God's favor. We all come to God in His mercy and "enter into the joy of our Lord"—as the Paschal Homily of St. John Chrysostom declares—and "enjoy the riches of His goodness. Let no one grieve poverty; for the universal Kingdom has been revealed."[196] Neither those who fast and who are devout, nor those who do not fast, nor those who have just shown up at Pascha are excluded from the mercy of God and the joy of the Resurrection that reveals the Kingdom of God. But that old unease with different piety is still around, because people look for piety as a clue that others belong to their shared Faith.

When it comes to gauging the devotion of people with disabilities, this reliance on pious expressions can be misleading. People accustomed to spotting a fellow Orthodox believer by shared fasting can be confused when a disability requires their fellow Christian not to fast or to fast differently. Yet even the great ascetics in early monasticism could not always eat the pulses and greens and dry bread that most of their fellow monks ate while fasting.[197]

Someone looking for piety could misinterpret the noises made by children or adults with developmental disabilities as impious when the noises occur at a time when common piety models silence. Yet those sounds might be those persons' attempt to praise God from their hearts or might even be involuntary.

Pious people might misunderstand a lack of greeting as impious, but a hearing, speech, or language processing impairment could be the cause of the other person's quiet or lack of interaction. Pious members might misunderstand sporadic church attendance as impiety, when in fact the families are likely absent due to difficulties arising from disabilities.

In all of these cases and others, people use the standard of piety to measure shared faith. But in none of these cases does the family's ability to follow pious norms reflect their devotion. The devotion of families with disabilities is shown by presence rather than piety. This is why we are not called to be enforcers of piety, but bearers of mercy. For ourselves, we struggle in virtue. Toward others, we extend the mercy of God by making a place for them and meeting with love their devotion to God, which is shown by their presence, not always by their conformity to piety.

Taking Up the Cross
Often when considering the welcome of families with disabilities, we have let our desire for piety overcome the need for compassion toward fellow members of Christ's Body. We would prefer to deal with some people once they're already healed in the Resurrection, and we have not considered that they

are already holy in God's time. We have not considered that we have all entered the suffering of Christ in baptism, and we need not fear to embrace our fellow members of His Body who suffer. It is only through perfect communion with one another in Christ, through shared sacraments, prayer, humility, and love, that we also will experience salvation.

We have failed to see the witness of persons with disabilities as they shine forth the truth that nothing can separate us from the love of God. We have turned away from the call to empty ourselves in mutual humility and love so that we can share the mind of Christ, which reveals the gifts of the Holy Spirit in each of us. Most of all, we have forgotten the simple law of hospitality by which we meet God at the table.

This book has sought to make a beginning by showing the way around these obstacles, by pointing back toward Christ, of whose Body we are all members, and by shining a light on the presence of Christ with us in the life of families with disabilities and in the community of the whole Church. Like the disciples who asked the Lord about the man born blind, "Who sinned, this man or his parents, that he was born blind?" we hear the Lord reply, "It was not that this man sinned, or his parents, but that the works of God might be made manifest in him." The works of God are made manifest in us when we as a community imitate the Savior's love and humility in making space, teaching so that everyone can learn, practicing prayers that all can pray, ministering to one another, and welcoming one another into fellowship as we welcome Christ.

Like the disciples, we will still make mistakes, sometimes asking misguided questions or making assumptions that hold back the children whom the Savior wishes to bless. But we have made a turn, despite our limits. The path is laid out before us, constrained by the love of Christ, and we can follow it together as a whole Church, including the twenty percent of us who live with disabilities. In this calling, as in all callings, our Lord is the Way.

To live in the Kingdom of God is to know ourselves and one another in Christ as members of His Body. We are all living in the Passion of Christ, and we are all living in the foretaste of His Resurrection. This mixture of sorrow and joy can only be navigated by clinging to God in love and pouring out love toward our neighbors. We must make room for families with disabilities in our teaching, our leadership, and, most importantly, in our friendships. We are all members of Christ's Body, and Christ is our Head. Look at Him. Copy Him. Love as He loves, for of such is the Kingdom of God.

Acknowledgments

I WOULD LIKE TO BEGIN by thanking the many hundreds of Orthodox Christian families who reached out to me over the past four years about the needs that prompted this book. Some responded to surveys and social media questions. Some messaged me in the middle of the night with frantic questions, wondering if I knew how to help with a situation that was troubling their special-needs family. We are on this journey into God together, and I am grateful to be able to bear witness with you to the grace of our Lord Jesus Christ at work among families with disabilities.

To the beloved parishes who have welcomed my family: St. Barbara Greek Orthodox Church in Durham, North Carolina, the Annunciation Greek Orthodox Cathedral in Houston, Texas, and The Forty Holy Martyrs of Sebaste Antiochian Church in Sugar Land, Texas. Thak you also to our Abouna, the V. Rev. Joseph Gereige, who has led the way in welcoming us at Forty Holy Martyrs.

To my dear friends who have talked with me about this book for so long, especially Elina, Nikki, Courtney, Elena, Tonya, Kayla, Jamey, Dawn, Michelle, Allison, Nicole, Monica, Jessica, Ksenia, Rebekah, Georgia, Janna, Blanca, and members of groups where we have shared so much of our lives, thank you. I remember you always with gratitude and love in my prayers.

This book could not have come to fruition without the help of other laypersons who have worked tirelessly to gather and share resources on living faithfully with disabilities. Some of these persons, like Maria Evangelou, Monica Spoor, Matthew and Summer Griffith, Lisa Wuertz, and Victoria Marckx, are featured in this book. Others, like Matushka Wendy Cwiklinski and William Gall, host online spaces that help connect the faithful with support and resources for Orthodox Christian life with disabilities. The resource person who has helped me the most with encouragement and tracking down sources is my friend Charlotte Riggle, whose blog (charlotteriggle.com) offers encouraging posts almost every week on life with disabilities. Her friendship, insights, and connections with other Orthodox Christians living with disabilities have made more difference to me than I can say.

I could not have written this book without the careful guidance, conversations, and blessing of my dear spiritual father, the Very Reverend Father Stavroforos Mamaies. My heartfelt thanks go out to him. I am also grateful to the faithful and loving clergy of the Annunciation Greek Orthodox Cathedral, especially the presiding priest, the Reverend Father Michael Lambakis, who helped me find a liturgical reference that shaped some of this book.

Several other clergymen helped me with prayers and resources for this book. I am grateful especially to the Reverend Father Marty Watts and the Reverend Father Christopher Foley, who shared in these pages some of their insights on guiding families with disabilities. For every layperson who shared with me a story of welcome for their family with disabilities, there are faithful clergymen who have guided their parishes in the way of Christ. Though they are not all named in this book, they have my gratitude.

Writing a book on theology is the work of years, and my family was on the writing journey with me. I'm grateful to my sister Alyssa for helping me with childcare and fleshing out ideas as I pressed to finish writing this book while balancing the demands of special-needs family life. I'm grateful to my Children of Joy, who were patient with me writing so many evenings and whose joy in Christ has caught me, too. Most of all, I am grateful to my beloved husband, Andrew Kinard, whose insight, wisdom, proofreading, and prayerful patience have helped me in this writing and parenting journey. I could not have written this book without him.

A holy icon pattern shows the Theotokos extending her cloak over all of the sick and poor and disabled who come to her and to the Church for protection. I have felt that protection daily in my prayers and study as I have written this book. Though it might seem a foregone conclusion that I could not have written this book without the prayers of the Holy Theotokos, gratitude and joy demand that I say thanks here as well. Alongside her, many patron saints have taught me through their prayers and the words of wisdom preserved by the Church through the ages. It is truly by their prayers that I was able to say anything good.

Above all, I wish to acknowledge our Lord Jesus Christ, who came and got me. I wrote this book while gazing at the icon of Christ the Bridegroom, and I hope His love and humility have shaped my words. With the Apostle Paul, I am persuaded "that neither death, nor life, nor angels, nor principalities, nor things present, nor things to come, nor powers, nor height, nor depth, nor anything else in all creation, will be able to separate us from the love of God in Christ Jesus our Lord" (Rom. 8:38-39).

In the Risen Christ,
Summer Kinard
Sunday of the Blind Man, 2019

Bibliography

Akathist to the Mother of God, Nurturer of Children. Safford, AZ: St. Paisius Orthodox Monastery, 2001.

Ambrose of Milan. *Saint Ambrose: Seven Exegetical Works.* Translated by Michael P. McHugh. Washington, D.C.: Catholic University of America Press, 2003.

Archangel Michael Greek Orthodox Church. "The Challenge Liturgy Ministry." https://archangelmichaelchurch.org/challenge-liturgy/ (accessed April 1, 2019).

Assembly of Canonical Orthodox Bishops of the United States of America. "Disability and Communion." http://www.assembly-ofbishops.org/news/scoba/disability-and-communion (accessed April 15, 2019).

Athanasius. *The Life of St. Anthony the Great.* Willets, CA: Eastern Orthodox Church, 1994.

———. *On the Incarnation.* Translated by A Religious of C.S.M.V. Crestwood, NY: St. Vladimir's Seminary Press, 2000.

Augustine. *The City of God Against the Pagans.* Cambridge Texts in the History of Political Thought. Translated by R. W. Dyson. Cambridge: Cambridge University Press, 2002.

———. *The Confessions.* Translated by Maria Boulding. New York, NY: Vintage Books, 1998.

———. *Confessions: Books IX XIII.* Loeb Classical Library, Vol. 27. Translated by William Watts. Cambridge, MA: Harvard University Press, 1979.

———. *The Literal Meaning of Genesis.* Translated by John Hammond Taylor. Vol. 1 of 2 vols. New York, NY: Newman Press, 1982.

———. *On Genesis: Two Books on Genesis Against the Manichees.* Translated by Roland J. Teske. Washington, DC: Catholic University of America Press, 1991.

———. *The Teacher, The Free Choice of the Will, Grace and Free Will.* Translated by R. P. Russell. Vol. 59. Washington, DC: Catholic University of America Press, 1968.

———. *The Trinity*. The Works of Saint Augustine: A Translation for the 21st Century. Edited by John E. Rotelle. Translated by Edmund Hill. Brooklyn, NY: New City Press, 1991.

Bonhoeffer, Dietrich. *Creation and Fall: A Theological Exposition of Genesis 1–3*. Edited and translated by Martin Ruter and Ilse Todt. Minneapolis: Fortress Press, 1997.

Branch-Smith, Brittany. "Church Access for the Deaf." *Frederick News-Post*, January 1, 2014. fredericknewspost.com/news/lifestyle/church-access-for-the-deaf/article_917b8ae6-bf5c-5108-97fa-3abe-f9193b7d.html (accessed May 1, 2019).

Briggs, David. "Study: U.S. Churches Exclude Children with Autism, ADD/ADHD." The Association of Religion Data Archives. http://blogs.thearda.com/trend/featured/study-u-s-churches-exclude-children-with-autism-addadhd/ (accessed April 1, 2019).

Brown, Peter. *The Body and Society: Men, Women, and Sexual Renunciation in Early Christianity*. New York: Columbia University Press, 1988.

Caldwell-Harris, C., C.F. Murphy, T. Velazquez, and P. McNamara. "Religious Belief Systems of Persons with High Functioning Autism." Proceedings of the Annual Meeting of the Cognitive Science Society (2011). https://escholarship.org/uc/item/6zh3j3pr (accessed May 1, 2019).

Callahan, V. *St. Gregory of Nyssa: Ascetical Works*. Washington, D.C.: Catholic University of America Press, 1967.

Catechism of the Catholic Church. New York: Doubleday, 1997.

Chryssavgis, John. "The Body of Christ: A Place of Welcome for All People, Including People with Disabilities." New York: Greek Orthodox Archdiocese of America, 2017.

Cuncic, Arlin. "How to Practice Self-Regulation." https://www.verywellmind.com/how-you-can-practice-self-regulation-4163536 (accessed August 15, 2019).

Cyril of Jerusalem. *St. Cyril of Jerusalem's Lectures on the Christian Sacraments: The Protocatechesis and the Five Mystagogical Catecheses*. Edited by F.L. Cross. Crestwood, NY: St Vladimir's Seminary Press, 1995.

Cyril of Jerusalem. *The Works of Saint Cyril of Jerusalem*. The Fathers of the Church: A New Translation. Translated by Leo P. McCauley and Anthony A. Stephenson. Vol. 1 of 2 vols. Washington, DC: Catholic University of America Press, 1970.

Freeman, Stephen. *Everywhere Present: Christianity in a One-Storey Universe*. Chesterton, IN: Conciliar Press, 2010.

Fish Eaters website. "Mary Gardens." https://www.fisheaters.com/marygardens.html (accessed May 1, 2019).

Food Allergy Research & Education website. https://www.foodallergy.org (accessed May 4, 2019).

Goleman, Daniel. "Brain's Design Emerges As a Key to Emotions." *The New York Times*, August 15, 1989, sec. Science Times. https://www.nytimes.com/1989/08/15/science/brain-s-design-emerges-as-a-key-to-emotions.html (accessed Aug. 19, 2019).

Grant, Robert M. *Irenaeus of Lyons*. London: Routledge, 1997.

Grcevich, Stephen. "It's the Hidden Disabilities That Keep Kids out of Church." *Church4EveryChild* (blog). July 23, 2018. https://church4everychild.org/2018/07/23/its-the-hidden-disabilities-that-keep-kids-out-of-church/ (accessed April 1, 2019).

Grcevich, Stephen. "What are the stats on disability and church?" *Church4EveryChild* (blog). February 9, 2016. https://church4everychild.org/2016/02/09/what-are-the-stats-on-disability-and-church/#_edn1 (accessed April 1, 2019).

Gregory Palamas. *Miracles of the Lord: Sermons by Saint Gregory Palamas*. Edited by Christopher Veniamin. Dalton, PA: Mount Thabor Publishing, 2013.

Gregory of Nyssa. *St. Gregory Ascetical Works*. The Fathers of the Church: A New Translation. Translated by Virginia Woods Callahan. Vol. 58. Washington, DC: Catholic University of America Press, 1967.

———. *The Lord's Prayer and The Beatitudes*. Translated by Hilda C. Graef. New York: Paulist Press, 1954.

——— and Edward Rochie Hardy. "Address on Religious Instruction." In *Christology of the Later Fathers*. Louisville, KY: Westminster John Knox Press, 2006.

Hardy, Edward Rochie. *Christology of the Later Fathers*. Louisville, KY: Westminster John Knox Press, 2006.

———. "Dogmatic Letters of Nestorius and Cyril of Alexandria." In

Christology of the Later Fathers. Louisville, KY: Westminster John Knox Press, 2006.

Ignatius of Antioch. *The Epistle of Ignatius to the Ephesians*. http://www.newadvent.org/fathers/0104.htm (accessed May 1, 2019).

John Chrysostom. *St. John Chrysostom: Baptismal Instructions*. Translated by Paul William Harkins. New York: Paulist Press, 1963.

———. *Chrysostom: On the Priesthood, Ascetic Treatises, Select Homilies and Letters, Homilies on the Statues*. Nicene and Post-Nicene Fathers: A Select Library of the Christian Church, Series One. Edited by Philip Schaff. Vol. 9. Peabody, MA: Hendrickson Publishers, 1999.

———. "Wisdom for the Day: St. John Chrysostom, Prayers for Every Hour of the Day." https://stbarnabasoc.org/wisdom-day-st-john-chrysostom/(accessed April 15, 2019).

John Climacus. *The Ladder of Divine Ascent*. Translated by Archimandrite Lazarus Moore. New York: Harper & Brothers, 1959.

John of Damascus. *Writings*. Translated by Frederic H. Chase, Jr. Washington, D.C.: Catholic University of America Press, 1958.

John of Kronstadt. *My Life in Christ: The Spiritual Journals of St. John of Kronstadt*. Parts 1 and 2. 2 Volumes. Edited by Nicholas Kotar. Jordanville, NY: Holy Trinity Publications, 2015.

Kinard, Summer. Website. https://summerkinard.com/

———. "The Church as Memory Palace." Accessed August 16, 2019. http://myocn.net/the-church-as-memory-palace/

Larchet, Jean-Claude. *The Theology of Illness*. Translated by John and Michael Breck. Crestwood, NY: St. Vladimir's Seminary Press, 2002.

Library of Congress National Library Service for the Blind and Physically Handicapped. Talking Books Catalog. https://www.loc.gov/nls/braille-audio-reading-materials/online-catalog-search/ (accessed May 1, 2019).

Louth, Andrew. *Maximus the Confessor*. London: Routledge, 2010.

Lubac, Henri de, Mark Sebanc, and E. M. Macierowski. *Medieval Exegesis: The Four Senses of Scripture*. Vol. 1 of 4 vols. Grand Rapids, MI: W.B. Eerdmans, 1998.

Mahler, Kelly. *Interoception: The Eighth Sensory System*. Lenexa, KS:

AAPC Publishing, 2017.

Maican, Petre. "Image and Likeness and Profound Cognitive Disability: Rethinking Patristic Categories." https://publicorthodoxy. org/2019/07/02/image-likeness-cognitive-disabilities/ (accessed July 12, 2019).

Marckx, Victoria. "'Let ALL the Little Children Come,' Including Those Who Need Gluten-Free Food." https://charlotteriggle.com/ let-all-little-children-come-including-gluten-free/ (accessed April 1, 2019).

Maximus the Confessor. *On the Cosmic Mystery of Jesus Christ: Selected Writings from St. Maximus the Confessor.* Translated by Paul M. Blowers and Robert Louis Wilken. Crestwood, NY: St. Vladimir's Seminary Press, 2003.

National Professional Development Center on Autism Spectrum Disorder. "What are evidence-based practices?" https://autismpdc. fpg.unc.edu/evidence-based-practices (accessed May 1, 2019).

Nellas, Panayiotis. *Deification in Christ: Orthodox Perspectives on the Nature of the Human Person.* Translated by Norman Russell. Crestwood, NY: St. Vladimir's Seminary Press, 1997.

Norenzayan A, W.M. Gervais, and K.H. Trzesniewski. "Mentalizing Deficits Constrain Belief in a Personal God." PLOS ONE 7(5): e36880 (2012). https://doi.org/10.1371/journal.pone.0036880 (accessed May 1, 2019).

Orthodox Marketplace Braille Divine Liturgy and Prayer Books. https://www.orthodoxmarketplace.com/esss/category/braille (accessed May 1, 2019).

Palmer, Constantina. *The Scent of Holiness: Lessons from a Women's Monastery.* Chesterton, IN: Conciliar Press, 2012. Kindle edition.

———. *The Sweetness of Grace: Stories of Christian Trial and Victory.* Chesterton, IN: Ancient Faith Publishing, 2017.

Palmer, G.E.H., Philip Sherrard, and Kallistos Ware, ed./trans., *The Philokalia.* Volume One. London: Faber and Faber, 1979.

Papadeas, Fr. George L., trans., *Greek Orthodox Holy Week and Easter Services.* Daytona Beach, FL: Patmos Press, 2016.

Papavassiliou, Vassilios, ed. *The Ancient Faith Prayer Book.* Chesterton, IN: Ancient Faith Publishing, 2014.

Parsells, Emily. "Our Mother of God Garden." *Charming the Birds* (blog). June 26, 2008. http://www.charmingthebirdsfromthetrees.com/2008/06/our-mother-of-god-garden.html. (accessed May 17, 2019).

Porphyrios. *Wounded by Love: The Life and the Wisdom of Saint Porphyrios.* Edited by the Sisters of the Holy Convent of Chrysopigi. Limni, Evia, Greece: Denise Harvey, 2005.

Rice, David Talbot. *Art of the Byzantine Era: David Talbot Rice.* London: Thames and Hudson, 1963.

Rilke, Rainer Maria. *Rilke's Book of Hours: Love Poems to God.* Translated by Anita Barrows and Joanna Macy. New York: Riverhead Books, 2005.

Rogers, Sally J., Geraldine Dawson, and Laurie A. Vismara. *An Early Start for Your Child with Autism: Using Everyday Activities to Help Kids Connect, Communicate, and Learn.* New York: The Guilford Press, 2012.

Salaris, Steven. "So why do 60% of our college youth leave Orthodoxy?" *Orthodox Christian Laity* website. Last modified on March 1, 2009. https://ocl.org/so-why-do-60-of-our-college-youth-leave-orthodoxy/

Special School District of St. Louis County. "Sensory Diet." https://www.ssdmo.org/cool_tools/inclusive/Resources/trying_to_make_sense_resources.pdf (accessed April 15, 2019).

Spoor, Monica. *Spirituality on the Spectrum: Having Autism in the Orthodox Church.* The Netherlands: Brave New Books, 2017.

Theodore the Studite. *On the Holy Icons.* Translated by Catharine P. Roth. Crestwood, NY: St. Vladimir's Seminary Press, 2001.

Vost, Kevin. *Memorize the Faith!* Manchester, NH: Sophia Institute Press, 2006.

Ward, Benedicta, ed., trans. *The Sayings of the Desert Fathers.* Kalamazoo, MI: Cistercian Press, 1984.

Westminster Study Bible: The Holy Bible, Revised Standard Version. Containing the Old and New Testaments. New York: Collins Clear-Type Press, 1965.

Williams, Benjamin D. and Harold B. Anstall. *Orthodox Worship: A Living Continuity with the Synagogue, the Temple, and the Early Church.*

Chesterton, IN: Ancient Faith Publishing, 2018.

Winner, Michelle Garcia. *Thinking About You, Thinking About Me.* 2nd ed. San Jose, CA: Think Social Publishing, 2007.

Works on the Spirit: Athanasius and Didymus. Translated by DelCogliano, Mark, Andrew Radde-Gallwitz, and Lewis Ayres. Crestwood, NY: St Vladimir's Seminary Press, 2011.

Wuertz, Lisa. "Of red deserts and blue skies." *Living Liturgically* (blog). March 26, 2018. https://livingliturgically.com/2018/03/26/of-red-deserts-and-blue-skies/ (accessed May 1, 2019).

Endnotes

1 This family-centered approach is also taken by Fr. John Chryssavgis in his pamphlet for the Greek Orthodox Archdiocese, "The Body of Christ: A Place of Welcome for All People, Including People with Disabilities" (New York: Greek Orthodox Archdiocese of America, 2017), which I read after I had already written a large part of this book. It affirms that families of persons with disabilities are frequently excluded and their physical and emotional burdens unrecognized. It's important to note that I will not refer to anyone in this book as an "individual," as that language is drawn from a reductionist view of human nature and community that does not reflect the way that God made us or redeems us. Rather, I use the terms "person," "persons," "humans," and "people." Note that I use the term "people" in the vernacular sense as a plural form of "person," rather than its formal meaning of a particular group with shared bonds, as in the biblical usage, "a people."

2 In his review of Dr. Andrew Whitehead's landmark study on church attendance and disabilities, Dr. Stephen Grcevich points out that disability ministries, which usually focus on children with physical and intellectual disabilities, are not reaching the most-excluded sector of persons with disabilities. Rather, "Dr. Whitehead's interpretation of the study results was that conditions that negatively impact upon social interaction or communication are those that result in the greatest impact upon church attendance." "It's the hidden disabilities that keep kids out of church," *Church 4 Every Child* (blog), July 23, 2018, accessed April 1, 2019, https://church4everychild.org/2018/07/23/its-the-hidden-disabilities-that-keep-kids-out-of-church/.

3 David Briggs, "Study: U.S. Churches Exclude Children with Autism, ADD/ADHD," The Association of Religion Data Archives, July 9, 2018, accessed April 1, 2019, http://blogs.thearda.com/trend/featured/study-u-s-churches-exclude-children-with-autism-addadhd/.

4 Stephen Grcevich, "What are the stats on disability and church?" *Church 4 Every Child* (blog), February 9, 2016, accessed April 1, 2019, https://church4everychild.org/2016/02/09/what-are-the-stats-on-disability-and-church/#_edn1.

5 Assembly of Canonical Orthodox Bishops of the United States of America, "Disability and Communion," June 25, 2009, accessed April 15, 2019, http://www.assemblyofbishops.org/news/scoba/disability-and-communion.

6 Divine simplicity does not mean naivety or acting like a simpleton. God is simple in the sense of being of a whole, not made of composite parts.

7   Thus that beautiful line in the "Late have I loved thee" poem in Augustine's *Confessions 10.27, "Fragasti, et duxi spiritum, et anhelo tibi"*: "Thou didst most fragrantly blow upon me, and I drew in my breath and I pant after thee." Augustine, *Confessions Books IX–XIII*, Loeb Classical Library, trans. William Watts (Cambridge, MA: Harvard University Press, 1979), 146.

8   Saint John of Kronstadt expresses this well when he says, "For by God's grace I become miraculously changed in the church. . . . At such times, we see everything clearly; we look upon everything correctly; we feel friendship and love toward everyone, even toward our enemies, readily excusing and forgiving everyone. O, how blessed is the soul when it is with God! Truly the Church is paradise on earth." John of Kronstadt, *My Life in Christ*, vol. 2, trans. Nicholas Kotar (Jordanville, NY: Holy Trinity Publications, 2015), 12.

9   Thus St. John Chrysostom tells us in his Twelfth Baptismal Instruction, "Even if a man be lame, or his eyes have been torn out, or he be disabled in body, or has fallen into the most extreme weakness, none of these things prevents grace from coming into the soul." John Chrysostom, *Baptismal Instructions*, Ancient Christian Writers, No. 31, trans. Paul William Harkins (New York: Paulist Press, 1988), 181–182.

10   John of Kronstadt, *My Life in Christ*, vol. 2, 13.

11   Gregory of Nyssa, "On the Soul and the Resurrection," in *St. Gregory Ascetical Works*, The Fathers of the Church: A New Translation, trans. Virginia Woods Callahan (Washington, DC: Catholic University of America Press, 1967), vol. 58, 258.

12   Assembly of Canonical Orthodox Bishops of the United States of America,"Disability and Communion," section 1.

13   Misleading questions are like the serpent's question in the Garden of Eden. "Did God really say . . .?" was already a nonsense question before the serpent finished his sentence, because it pretends that God did not know what they were talking about or would not have answered and readily guided any asker in the right way. No matter what is asked in these sorts of questions, they are presumptive and lead astray. Rather we must start with acknowledging that God is with us and give thanks for what He has given us.

14   Chryssavgis, John, " The Body of Christ: A Place of Welcome for All People, Including People with Disabilities," 4.

15   2 Corinthians 12:9 gives us a succinct view of a person with a disability who is living a life filled with sanctity. Saint Paul describes his own answer from God, who did not remove his burden but gave him strength instead:"But he said to me, 'My grace is sufficient for you, for my power is made perfect in weakness.' I will all the more gladly boast of my weaknesses, that the power of Christ may rest upon me."

16 From the Nicene Creed

17 Saint Theodore the Studite in *On the Holy Icons,* section 43, tells us, "Christ is circumscribed even after His resurrection. Listen to Him speaking to His own disciples, when after the resurrection they thought they saw Him as a spirit: 'See my hands and feet, that it is I myself,'" and "after the resurrection also he was contained by circumscription, because He had not lost the properties of His human nature" (trans. Catharine P. Roth, Crestwood, NY: SVS Press, 2001, 70). This shows us that God does not abandon human nature either in suffering or glory, and we who live with disabilities suffer with God and will share the glory of God.

18 "Will I be autistic in the resurrection? Will my friend have cerebral palsy? Will my loved one be able to hear? Will the hands and feet cut off to avoid sin (Matt. 18:1–11) be restored?" These questions, though not wholly misdirected, are yet distractions from looking to Christ, the true goal of our holy imaginations and our imitation.

19 Augustine, *The City of God Against the Pagans,* XXII.19, trans. R.W. Dyson (Cambridge: Cambridge University Press, 2002), 1148–1149. "What are we to think of the Almighty Artist? Will He not be able to remove and abolish all deformities of the human body, whether common ones or rare and monstrous, which, though in keeping with this wretched life, are not consistent with the future happiness of the saints?" In keeping with the truth that God will restore and change us in the resurrection, St. Augustine teaches that God will not be limited in bringing happiness to people, no matter which type of disability they bear in the present life.

20 Ibid., 1149–1150. Saint Augustine distinguishes between blemishes and the marks of virtue borne on the bodies of martyrs who suffered for Christ's sake. It might be that disabilities, when they are the occasion of virtue that bears witness to Christ's presence and salvation, will leave marks on resurrected bodies that are not blemishes.

21 Ibid., 1168.

22 Chryssavgis, John, "The Body of Christ: A Place of Welcome for All People, Including People with Disabilities,"6.

23 In its statement, "Disability and Communion," the Assembly of Canonical Orthodox Bishops of the United States of America tells us, "Persons with disabilities comprise the largest minority group in the United States, with almost 20% of the population facing disability in one form or another."

24 St. Athanasius, *The Life of St. Anthony the Great* (Willets, CA: Eastern Orthodox Church, 1994), 54.

25 Ibid.

26 In his sermon "The Paralytic Let Down Through the Roof," St. John

Chrysostom engages this metaphor of the three children in the furnace as a model for disability. In "Select Homilies," *Nicene and Post-Nicene Fathers,* ed. Philip Schaff (Peabody, MA: Hendrickson Publishers, 1999), vol. 9, 212.

27   Innumerable sermons explain the spiritual meaning of disabilities in terms of virtues. I chose to highlight St. Cyril of Jerusalem, St. Gregory of Palamas, and St. John Chrysostom (the fiery furnace metaphor) because they give some of the most eloquent and succinct examples of this way of reading Scripture in light of the Resurrection and the presence of the Holy Spirit with us now.

28   Gregory Palamas, "On the Healing of the Paralyzed Man in Capernaum I" in *Miracles of the Lord: Sermons by Saint Gregory Palamas*, ed. Christopher Veniamin (Dalton, PA: Mount Thabor Press, 2013), 7.

29   Gregory Palamas, "On the Healing of the Blind Man," *Miracles of the Lord*, 32.

30   Cyril of Jerusalem, "Sermon on the Paralytic" in *The Works of Saint Cyril of Jerusalem*, trans. Leo P. McCauley and Anthony A. Stephenson (Washington, DC: Catholic University of America Press, 1969), vol. 2, 209–222.

31   Cyril of Jerusalem, "Sermon on the Paralytic" in *The Works of Saint Cyril of Jerusalem,* 215–217.

32   Ibid., 220.

33   Ibid., 221.

34   This connection and the reference to Abba Agathon are drawn in Fr. John Chryssavgis, "The Body of Christ: A Place of Welcome for All People, Including People with Disabilities," 5.

35   Larchet, Jean-Claude, *The Theology of Illness* (Crestwood, NY: SVS Press, 2002), 59. Though the issues arising from illness and disability do not overlap entirely, in many places they contain similar calls to action. One such similarity is the view that weakness of body is a gift that prepares the soul to seek what is holy.

36   Gregory Palamas, "Healing of the Paralyzed Man in Capernaum I," *Miracles of the Lord,* 5.

37   Nellas, Panayiotis, *Deification in Christ: Orthodox Perspectives on the Nature of the Human Person* (Crestwood, NY: SVS Press, 1997), 151–152.

38   Augustine, *Free Choice of the Will* 3.23.66 in *The Teacher, The Free Choice of the Will, Grace and Free Will*, trans. R. P. Russell (Washington, DC: Catholic University of America Press, 1968), 225.

39   "O Heavenly King, Comforter, Spirit of Truth, everywhere present and filling all things. . ." *The Ancient Faith Prayer Book*, ed. Vassilios Papavassiliou (Chesterton, IN: Ancient Faith Publishing, 2014), 7.

40   Cyril of Jerusalem, "Mystagogical Lecture V" in *St. Cyril of Jerusalem Works,* vol. 2, trans. Leo P. McCauley and Anthony A. Stephenson

(Washington, D.C.: Catholic University of America Press, 1970), 186.

41 Freeman, Stephen, *Everywhere Present: Christianity in a One-Storey Universe* (Chesterton, IN: Conciliar Press, 2010), 8.

42 Cyril of Jerusalem, Mystagogical Catechesis II, "On the Rites of Baptism," in *St. Cyril of Jerusalem Lectures on the Christian Sacraments*, ed. F.L. Cross (Crestwood, NY: SVS Press, 1995), 61–63. Here St. Cyril illuminates the mystery of salvation in baptism, that we enter the likeness of Christ's sufferings without having to partake fully of them but receive the fullness his salvation.

43 Rilke, Rainer Maria, *The Book of Pilgrimage* II.1, trans. Anita Barrows and Joanna Macy, in Rilke's *Book of Hours* (New York: Riverhead Books, 2005), 135.

44 The interview upon which this chapter is based took place over the phone in January 2017 between Garrison and Charlotte Riggle, an Orthodox Christian children's book writer and blogger who offers many posts about faith and disabilities. Charlotte also compiled the interview into its present form, which Garrison has approved. The interview and summary were carried out with the intention of sharing Garrison's story in this book, and this chapter is included with both Charlotte and Garrison's permission.

45 "Wisdom for the Day—St. John Chrysostom," St. Barnabas Orthodox Church (website), November 6, 2013, accessed April 20, 2019, https://stbarnabasoc.org/wisdom-day-st-john-chrysostom/.

46 Editor's note: In fact, autistic families are more excluded than most families with disabilities.

47 Cyril of Jerusalem, "Mystagogical Lecture V," section 19, in *St. Cyril of Jerusalem Works*, vol. 2, ed. Leo McCauley and Anthony Stephenson (Washington, D.C.: Catholic University of America Press, 1970), 202.

48 Athanasius, *On the Incarnation of the Word*, section 54, trans. and ed. A Religious of C.S.M.V. (Crestwood, NY: SVS Press, 2000), 93.

49 Athanasius, *On the Incarnation of the Word*, section 11, 38.

50 Saint Augustine tells us, "To Him as the Word belongs the perfecting of created being, which is called back to Him to be formed by a union with its Creator and by an imitation, in its own way, of the Divine Exemplar." *The Literal Meaning of Genesis*, vol. 1 (New York: Paulist Press, 1982), 24. In other words, imitation of Christ leads to union with God, because the Word is "eternally and unchangeably united with the Father, [and] is of necessity identical in nature with Him." The idea of an exchange of characteristics between God and man, or the *communicatio idiomatum*, is most developed in St. Athanasius's *On the Incarnation of the Word*, but other Fathers shared his thinking. Christ as fully God and fully human is the way that we humans know God and can take on His characteristics. Saint Maximus is probably the best at showing that this

is done through love. When he speaks of humans becoming like God, the love of God is what deifies us (makes us like God): "Love is therefore a great good, and of goods the first and most excellent good, since through it God and man are drawn together in a single embrace, and the creator of humankind appears as human, through the undeviating likeness of the deified to God in the good so far as is possible to humankind." "Letter 2: On Love" in Andrew Louth, *Maximus the Confessor* (London: Routledge, 1996), 90.

51   I have not forgotten that this advice comes in the context of the kenotic Christ, and we will look more closely at humility and self-emptying in the last two sections of the book.

52   Saint Gregory of Nyssa describes *theosis* across many of his works as participating in God through the sacraments and drawing near to Him in love through prayer; he also describes virtues as the way that we imitate God and with Him restore the His image in us. However, St. Cyril of Jerusalem says this most succinctly in his fifth Mystagogical Lecture: "For truly One only is holy—holy, that is, by nature; yet we also are holy, not, indeed, by nature, but by participation, training, and prayer." Cyril of Jerusalem, "Mystagogical Lecture V," in *St. Cyril of Jerusalem Works*, vol. 2, 202.

53   Cyril of Jerusalem, "Mystagogical Lecture IV," section 3, in *St. Cyril of Jerusalem Works*, vol. 2, 182.

54   Gregory of Nyssa, Sermon 3 on the Beatitudes, "Blessed are they that mourn, for they shall be comforted," in *The Lord's Prayer and The Beatitudes*, trans. Hilda Graef (New York: Paulist Press, 1954), 116.

55   Athanasius, *On the Incarnation of the Word*, 38.

56   Ibid., 44.

57   Ambrose, "Jacob and the Happy Life" 9.37 in *Saint Ambrose: Seven Exegetical Works*, trans. Michael P. McHugh (Washington, D.C.: Catholic University of America Press, 2003), 169.

58   See Luke 18:2, the unrighteous judge.

59   Irenaeus, *Against Heresies* IV.20.7 in *St. Irenaeus of Lyons*, Robert M. Grant (London: Routledge, 1997), 153.

60   Augustine, *Confessions,* trans. Maria Boulding (New York: Vintage Books, 1997), 3. "You arouse us so that praising you may bring us joy, because you have made us and drawn us to yourself, and our heart is unquiet until it rests in you."

61   "Thou dost show me the path of life; in thy presence there is fulness of joy, in thy right hand are pleasures forevermore" Psalm 16:11, RSV. These pleasures from the presence of God are not fleeting nor dependent on bodily abilities. Rather, the pleasure is the joy in the presence of God, because in typical psalmic poetry, the first part of the verse explains the second.

62 Cyril of Jerusalem, "Catechesis XII" in *The Works of Saint Cyril of Jerusalem*. Translated by Leo P. McCauley and Anthony A. Stephenson. Vol. 2. The Fathers of the Church: A New Translation (Washington: Catholic University of America Press, 1970) 236.

63 *The Sayings of the Desert Fathers*, ed., trans. Benedicta Ward (Kalamazoo, MI: Cistercian Press, 1984), 25. This story is also summarized in Fr. John Chryssavgis, "The Body of Christ: A Place of Welcome for All People, Including People with Disabilities," 8.

64 Though I had written this before the publication of Fr. John Chryssavgis's pamphlet, it's important to note that it also relates this lesson from the story of the man born blind. This pamphlet has many useful tips for making welcome, which I will share along with those brought to me by Orthodox Christians living with disabilities.

65 The Assembly of Canonical Orthodox Bishops of the United States of America, "On Disability and Communion."

66 Chryssavgis, John, "The Body of Christ: A Place of Welcome for All People, Including People with Disabilities," 8.

67 Ibid., 9.

68 Ibid.

69 Several people independently recommended to me that each church would benefit from a disability ministry coordinator or advocate, and especially that the ideal person for such a position is someone who is himself disabled or familiar with treating people with disabilities respectfully. Father John Chryssavgis points out that this advocate could even work to help coordinate ministries over several parishes for special services ("The Body of Christ," 7). As you will see in a later chapter in this section of the book, "Spotlight: Special Needs Liturgy and Community Gathering," that is exactly the model that is being implemented currently in several parishes in the New York City metropolitan area.

70 Here I deviate from Fr. John Chryssavgis' advice to use "person first" language, such as "person with visual impairment," because members of different communities of people with disabilities use different approaches to language. Some people call themselves "disabled," "autistic," "deaf" or "Deaf," or "blind," and others say they have a child "with autism," "with hearing impairment," "with impaired vision," or "with cerebral palsy," for instance. There is no hard-and-fast rule for anyone to know how someone will prefer to speak of her disability. If you follow the lead of the person with a disability, she will tell you how she describes herself. For instance, I and most other adults "with autism" call ourselves "autistic," since autism is a brain difference, not an illness or epidemic. Some people, however, find the phrase "person with autism" respectful. The only words to avoid for sure are ones most often used in mockery or insult, such as "moron," "dumb," and "lame."

71   John Climacus, *The Ladder of Divine Ascent*, Step 26.53, trans. Archimandrite Lazarus Moore (New York: Harper & Brothers, 1959), 95.

72   In their statement on "Disability and Communion," the Assembly of Canonical Orthodox Bishops of the United States of America advise recognizing, loving, and respecting persons with disabilities, including those with service dogs. They do not specify exactly how to include service dogs, and different jurisdictions have different biases surrounding dogs. I mentioned the recommendation of several priests who allow guide dogs to help blind people in church services, which is that they treat the dog like a medical prescription rather than a regular animal. This seems to reflect the way that blind Christians explained to me the months of training and lifelong reliance between guide dogs and the blind people they help.

73   Father John Chryssavgis gives this helpful advice in his pamphlet, "The Body of Christ."

74   I am grateful to Laura Theodora Collins for telling me about Braille Divine Liturgy and prayer books. They are available for purchase online from the Orthodox Marketplace.

75   Laura Theodora Collins shared this tip.

76   Laura Theodora Collins pointed out these resources to me. You can access the Talking Books catalog and search for Orthodox Christian titles at the Library of Congress National Library Service for the Blind and Physically Handicapped, https://www.loc.gov/nls/braille-audio-reading-materials/online-catalog-search/.

77   An Orthodox Christian named Josefina, whose genetic condition causes hearing impairment, shared many of these tips with me.

78   Branch-Smith, Brittany, "Church Access for the Deaf," *Frederick News-Post*, January 1, 2014. fredericknewspost.com/news/lifestyle/church-access-for-the-deaf/article_917b8ae6-bf5c-5108-97fa-3abef9193b7d.html.

79   For instance, book discussions in the "Take Up and Read Orthodox and Catholic Reading Room" group on Facebook are organized by comment threads. Live meetups in Slack, in Facebook groups or events, on Twitter hashtag streams, or on other online, threaded chat services allow participants with internet access to post questions, ideas, and replies by typing rather than speaking. This removes the handicap of several types of impairments, since the person typing and reading (visually or with a screen reader) does not miss out on the discussion or have to wonder who said what.

80   Assembly of Canonical Orthodox Bishops of the United States of America, "Disability and Communion," Point 4: Pastoral Ministry, Practical Implications.

81   Grcevich, Stephen, "It's the hidden disabilities that keep kids out of church."

82 My godson's mother, Courtney Napier, learned about the not-book club model from her friend Katie Thompson.

83 Cyril of Jerusalem, Mystagogical Lecture IV.3 in *The Works of St. Cyril of Jerusalem,* vol. 2, trans. Leo McCauley and Anthony Stephenson (Washington, D.C.: Catholic University of America Press, 1970), 182.

84 For example, the Ladies' Philoptochos of the Greek Orthodox Metropolis of Atlanta sponsors Christ the Good Shepherd summer camp for autism families. I have had the joy of being part of that experience with my family. The camp setting, trained volunteers, catering to sensory needs, and welcoming clergy made the prayer services and Divine Liturgy some of the most joyful of our family's experience. However, camp settings are not replicable to most churches, so I wanted to find an example of an average-sized parish making welcome through a special-needs Divine Liturgy.

85 "The Challenge Liturgy Ministry," The Archangel Michael Greek Orthodox Church, accessed April 1, 2019, https://archangelmichaelchurch.org/challenge-liturgy/.

86 This emphasis on behavior rather than attention has also long been a bias in therapeutic interventions for people with communication challenges. However, over the past thirty years, we have discovered that learning is most effective when teachers try to gain and manage attention rather than focusing primarily on certain behaviors. Winner, Michelle Garcia, Introduction, *Thinking About You, Thinking About Me,* 2nd ed. (San Jose, CA: Think Social Publishing).

87 As Fr. John Chryssavgis explains on page 3 of "The Body of Christ: A Place of Welcome for All People, Including People with Disabilities," handicaps are not necessary. Rather, he explains, "Handicaps are actually the barriers that we create for people with disabilities by excluding them socially and physically."

88 Goleman, Daniel, "Brain's Design Emerges As a Key to Emotions," *The New York Times,* August 15, 1989. This article explains the discovery that people feel emotions before they think, not afterward.

89 Mahler, Kelly, *Interoception: The Eighth Sensory System* (Lenexa, KS: AAPC Publishing, 2017), 2–7.

90 Rogers, Sally, et al., *An Early Start for Your Child with Autism* (New York: Guilford Press, 2012), 220–221. The chapter "The Joint Attention Triangle: Sharing Interests with Others" explains how to share interests through gestures like giving an object, pointing, and showing objects. These activities are of course common in interactive teaching and even in the Divine Liturgy. We will talk more about this in Chapter 13 of this book.

91 Mahler, *Interoception,* 24–25. This section of the book explains the role of an inner part of the brain called the insula in the formation of gut

feelings based on sensory input.

92   Saint Augustine discusses joint attention in its purest and highest form
      in his *The Trinity* 8.12, where he shows us that love is only known fully
      when we are loving someone. This pattern of love is not meant to define
      the Persons of the Trinity, but it is a threefold pattern that reminds
      us that we are made in God's Trinitarian image. Augustine, *The Trinity*
      (Brooklyn, NY: New City Press, 1991), 253-255.

93   Here I am thinking of the marvelous thesis of St. Augustine's *Confes-
      sions* 1.1.1, "You arouse us so that praising you may bring us joy, because
      you have made us and drawn us to yourself, our heart is unquiet until it
      rests in you." *Confessions*, 3.

94   See, for instance, the way that St. Irenaeus describes the Virgin Mary as
      the Second Eve, untying the knot of Eve's sin. In this section, he applies
      a pattern of reading called typology to highlight the ways that God
      saves by matching up with our needs. Irenaeus, *Against Heresies* 3.22.4, in
      Robert Grant, *Irenaeus of Lyons*, 140-141.

95   A summary of the four levels of interpreting Scripture in the medie-
      val period is found in Henri de Lubac's *Medieval Exegesis*: "The letter
      teaches events, allegory what you should believe. Morality teaches what
      you should do, anagogy what mark you should be aiming for." Henri
      de Lubac, *Medieval Exegesis: The Four Senses of Scripture* (Grand Rapids,
      MI: Eerdmans, 1998), 1. De Lubac also mentions the reception of St.
      Jerome's metaphor of Holy Scripture later in chapter one of the first
      volume of *Medieval Exegesis*.

96   *The Catechism of the Roman Catholic Church* inherits the tradition of
      advancing from the literal to the spiritual senses of Scripture, with the
      spiritual senses divided into the allegorical, the moral, and the heavenly
      levels. See the *Catechism*, sections 115-119 (New York: Doubleday, 1997),
      38-39. Catholic readers will recognize this arrangement with the literal
      meaning given first. However, we will be using the order that St. Augus-
      tine laid out, because we are only able to know anything about God or
      the Scriptures because of Christ.

97   Thus, when St. Augustine explains the first words of Genesis, he tells
      us that Christ is the beginning. "God made heaven and earth in the
      beginning, not in the beginning of time, but in Christ. For he was the
      Word with the Father, through whom and in whom all things were
      made." Augustine, *On Genesis Against the Manichees* 1.2.3 (Washington,
      D.C.: Catholic University of America Press, 1991), 49.

98   Augustine, *The Literal Meaning of Genesis*, 19.

99   Father Steven Salaris explains the problem of sixty percent of young
      people leaving the Faith and brings up "failed models of Christian
      education" as one of the factors contributing to the decline in his web
      article "So why do 60% of our college youth leave Orthodoxy?" *Orthodox*

Christian Laity, accessed April 2, 2019, https://ocl.org/so-why-do-60-of-our-college-youth-leave-orthodoxy/.

100 Maximus the Confessor, "Ad Thallasium 61" in *On the Cosmic Mystery of Jesus Christ,* trans. Paul M. Blowers and Robert Louis Wilken (Crestwood, NY: SVS Press, 2003), 143.

101 John of Kronstadt, *My Life in Christ,* part 2, 222.

102 Saint Athanasius, in his work *On the Incarnation of the Word,* makes it plain that God became man to meet our senses so that we can become like God. If we teach to engage the senses, we are only imitating God, who teaches us the same way. We see this put plainly in section 15, where St. Athanasius says, "The Saviour of us all, the Word of God, in His great love took to Himself a body and moved as Man among men, meeting their senses, so to speak, half way. He became Himself an object for the senses, so that those who were seeking God in sensible things might apprehend the Father through the works which He, the Word of God, did in the body." *On the Incarnation of the Word,* 43.

103 Saint John of Damascus explains memory as "the retention of sensation and thought." The input from the senses forms "a mental impression." While St. John explains intellectual objects as separate from sensory (sensible) memories, I believe that his explanation fits well with modern brain science's explanation of attention. The "mental impressions" formed by sensory input are like channels through which thoughts travel, the way impressed wax forms a channel down which water or melting wax might flow. John of Damascus, *Orthodox Faith: Book Two,* Chapter 20 in *Writings* (Washington, D.C.: Catholic University of America Press, 1999), 245.

104 In his *Confessions* 10.8.12–10.9.16, St. Augustine gives an elaborate description of the "fields and vast mansions of memory," where sense perceptions are used to layer memories upon memories throughout the spaces that he remembers. Later Western thinkers such as Thomas Aquinas elaborated on the method, and this technique for memorizing the Faith has come into vogue again in the recent past with books such as *Memorize the Faith!* by Kevin Vost (Bedford, NH: Sophia Institute Press, 2006) and pop cultural references such as an episode of *Sherlock.* However, the technique is ancient and was widely used both before and after St. Augustine's time.

105 The truth of God as a place for us is a refrain throughout the Psalms, and the heavenly vision of Jesus going to prepare a place for us in His Father's house with many mansions (John 14) carries this image to its eschatological end. God is not only with us but actually a place for us. Saint Gregory of Nyssa tells us in "On the Soul and Resurrection" that "God becomes a place to those who are worthy and a home and a garment and nourishment and drink and light and wealth and a

kingdom and every idea and name we have for what makes up the good life." (*Ascetical Works*, 244.) This passage explains how God is all things and in all things, and it does so by way of encouraging those who suffer bodily misfortunes in this life. This hope of having God as our place encourages us to live virtuously and in prayer now as though this truth were fully manifested.

106 In the space of about fifty years, many Church Fathers wrote commentaries on the literal meaning of Genesis or on the first six days of creation. For instance, St. Basil and St. Ambrose both wrote a commentary on the Hexameron (first six days), and St. Augustine wrote along the pattern of the first six days of creation in several commentaries, including the *Confessions, The Literal Meaning of Genesis*, and *On Genesis Against the Manichees*. His great work *The City of God* is a contemplation of history and his contemporary world from the viewpoint of the goal of the seventh day, sabbath rest. His *Confessions* is also framed around the pattern of the seven days of creation, with his memories formed around the creation of trees (the pear tree), his struggle of living like a wild beast (his carnal desires), his exploration of his human nature (Ambrose and Ossia), his recognition of himself in the image of God (his mother's death, the poetic outbursts on the love of God that sought him and drew him near), and his hope for the sabbath rest of clinging to God that he set out as his thesis at the beginning of his work (our hearts are restless until they rest in you). These many layers of meaning in one text serve the purpose of rescuing the speculative theories of Origen from Platonic indifference and the many dualistic heresies that were spinning out from the Origenist idea that the end is like the beginning. On one hand, sects were teaching cyclical holiness and profanity, and on others, sects were teaching that people could bypass the saving love of God to be perfect merely through their own efforts and by thinking about it hard enough. St. Augustine did much to guard against these heresies, which unfortunately rear their heads in our day, too. It's an additional benefit that teaching to the senses in order to affirm the presence of the Incarnate God also helps to protect the hearers from the excesses of the new Gnosticisms.

107 By the ninth and tenth centuries, imperial churches were built and painted specifically to engage the worshiper in the microcosms of salvation history and the world, "the church being regarded on the one hand as a sort of microcosm of the world outside, with heaven above and earth below, and on the other as the New Jerusalem, where Christ's life was lived anew from day to day. . . . [E]ach scene was thus intended to call to mind a particular place where He had sojourned on earth, and each had its appropriate place in the church." David Talbot Rice, *Art of the Byzantine Era* (New York: Oxford University Press, 1963), 88.

108 Thus, in "On the Soul and the Resurrection," St. Macrina tells her brother St. Gregory, "It is said by the wise that man is a microcosm, encompassing in himself the elements by which he is made complete." Gregory of Nyssa, *Ascetical Works,* 204.

109 God makes Himself accessible to our senses in order for us to know Him, because "knowledge of their Maker is for men the only really happy and blessed life." Athanasius, *On the Incarnation of the Word*, 38.

110 In several places, including Catechesis IV.10, St. Cyril writes that his lectures are given at the site of Christ's Crucifixion. Cyril, *The Works of Saint Cyril of Jerusalem,* vol. 1, 124.

111 Summer Kinard, "The Church as Memory Palace." Accessed August 16, 2019. http://myocn.net/the-church-as-memory-palace/

112 John of Kronstadt, *My Life in Christ*, 59. I quoted only the beginning of the passage, but St. John goes on to mention the events of salvation history that he sees in the temple (the Church). These events assure him of God's love.

113 Again, St. John of Kronstadt gives us an assurance that we can know God in space, this time by speaking of the Holy Spirit. "We 'have been made to drink into one Spirit' (1 Cor. 12:13). From this you see that the Spirit of God surrounds us on all sides, like water or air. 'The Spirit of the Lord fills the world (Wis 1:7).'" Op. cit.., 224.

114 Gregory of Nyssa, *Ascetical Works*, 244.

115 John of Kronstadt, *My Life in Christ*, 220.

116 Athanasius, *On the Incarnation of the Word,* section 15, 43.

117 I am familiar with sensory diets through extensive therapeutic work with my children. I used the following helpful sensory diet explanation and checklist as inspiration for the one that you see in this chapter: Special School District of St. Louis County, "Sensory Diet," accessed April 15, 2019, https://www.ssdmo.org/cool_tools/inclusive/Resources/trying_to_make_sense_resources.pdf.

118 Arlin Cuncic, "How to Practice Self-Regulation," Accessed August 15, 2019, https://www.verywellmind.com/how-you-can-practice-self-regulation-4163536 .

119 A version of these instructions was published on Summer Kinard's website as "Accessible Prayer Corner Tutorial," March 28, 2019, accessed May 1, 2019, https://summerkinard.com/2019/03/28/accessible-prayer-corner-tutorial/.

120 Sensory bins are waterproof plastic trays or shallow rectangular containers filled with a large quantity of a tactile item. Children gather around it in order to play with the items inside. In outdoor spaces, water tables or paddling pools serve as sensory bins as well.

121 Felt candles that can be used in pretend play or on birthday cakes are available from online sources such as Etsy, or you can make them

yourself. The idea is to sew a felt pocket in the shape of a candle with room for a lollipop stick inside, with an orange felt flame shape sewn to the top. For specific resources, see the blog post where I first introduced this idea: "Accessible Prayer Corner Tutorial," https://summerkinard.com/2019/03/28/accessible-prayer-corner-tutorial/.

122 Ignatius of Antioch, *Epistle to the Ephesians* 15, accessed May 1, 2019, http://www.newadvent.org/fathers/0104.htm.

123 The universal Church is the household of God with Christ as its Head. This is a welcome word to those who cannot speak, because the ongoing guidance of Christ with us assures that even nonverbal Christians can keep the Faith of the Church. St. Irenaeus, *Against Heresies* I.10.2 in Robert M. Grant, *Irenaeus of Lyons*, 71.

124 Irenaeus, *Against Heresies* III.22.4 in Robert M. Grant, *Irenaeus of Lyons*, 140–141.

125 Ward, *The Sayings of the Desert Fathers*, 131.

126 The National Professional Development Center on Autism Spectrum Disorder, "What are Evidence-based Practices?" Accessed on May 1, 2019, https://autismpdc.fpg.unc.edu/evidence-based-practices.

127 When St. Anthony the Great advised his listeners to fight demons with the sign of the cross, he said, "For they are cowards, and utterly dread the sign of our Lord's Cross, since it was on the Cross that the Saviour despoiled them and exposed them." Athanasius, *The Life of St. Anthony the Great* (Willits, CA: Eastern Orthodox Books, 1994), 50.

128 Saint John Chrysostom tells the candidates for baptism in his Baptismal Instructions that the sign of the cross is an "impregnable tower" (191) and a spiritual weapon to protect them on every side. "The devil will not dare look upon such a sight" (169) of one with the sign of the cross, because of "the lightning flash which leaps forth from it and blinds his eyes" (52). Making the sign of the cross is like shooting spiritual lightning at the devil. Tell that to your Sunday school children if they seem bored. John Chrysostom, *Baptismal Instructions*, 52, 169, 191.

129 A BoardMaker version of the Lord's Prayer is available to print from my website: https://summerkinard.com/2017/04/01/how-to-sort-autism-facts-from-fads/. Updates to this prayer and other prayer resources will be posted on the website: www.summerkinard.com/special-needs-resources/.

130 A BoardMaker version of the Jesus Prayer as a matching prayer is available to print from my website: https://summerkinard.com/2019/05/14/non-verbal-prayer-the-jesus-prayer-matching/.

131 Spoor, Monica, *Spirituality on the Spectrum: Having Autism in the Orthodox Church* (The Netherlands: Brave New Books, 2017), 39–40. Excerpted with permission.

132 A guide to nonverbal prayer with printable prayer maps and holy icon

circles to place on them is included on my website: "Non-Verbal Prayer 3 Ways," May 4, 2019, accessed May 17, 2019, https://summerkinard. com/2019/05/04/non-verbal-prayer-3-ways/.

133 Psalm 141:2: "Let my prayer be counted as incense before thee, and the lifting up of my hands as an evening sacrifice." We sing that refrain in Great Vespers and in the Presanctified Liturgy throughout Lent in church with incense. It also inspired using a prayer silk for places where incense might not be suitable. This prayer method includes people from all abilities in a group prayer that teaches through movement.

134 Julianna told me that she was inspired by a blog post on Mat. Emily Parsells's site, *Charming the Birds from the Trees*. Of note, this post features a small container garden to the Theotokos, which shows that this idea can be adapted to any available space. "Our Mother of God Garden," June 26 (year not given), accessed May 17, 2019, http://www. charmingthebirdsfromthetrees.com/2008/06/our-mother-of-god-garden.html.

135 Julianna directed me to this long list of plants that have associations with the Theotokos. "Mary Gardens," *Fish Eaters* (blog), accessed May 1, 2019, https://www.fisheaters.com/marygardens.html.

136 John Chrysostom, Twelfth Baptismal Instruction section 29, *Baptismal Instructions*, 181–182.

137 Gregory of Nyssa, Sermon 1 On the Beatitudes in *St. Gregory of Nyssa: The Lord's Prayer and The Beatitudes*, 90.

138 Gregory of Nyssa, "To Call Oneself a Christian," in *St. Gregory: Ascetical Works*, 89.

139 *On the Incarnation of the Word*, section 11, 38.

140 We see in many places in the Orthodox Latin and Greek Fathers that the imitation of Christ in virtues leads to union with God; for instance, St. Augustine's *The Literal Meaning of Genesis*, and in St. Gregory of Nyssa: "the end [aim] of the life of virtue is to become like God" (Sermon 1 On the Beatitudes in *St. Gregory of Nyssa: The Lord's Prayer and The Beatitudes*, 89). I could fill a page with footnotes to similar references through many Fathers, but let these suffice.

141 John Chrysostom, Twelfth Baptismal Instruction, section 26, *Baptismal Instructions*, 181.

142 Theodore the Studite, *On the Holy Icons*, section 45, trans. Catharine P. Roth (Crestwood, NY: St Vladimir's Seminary Press, 2001), 94.

143 Dietrich Bonhoeffer, in *Creation and Fall: A Theological Exposition of Genesis 1–3* (trans. Martin Ruter and Ilse Todt, Minneapolis: Fortress Press, 1997, 99ff), also writes about human creation as male and female in terms of limits, but I have used the term differently than he in an important way. He speaks of limits as allowing us to know that someone else is other than ourselves and of love as what helps us to bear the

limits of our bodies as male and female. However, "other" is not my reference point in the way he means, because "self" is not a category in the way that he means. We only know ourselves through loving God and our neighbors, or more accurately, our selves are only discernable in that loving which imitates God in loving Him and our neighbors. (See the section of "Four Levels of Scripture and Attention" on triadic attention, page 120). The primary reference is the love of God, not the idea of oneself. Therefore the limit is not a problem that love must overcome but a gift given by God in his love in order to lay at our feet the path of salvation. Limits mark the boundaries of our personal journey in the Way of Christ.

144 John Chrysostom, Twelfth Baptismal Instruction, section 26, *Baptismal Instructions*, 181.

145 In *The Body and Society*, Peter Brown describes the biological science current in the second through fifth centuries that saw women as "failed males" (New York: Columbia University Press, 1988, 10). What is extraordinary in this context is that the Fathers made the radical claim that women were still women in the resurrection, completely overturning the Roman idea that men were the exemplary definition of humanity. God, not males, is the one who shows us what it means to be human.

146 Thus St. Augustine tells us in *The City of God* XXII.17 that femaleness is not a flaw to be corrected in the resurrection, but a trait that will be revealed to all in a "new beauty," when sin no longer clouds our relationships with one another. Rather than going along with the lie that women are defective males, St. Augustine tells us, "He, then, who instituted two sexes will restore them both." St. Augustine, *The City of God*, 1145.

147 Though the debate about whether to baptize or confirm persons with cognitive or developmental disabilities is a perennial one in Protestant circles, this attitude of treating abilities—rather than God's providence and mercy in creating people in His image—as the standard for full inclusion in the Church has lately even crept into some Orthodox scholarship. See for instance, Petre Maican's essay, "Image and Likeness and Profound Cognitive Disability: Rethinking Patristic Categories" on the Public Orthodoxy site, accessed July 12, 2019, https://publicorthodoxy.org/2019/07/02/image-likeness-cognitive-disabilities/ .

148 Thus, in his "Address on Religious Instruction," St. Gregory of Nyssa explains how humans, being made in the image of God, all have free will. They are not bound to necessity but are free to cling to God. We are made to have communion with God, and that communion with God is natural to us all. Hardy, Edward R., *Christology of the Later Fathers*, Library of Christian Classics, Book 3 (Louisville, KY: Westminster John

Knox Press, 2006), 276–277.

149 Nor was Christ limited in his divine nature when He became man. We are members of Christ's Body. The holiness of Christ was not diminished by his Incarnation, and our sanctification is not diminished by the limits of our bodies with disabilities.

150 Augustine, *The Free Choice of the Will*, section 67, trans. Robert Russel (Washington, D.C.: Catholic University of America Press, 1968), 226.

151 Ibid., 226–227.

152 Saint Gregory of Nyssa, in "On the Soul and Resurrection," tells us, "Since it is the nature of evil not to exist apart from choice, when all choice resides in God, evil will disappear completely because there will be nothing left to contain it." *St. Gregory: Ascetical Works*, 242. Whereas our natures are in the image of God and good, evil cannot exist apart from choice. That means that someone who does not have the capacity to choose on his own cannot choose to do evil. But since a person can receive grace and faith and love by nature and through the gifts of God and of fellow members in Christ's Body, there is no hindrance to holiness. This is also why St. Augustine tells us in *The Free Choice of the Will* 3.22.64 that being unable to do something is not deserving of condemnation, unlike doing something wrong or inadequately due to a perverse will (223, paraphrase). And again, St. Gregory of Nyssa tells us in "To Call Oneself a Christian" that "not being separated by choice from God is the same as living in heaven." *Ascetical Works*, 87.

153 See previous discussion in the first section of this book, "Illness Versus Disability."

154 Gregory of Nyssa, Sermon 1 On the Beatitudes in *St. Gregory of Nyssa: The Lord's Prayer and The Beatitudes,*, 90.

155 St. Maximus the Confessor, "Letter 2: On Love," in *Maximus the Confessor*, 88, 91.

156 John Chrysostom, "Twelfth Baptismal Instruction," section 15, *Baptismal Instructions*, 177. What makes our bodies beautiful is virtue.

157 Ibid., 187.

158 Palmer, Constantina, *The Scent of Holiness: Lessons from a Women's Monastery* (Chesterton, IN: Conciliar Press, 2012), Kindle edition.

159 Saint John Chrysostom's *Baptismal Instructions* advise against the spiritual harm of going to see spectacles in contrast to the Divine Liturgy. Not only is the subject matter of the spectacles of his day (violent sports, public deaths, and lewd theater) problematic, but watching spectacles trains people away from love of neighbor and worship of God.

160 I experienced this myself as an autistic Christian. When I was told, "Do not judge your neighbor," I struggled to figure out how to reconcile that negative advice with the fact that I was able to notice untruths and

brokenness. That struggle led me to spend too much time thinking about the deviations from the good that I saw around me. However, when I was told, "Love your neighbor as a fellow member of Christ's Body," I became less confused and was able to follow the other advice, too. The temptation to judge fell away as I realized that Christ is the Head of His Body and can be trusted to put us all in proper order.

161 Porphyrios, *Wounded By Love*, ed. Sisters of the Holy Convent of Chrysopigi (Limni, Evia, Greece: Denise Harvey, 2005), 135.

162 Ibid., 136.

163 Gregory of Nyssa, "To Call Oneself a Christian," in *St. Gregory: Ascetical Works*, 89.

164 Two recent studies have shown that many high-functioning (meaning verbal) autistics are atheists because they cannot connect with the abstract ideas of faith. When I read these studies as a teacher and as a "high-functioning autistic" myself, I see what the researchers did not: that the failure to believe was due to a failure to engage attention and reason through concrete examples. To reach these people and many others with learning challenges, churches must intentionally begin to form habits through the senses and repetition. These studies, for reference, are Norenzayan, A., W.M. Gervais, and K.H. Trzesniewski, "Mentalizing Deficits Constrain Belief in a Personal God," PLOS ONE 7(5) (2012): e36880, accessed May 1, 2019, https://doi.org/10.1371/journal.pone.0036880; and Caldwell-Harris, C., C.F. Murphy, T. Velazquez, and P. McNamara, "Religious Belief Systems of Persons with High Functioning Autism," Proceedings of the Annual Meeting of the Cognitive Science Society (2011), 33, accessed May 1, 2019, https://escholarship.org/uc/item/6zh3j3pr. Notably, the deficits in mentalizing are the most consistent predictor in not believing in God, and this deficit is more prevalent in men as well as in autistics. This is an evocative deficit, considering the traditional role of religion in forming habits, especially in men. These habits were called *vir*tues because they were what a man (*vir*) aimed to be. Perhaps the recovery of teaching in order to form habits rather than to cover lots of subjects will not only include people with disabilities, but will also make church teaching more accessible to men. Being a man is not a disability, but we might be creating handicaps for men's belief in God by neither teaching concretely nor repeating lessons with increasing depth.

165 Athanasius, *On the Incarnation of the Word*, section 15.

166 Larchet, Jean-Claude, *The Theology of Illness*, 74.

167 Palmer, *The Sweetness of Grace*, 47–48.

168 Cyril of Jerusalem, "Mystagogical Lecture V," 196.

169 Augustine, "The Free Choice of the Will," 225.

170 Irenaeus of Lyons, *Against Heresies* IV.20.7 in Grant, *Irenaeus of Lyons*,

153.

171 Athanasius, *The Life of St. Anthony the Great*, 118.

172 John of Kronstadt, *My Life in Christ*, Part 2, 19.

173 Irenaeus of Lyons, *Against Heresies* I.10.2 in Grant, *Irenaeus of Lyons*, 71.

174 Didymus the Blind, *On the Holy Spirit* II.10 in *Works on the Spirit: Athanasius and Didymus*, trans. Mark DelCogliano et al. (Crestwood, NY: SVS Press, 2011), 146.

175 John of Kronstadt, *My Life in Christ*, part 2, 69.

176 Ibid., 65.

177 Ambrose, *Jacob and the Happy Life 9.37* in *St. Ambrose: Seven Exegetical Works*, trans. Michael P. McHugh (Washington, D.C.: Catholic University of America Press, 2003), 169.

178 From Socrates, *Hist.* IV, c. 25, quoted in Athanasius, *The Life of St. Anthony the Great*, 94.

179 I summarized the beginning of the verse for brevity. The full passage reads: "For I am sure that neither death, nor life, nor angels, nor principalities, nor things present, nor things to come, nor powers, nor height, nor depth, nor anything else in all creation, will be able to separate us from the love of God in Christ Jesus our Lord" (Rom. 8:38–39).

180 Chryssavgis, John, "The Body of Christ: A Place of Welcome for All People, Including People with Disabilities," 6.

181 I share this story with the approval and permission of my daughter, my family, and the Christian education director who was so kind.

182 Assembly of Canonical Orthodox Bishops of the United States of America, "Disability and Communion," point 4,.

183 Monica was not the only parent of a child with disabilities who told me how much this Akathist helps them. In my family, too, I often listen to a recording of this prayer and sing along. Asking the Theotokos to "raise my children" reminds me and many other parents that we and our children are members of Christ's Body, looked after by His saints and especially His Mother. *Akathist to the Mother of God, Nurturer of Children* (Safford, AZ: St. Paisius Orthodox Monastery, 2001).

184 Our experience of Christ in the Eucharist transforms time and space, and this transformation carries out into the whole life of the community. See Panyiotis Nellas, *Deification in Christ* (Crestwood, NY: SVS Press, 1997), 151–152.

185 Assembly of Canonical Orthodox Bishops of the United States of America, "Disability and Communion."

186 Ibid, point 3.

187 Gregory of Nyssa, *The Life of Saint Macrina*, in *St. Gregory: Ascetical Works*, 182.

188 The daughter of the military man was healed through prayer and hospitality. Ibid, 188–190.

189 In "The Body of Christ: A Place of Welcome for All People, Including People with Disabilities," 4–6, Fr. John Chryssavgis talks about the physical as well as emotional burdens placed on families with disabilities. Speaking of these burdens, he writes, "When we are not aware of this reality, we place an additional challenge on families" (5).

190 Assembly of Canonical Orthodox Bishops of the United States of America, "Disability and Communion," point 2.

191 Second Baptismal Instruction, section 30, in *St. John Chrysostom: Baptismal Instructions*, 54.

192 *Baptismal Instructions*, 97–98.

193 John of Kronstadt, *My Life in Christ*, part 1, 252.

194 This essay originally appeared as a guest post on www.charlotteriggle. com titled, "'Let ALL the Little Children Come,' Including Those Who Need Gluten-Free Food." https://charlotteriggle.com/let-all-little-children-come-including-gluten-free/. This essay has been edited and reprinted with permission from Charlotte Riggle and Victoria Marckx.

195 I consulted the *Food Allergy Research & Education* website (https://www. foodallergy.org) for some of the information about the names and types of foods that cause the top eight food allergies (accessed May 4, 2019). I also suffer from multiple severe food allergies and have worked with children with severe allergies, so much of this knowledge is from personal experience. Any questions about food allergies should be directed to a qualified medical professional.

196 *Greek Orthodox Holy Week & Easter Services*, trans. Fr. George Papadeas (Daytona Beach, FL: Patmos Press, 2016), 481.

197 Palmer, G.E.H., Philip Sherrard, and Kallistos Ware, eds., trans., *The Philokalia*, vol. 1 (London: Faber and Faber, 1979), 73–74. Here St. John Cassian relates in his discourse "On Control of the Stomach" from his "On the Eight Vices," that the holy Fathers had not given only a single rule for fasting, because not everyone could eat the same types of foods or in the same quantities. Rather, they advised eating without satisfying hunger as a way to control the stomach.

About the Author

A S AN AUTISTIC MOTHER REARING autistic children in the Faith, Summer Kinard knows firsthand many of the gifts and challenges of life with disabilities. She brings her extensive background in patristic theology and catechesis (B.A. in religion, M.Div., Th.M. in early church history and theology) to skillfully weave together the healing patterns of Holy Tradition with the daily patterns of life with disabilities. Summer has become acquainted with hundreds of Orthodox families with disabilities through sharing on her website the resources she has developed to make faith accessible to them. At a time when at least twenty percent of people live with disabilities and two percent are autistic, there is an urgent need to apply Church teachings to questions about the care and inclusion of persons with disabilities as full members of Christ's Body. Summer brings the grace, kindness, and insight of an experienced teacher and mother to begin answering those questions. Summer Kinard is an Antiochian Orthodox Christian in the Diocese of Wichita and Mid-America. She lives with her husband, Andrew, and five children in Texas.

Ancient Faith Publishing hopes you have enjoyed and benefited from this book. The proceeds from the sales of our books only partially cover the costs of operating our nonprofit ministry—which includes both the work of **Ancient Faith Publishing** and the work of **Ancient Faith Radio**. Your financial support makes it possible to continue this ministry both in print and online. Donations are tax-deductible and can be made at **www.ancientfaith.com.**

To view our other publications,
please visit our website: **store.ancientfaith.com**

Bringing you Orthodox Christian music, readings,
prayers, teaching, and podcasts 24 hours a day
since 2004 at
www.ancientfaith.com